BORN TO LOVE

*

To Jesus in the Blessed Sacrament,
To our Blessed Lady, our Queen and Mistress;
To our Mother Foundress and to our
departed Sisters, to those
now living and yet
to come,
this biography is
humbly, lovingly and gratefully
dedicated in this, the Centenary year
of the Poor Servants of the Mother of God.
May our Lady, the first Christ-bearer,
be always our Model,
as we try to draw souls ever nearer to Her Divine Son.

BORN TO LOVE

by

Mother M. Geraldine, S.M.G.

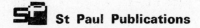 St Paul Publications

DECLARATION

In conformity with the decree of Pope Urban VIII, dated March 17, 1625, we declare that if in the course of this work we should give the name of Saint to those not officially recognized as such, and if we make mention of such facts and revelations as might bear the character of the miraculous or prophetic, we do not in any way presume to take upon ourselves to express, on either persons or facts, a judgement which is reserved to the Church, nor in any way whatsoever to forecast decisions which belong to her alone.

NIHIL OBSTAT: John M. T. Barton, S.T.D., C.B.S.,
             Censor

IMPRIMATUR: Victor Guazzelli, *V.G.*
Westminster, 2. iii. 1970

The Nihil obstat *and* Imprimatur *are a declaration that a book or pamphlet is considered to be free from doctrinal or moral error. It is not implied that those who have granted the* Nihil obstat *and* Imprimatur *agree with the contents, opinions or statements expressed.*

SBN 85439 031 6

Printed in Great Britain by the Society of St Paul, Langley, Bucks.

CONTENTS

GENERAL ACKNOWLEDGMENT AND REFERENCES

To His Eminence Cardinal Heenan for his Preface and his Paternal interest in the Book. — His Grace Archbishop Beck of Liverpool for freedom of reference to his Masterpiece: "The English Catholics and the Restoration of the Hierarchy, 1850-1950". — His Paternity Very Reverend Father General, S.J. (Aruppi) for "general permission" for Fathers' names and our continual spiritual help from the Society for 100 years. — The Rev. Father Jude Mead, C.P., of Baltimore, for "Shepherd of the Second Spring" (Blessed Dominic Barberi), St. Anthony's Guild Press, Paterson, New Jersey, U.S.A. — Rev. Father Superior, C.P., Passionist Retreat, Highgate, London, for reference to Rev. Fr. Ignatius Spencer, C.P. (Hon. George), by Fr. Urban Young, C.P., Burns & Oates, Ltd. — Mr. H. P. Commager, for "World War II' (in Tuscany), Pocket Book Edition, 1230, 6th. Ave., N.Y., U.S.A. — The Executors of the British Museum, for permission for Facsimile of Receipt, signed "Fanny Taylor" re "Dream of Gerontius". —

Eastern Hospitals and English Nurses, by Fanny M. Taylor. — Irish Homes and Irish Hearts, by Fanny M. Taylor. — Regina Prophetarum, by Sister M. Campion, S.M.G., Rome. — Memoir of Father Dignam by Mother Magdalen Taylor, B.O.W., London. — Meditations by Father Dignam by Mother Magdalen Taylor, B.O.W., London. — Conferences by Father Dignam by Mother Magdalen Taylor, B.O.W., London. — Inner Life of Lady Georgiana Fullerton by Mother Magdalen Taylor, B.O.W., London. — "Mother as we knew her", S.M.G. Archives. — A Shrine and a Story - St. Joseph's, Portland Row, Dublin. — Related incidents by contemporary Sisters, S.M.G. — Life of Mother Magdalen Taylor by Father F. Devas, S.J., B.O.W., London. — Mother Magdalen Taylor by Mary Angela Dickens, C.T.S., London.

Miss Louise Alexander, D.L. — Mrs. Cone — Mrs. McKinley Bryan — Mrs. Melva Price of Greensboro and High Point respectively. — Mr. W. C. Bennett and Mr. Keith Barish of Florida. — Mr. W. McSweeney, New York. — Mr. Frank Cullen-Brophy of Arizona, U.S.A.

The Fathers and Brothers of the S.S.P. Publications deserve our deep gratitude for their zealous interest in, and dedication to detail in the printing and publishing of this work.

Grateful mention must be made of the devoted "Blue Ladies" of Maryfield Nursing Home, High Point, North Carolina; also the Nursing and Maintenance Staffs. These latter, like the woman of Gospel fame (Luke 21 : 1-4) wished and insisted on subscribing, out of their necessity towards printing and publication expenses.

Last, but not least, I thank our Reverend Mother General and our S.M.G. Sisters for their kind encouragement and loving, impatient interest to see the Book a printed fact. In particular is Sister Maria Campion, S.M.G. of Maryfield, High Point, N. Carolina, to be thanked for her labour of love in her very correct typing of the MS. "Born to Love".

PREFACE

This elegantly written and absorbingly interesting life of Fanny Taylor does not need the support of a preface. I have accepted the invitation of Mother Geraldine to write this preface because of our friendship and as a sign of gratitude for the apostolate of the Poor Servants of the Mother of God in this country.

To call this account of Mother Magdalen's life interesting is to confess the inadequacy of words. It is an exciting narrative. It reads like an historical novel but, of course, in no sense is it a work of fiction. It is a sober record of amazing achievements. For a child from an English vicarage to become the foundress of an order of Catholic nuns is fanciful enough. If to this is added the fact that she was received into the Church in a first aid post at the height of the Crimean war it is apparent that hers is no commonplace story. It is, in fact, in many ways more remarkable than that of her friend Florence Nightingale.

I shall not spoil the reader's enjoyment by referring to any of the events so graphically and faithfully recorded here. I deliberately refrain from anticipating a single incident of this odyssey. It is enough to note that like most historic characters Fanny Taylor appears as one born out of due time. Thomas More had been described as a man for all seasons. Fanny Taylor is a woman for the second half of the twentieth century.

To-day both believers and those without any religious faith have grown conscious of our human duty to relieve poverty. The Third World, as it has come to be called, fascinates the rest of mankind and troubles its conscience. Fanny Taylor was troubled about the poor long before the habit became fashionable. She did not call her daughters "poor servants" for sentimental reasons. She wanted them to serve the poor in the spirit of the Mother of the Poor Man of Nazareth. Their love of the poor must first be shown by the example of poverty in their own lives.

This is not a book to attract only women readers. It will grip anyone with imagination. I am confident that it will inspire all who can recognise and cherish the kind of heroism which is unselfconscious and good humoured.

+ JOHN CARD. HEENAN
Archbishop of Westminster

2nd February 1970.

C h a p t e r 1.

CHILDHOOD AND CHANGE

Hidden from sight under the pulpit in Stoke Rochford Church, Lincolnshire, little Fanny, aged six, determined on that Sunday evening of Harvest Thanksgiving Day to find out, once and for all, what "stories" her father, the Reverend Henry Taylor, told his attentive congregation on those beautiful autumnal Sunday evenings. The Taylor children, of whom Fanny was the tenth and youngest, were not allowed to attend the evening services, theirs being after the morning's "Readings".

Against the beautifully carved pulpit were propped golden full-eared sheaves of corn; from delicately festooned Virginia creeper and other greens hung luscious bunches of grapes, fat rich plums, rosy juicy apples, etc., while along the aisle, at intervals of space, lay pretty little baskets of eggs. Little Fanny, thinking herself safe and secure in her nook, with her little hands clasped in her lap, waited breathlessly for the story. At the children's Scripture gatherings, she had learned of Adam and Eve, the shimmering serpent, about the animals and other creatures in the Ark (she wondered if God put lady-birds there). She knew of Bethlehem and the Holy Innocents, etc., but whatever could her Papa be telling those "big, big" people? They were "as big as Papa himself," thought Fanny.

It would be 1838, Queen Victoria was a year on the throne. England was pleased that the reign of the Georges was over, that all danger from Napoleon was of the past, and that prosperity and peaceful living were secure for the time. But were they? O'Connell had made noise at Westminster and had won his cause almost a decade before. There were feelings of tension in the air, the myths of Rome and the "Scarlet Woman" were still being whispered in gossiping circles and considered "dangerous". Meanwhile the great world rolled on and all was well.

Presently from the Sacristy came the Rector, with reverent, measured step, and mounted the pulpit, as he gave an affectionate look round at his flock and at the beautifully decorated Harvest Thanksgiving scene in the Church. After a moment's settling rustle on the part of his happy congregation, the Rector began the "Lesson" for the day, after which the organist struck up the notes for the Thanksgiving hymn, and then followed the sermon.

"Seek and you shall find" spoke the fine Oxford voice from the pulpit, while the men in their white-fronted shirts and black evening suits, and ladies young and old among the congregation looked up trustfully at their beloved Pastor, who always spoke to them hopefully of God's faithfulness to His divine promises. "Seek and you shall find," he repeated, little dreaming of the small parishioner beneath the pulpit, or that to no one else in his country congregation would his words apply more fully than to his own child. As if meditating on his text, and himself becoming spiritually inebriated by the thought of its impact on others of his attentive congregation, the zealous preacher a third time emphasized the reassuring words: "Seek and you shall find." Then tremulously fingering and re-adjusting his stole, as if this action were part of the dramatic opening, the Reverend Henry Taylor began his theme.

Little Fanny Taylor, having waited in vain for the "Once upon a time" of her father's tale, and not being interested in "Chapter and verse," crouched from her hiding-place and escaped through the open door.

Those were the days of frills and flounces, and, for children, long flowing frocks, prettily-frilled starched bonnets and buttoned high-shinned boots which make the Victorian children of the picture-books look like grandmothers in miniature to the children of today. Such a little woman did Fanny Taylor seem, as next morning she approached her father in his sunlit study, and, putting her tiny hand on his knee, looked up courageously, if guiltily, into that kindly austere face and popped the question: "Papa, what is 'seek'?" The child had known well in practice

2

what it meant to "hide", but "seek" was beyond her. For an instant her puzzled father thought: "Surely she was not in Church last night?" but nevertheless wisely answered her question: "To seek is to look for, to search for, to try to find out." "Ah!" exclaimed the precocious little guilty one, as she scampered off to search for lady-birds among the gooseberry bushes. While yet Mr. Taylor, folding his paper, was pondering curiously on his child's interrogation in the questioning sense of: "What a one, think you, shall this child be?" Fanny's conscience sent her tripping back to tell her father that she "did" a big lie last night (Fanny loved the word "big") and she blurted out the whole story of the preceding evening. Happy that her father knew and forgave her, she must needs unburden to her mother before lessons began in the nursery.

Home life at Stoke Rochford must have been ideally happy for that large family of seven girls and three boys. Much of it was spent out of doors. The Taylors were brought up fearless of snow, wind and rain, they were out in all weathers and, in later years, little Fanny could relate how she had released a fly from a spider's web, and she was known on one occasion to construct a little "Ark" in the shrubbery for her collection of "Creeping things," in which also she tended a little lame mouse, released from a trap which her father had set.

This love for all the wondrous little creations of God was characteristic of Fanny to the end of her days, when she would call a young Sister to the window to observe a crow or blackbird "listening" ere it beaked for its prey into the moist earth, and would exclaim: "Let us magnify the wisdom of God for this instinct." It is not recorded that she sympathised with the poor worm!

In her early childhood too, Fanny Taylor's lively imagination showed itself in the weaving of fanciful tales, which for want of an interested audience she would tell herself. Nor was the actress wanting in the Rector's youngest daughter. With her innate power of personifying, in her father's absence she would steal into church, climb the pulpit steps, take the book of "Notes for Sunday" and announce to the congregation of empty pews all the notices for the week, and this when as yet reading

3

was impossible for her, and Mr. Taylor's caligraphy in particular, which, as Mrs. Taylor used to say humourously to her husband: "Only you yourself can decipher!"

Sundays at the Rectory were strictly kept. The collects were recited by all, only sacred music was allowed, and Mrs. Heman's "Ave Sanctissima" was a favourite when the girls sang in chorus. "Surely," said Fanny in after years, "this Mother of Love and Compassion heard us sing to her, though we did not mean it, and her mighty prayer went up to her Son's throne as we sang 'Ora pro nobis!'"

Everyone knows, more or less, in this nuclear age of so-called progress, haste and restlessness, what calm, peace and freedom from anxiety reigned in a Victorian home, especially in the country, in the post-Napoleonic years of the early nineteenth century, and the home of the Taylors at Stoke Rochford was no exception. "Away, away from men and towns," as were the Rectory and the Church, Mr. Taylor was the undoubted master in both. As their devoted Pastor, he was loved by his people, whose joys and sorrows he shared so sympathetically, and Mrs. Taylor leant on her husband's strong and rich personality for almost every family decision. "Being of a naturally timid and gentle character herself," writes Father Devas, "Mrs. Taylor needed the strong prop that Mr. Taylor proved himself to be throughout their whole married life." But now, when Fanny was in her eighth year, came the crisis of her beloved father's increasing illness and his absence from home, advised, as he was, now to try one cure, now another, until in the spring of 1842 he returned home to die. The poet asks:

> "A simple child that lightly draws its breath
> And feels its life in every limb,
> What should it know of death?"

In "We are Seven," death brought no seeming separation, but Fanny Taylor saw Death with all its cruelly maturing effects as it forced the philosophy of its actual reality on her young mind. "Four tall black-suited men," she was heard to relate in after years, "waiting restlessly as if impatient to bear my father away." There was the hushed atmosphere of loneliness and

4

mourning, the sympathizing visits of grief-stricken parishioners, the slow procession to the Church, and then, most poignant of all, the black-veiled widow being comforted as the coffin was lowered, and all was over.

The Taylors had now to face the vacant rooms where every object told a story. There was the Rector's tall hat, the lonely library with its central table on which lay the large family Bible, and by chance, a shining linen clerical collar, which the Rector would never need again. As he laid his collar aside for the last time, little did the Rector think that down the years another Taylor of his blood and line, the Reverend Charles Taylor, C.S.S.R., would don a Roman Catholic priest's collar, and live and die in one of the great Orders of the Church, and that the great family of Taylors, down to the fourth and fifth generation which is now, should all be Catholics, having sought and found, with little Fanny, "the pearl of great price." Such are the ways of God, Whose Divine Spirit "breatheth where He wills" when souls are open to His all-conquering Breath and His Divine Grace.

Soon life for the Taylors ended at Stoke Rochford, and it is on record how and by what means the final exit was made. One can imagine those last days, last visits to the Church and its tombs, and then came the moment of departure, when one last, nostalgic, lingering look behind was the end. We know of the famous Grantham Inn, the gathering place for travellers by the stage-coach that made a daily journey from London, but railway travel was still in its tottering infancy and railway stations were few and far between. Fanny writes of the journey: "We drove some twenty miles to the nearest railway station. There were few railways in England in those days and this was quite a new line. It was thought a great event to travel by rail, and people deemed us very courageous! I had never been in a stage-coach, so I began my life of travelling by rail!"

Life at Stoke Rochford would go on. A new Rector had come to take over the Living and the Parish. Mrs. Taylor and her family faced London and the unknown, but the new Rector and the parishioners would see to it that a fitting memorial be erected to their late devoted Pastor, and to-day in the beautiful

5

sanctuary can be seen the tablet erected one hundred and twenty-five years ago, and which reads:

"The Reverend Henry Taylor, M.A.
18 years Rector of this Parish and of Ashby,
near Spilsby in this County.
Died 19th June, 1842, in his 65th year.
Hic Corpus, Ubi Anima.
Credo, Spero, Confido."

One hundred and twenty-five years also after the flight of the Taylors from Lincoln to London, Stoke Rochford was visited by Sisters of the Congregation founded by Fanny Taylor in 1869. What a surprise and a re-assuring joy of historic accuracy to read their account, even in 1966! "On the main road from Peterborough to Grantham there is a signpost announcing 'Stoke Rochford' on the left. Turning into this road, we glimpsed a little country village nestling in the valley below, in the centre of which rose a tower of an old and very beautiful stone church. This village was Mother Foundress's birthplace, and looking at the village in the distance, one felt that Stoke Rochford must have changed little since her day. It could also be easily understood why, as a child she spent so much time out of doors, and why she loved Nature so much in general. Leaving the road, we went through a gateway that led to another by-way, which in turn led to the village. The fine church was situated at the junction of these two roads, and this fact reminded us of Mother Foundress's reminiscences about the London stage-coach and the luggage conveyed from the City and met from the Rectory or the Park. We learnt that the Church dated back to Norman times. At first we could think we were mistaken, till we discovered a slab on the wall giving a list of departed Rectors, and surely enough, there was "Henry Taylor, M.A., 1824 - 1842." After further search, we found underneath the carpet, opposite the main altar, the flagstone covering his grave, with the above inscription clear and legible with the details hitherto quoted. We next visited the Presbytery, where the housekeeper was most kind, but unfortunately the Bishop of Grantham, who lives at the Presbytery, was away from home. We should have loved to have met His Lordship. The very kind housekeeper told us that the

6

present house dates to 1874, but was built exactly on the same plan as the old, described by Mother Foundress (and given in Father Devas's "Life" of her, page 5) except that the 1874 building is larger and the rooms more spacious."

Such is Stoke Rochford to-day, and though Fanny never returned to her native village where she spent the first ten years of her life, she loved to reminisce about it, and liked to think in after years that the grace of her conversion was due to the holy men and women who had lived in her native county in pre-Reformation times, and was proud of the very Catholic traditions of Lincolnshire — St. Guthlac and his holy sister Bega, who went on pilgrimage to Rome, St. Hugh and his swan, Ely, Boston, Thorney, Bury St. Edmunds, etc. To the merits and prayers of those monks and nuns of the Lincolnshire monasteries who suffered through the bitter periods of persecution, and to those of its older hermits and anchorites, Fanny Taylor liked to think she owed her conversion in great part.

One asks oneself, how ever did this child of ten, entirely accustomed to a quiet, happy home life in a village such as Stoke Rochford, become acclimatized to London life, even as early as 1842? Accustomed as little Fanny was to hedges and ditches and butterflies and lady-birds, and to rich Nature's various wonders, of which poets have sung, no wonder her sulking in Hyde Park and refusing to return home with her little brother, as the next chapter relates. But is there not a deeper reason for this growing power and force within her? She, for whom God had so many disappointments in store, was being educated by Him to serve others. She who had asked her father what "seek" meant was destined to "find" later, in the slums of London, Liverpool etc., children who never knew real child-life nor happiness such as she had known. Her great Mother's heart was in later life to find shelter and comfort for every form of human misery, and her spiritual daughters carry on her mission to-day in hospitals, schools at all levels, homes for the handicapped and the deprived, for the aged and lonely, for spastics and polio victims, and, in addition, Parish visiting, the instruction of converts and Catechism classes for those attending non-Catholic schools. The little Fanny of Stoke Rochford, who was to say towards the end of her life: "God will have our heart's love and the whole of it"

7

was truly "born to love," and that with a love which made her insert in her Rule, years after: "There is no work of mercy imposed by Holy Obedience that they can do for the poor of Jesus Christ, for which the Sisters shall not be cheerfully ready." and again, in the same chapter: "Just as we cannot reach Heaven except by using earthly things, the Sisters, to gain souls by works of mercy, ought to show themselves willing to render the lowliest services to those who are in distress." Lastly, and these lines echo the days in Miss Sellon's Sisterhood, and the cholera, when Fanny was only sixteen: "In case of pestilence breaking out in the neighbourhood in any of the houses of Mission, the Sisters shall show themselves full of devotion and alacrity."

Most interesting will it be to follow the unfolding of the story of the life of one on whom Our Lord had set His seal from the beginning to be, as Cardinal Newman says: "A link in a chain, a bond of connection between persons" to draw their souls ever more closely to His Divine Heart.

Arrived in London, the Taylors settled firstly in Cumberland Place, and soon we find Fanny at her "seeking" again — not lady-birds now, but street after street of that contrasting wonderland of a great city where, unimportant little Anglican as she was, she was destined to play so important a part in the years to be. That Fanny had imagination and daring, the incident at Stoke Rochford on Thanksgiving proves; that she had a strong will and its caprices, the following story reveals. Having found her initial bearings in her new surroundings, she would one day, with her brother Mortimer, explore further in Hyde Park. After some time, he wished to return home, she did not, they fell out. She would go further, until feeling herself alone and frightened, she turned back, sat on a doorstep and cried. Luckily a Quaker lady came along to her. Fanny grew more frightened until the lady asked: "Child, why dost thou cry?" Fanny told her tale and the lady offered to accompany her home. Just then, Mrs. Taylor appeared round the corner, and with a "terrified face," thanked the lady. Even in Victorian times it was a risk to wander alone, especially for a country child. Ever since that day, Fanny tells in later years, she had a great regard for Quakers, especially as she saw the lady take a coin from her pocket for a certain "Tommy Drew" who stood near by with "an organ and a monkey too!"

The family soon left Cumberland Place for Brompton, and soon too began to make their circle of friends in and about Kensington and London. Naturally Fanny's elder sisters began to contemplate their future. Emma in 1848 left to join Miss Sellon's Anglican Sisterhood at Devonport, and was very happy there. Thither followed Fanny at the age of sixteen, only to leave within a period of months, but this experience was not lost on her "seeking" mind. She could tell how useful and full of charity the Sisters were for the cholera victims at Bristol and Plymouth, where she herself had helped as a postulant in 1849.

During the next five years, her stay in Miss Sellon's Sisterhood helped her ever-growing zeal for the poor and suffering in London. At one time, impressed by the scarcity of schools for poor children and ragamuffins in the neighbouring slums, and seeing them grow up and develop in ignorance and vice, with other friends she began what was in those days styled a "Ragged School", and found she could coax her pupils to attend by a meal of bread and treacle. One has but to read Dickens to understand how necessary such work was at that time, in school, in slum, in workhouse and hospital. Lord Shaftesbury did much in his time for the "Ragged Schools", and in 1847 the Factory Act limited the working hours of women and children to ten hours a day — a concession then which later on was considered even cruel.

Social science as a study had not as yet a faculty, nor had psychiatry come into the open, but here was a girl in her late teens who was to discover for herself that every Nicholas Nickleby had a heart to be found, and with Madame Montessori of later years (who had also had to prove in her own case) that, granted the child is baptised, trust and responsibility make for maturity in the seemingly backward or wayward youngster.

In modern times, with almost every benefit at the disposal of the people for the furtherance of education, the preservation of the health of the nation, the care of the aged and the handicapped, it is difficult to realize the conditions of the poor, even as late as the 1850's. Let whoever would or could come forward to help a particular case, but the general interest was lacking.

Fanny Taylor and her companions, apart from the work of their school, were engaged in what would be described to-day as "an intensive apostolate of completely voluntary legionary social work" among the poor, without distinction of creed or class. They had also formed a study circle among themselves, where French had priority, and one or the other went for a period to Paris to "take home" good pronunciation.

Nor did Fanny Taylor omit Sunday School from her curriculum. Her father's Bible was her chief treasure, and from it she drew fruitful lessons and examples for her pupils. Fanny's own sisters, Ellen, Louisa and Charlotte were partners in her social campaign in London, until gradually the large family lessened; Louisa and Ellen both married, Louisa to a Mr. Colles, Vicar of Melton Mowbray, Ellen to a Mr. Nugent, who later set out for Australia, where he was to redeem his vast losses caused by some unfortunate investments in England, and from which the whole family suffered. Thither, four year later, George Taylor and his family emigrated, and made common cause with his brother-in-law in that great and tempting Continent, where every child of the line of the Reverend Henry Taylor was eventually to embrace the Faith of Our Lady's dowry and of old Catholic Lincolnshire. An exception was the Rector's second son, Lieutenant Richard Taylor, who was killed in India in 1849 in the 27th year of his age. Fanny's favourite brother, Mortimer, never married, and was received into the Church on his death-bed in 1894, the same year as his maiden sister Lucy, who remained staunch to her Anglican beliefs all her life. Fanny's and Charlotte's contacts are for another chapter, while history ceases at the age of fourteen for Harriet Taylor, whose grave-tablet is seen beside that of her father in Stoke Rochford Church.

Mrs. Taylor's interests were being whetted daily as her zealous daughters recounted their experiences each night at the supper table. She set aside a tiny makeshift workroom, and would work for hours at a stretch, transforming ladies' dresses and making as many as three or four little frocks from the hooped fashionable skirts of the time. Her old hand-machine of Stoke Rochford days had many memories for her, and the fact that her little frocks etc. were for the poor children of the slums did not lessen her care that they should be neat and becoming.

Her devoted daughters were happy to see their mother thus occupied, as she was by nature introspective, and somewhat lonely as one birthday after another came round, and Stoke Rochford's family feasts held precious memories for her, that only she herself could appreciate fully. Dr. Newman's sayings she treasured, and drew much comfort from the following, which she had by heart, and which probably her husband was given during his illness: "If I am in sickness, my sickness may serve Him, in perplexity, my perplexity may serve Him, if I am in sorrow, my sorrow may serve Him. He does nothing in vain. He knows what He is about. He may take away my friends, He may throw me among strangers, He may make my spirits sink, hide my future from me, still He knows what He is about."

Mrs. Taylor was very stable in her High Church beliefs, and was known to have "converted" many of her lady friends in the neighbourhood of St. John's Wood. She would be seen in Holy Trinity Church, lost in prayer, long before the Sunday service started, and no doubt God heard her prayer and blessed her yearnings.

Chapter 2.

GIRLHOOD AND GRACE

It must be remembered that from 1829 onward, London was alive with controversy about what Father Faber describes as "three hundred loveless years," since Henry VIII declared himself head of the English Church "as by Law established." Daniel O'Connell, the great Irish agitator, having been elected Member of Parliament for Clare, won the grudging assent of George IV to his Emancipation Bill for Catholics in Ireland, England, Scotland and Wales. Freedoms and Rights in Religion, Education and the Professions had hitherto been denied them on the ground that they were Papists. From 1830 to 1845 and the Oxford Movement, there was much doubt, contradiction and confusion in England. What a shock to English high society in 1830 to learn that a great scion of its aristocracy, Lord George Spencer, had not only "gone over to Rome" (to use his own phrase) but had entered the English College, Rome, to study for the Sacred Priesthood, determined to return and work until death for the conversion of his country. He little dreamt where Divine Grace was leading him, years before the Oxford Movement was born, or that he, who after his degree at Cambridge and during his "Grand Tour" had visited Rome and laughed at its "mummeries", should return there fully convinced of the Truth. The "Kindly Light" which will later lead Dr. Newman and the Oxonians into the "one true Fold" led George Spencer to find the future St. Paul of the Cross, Founder of the great Passionist Order, whose spiritual son he is destined to become, and who had offered his own life to God for the conversion of England. Spencer is also introduced to Father Dominic Barberi, who, in the designs of God is destined to guide Newman himself into the true Fold in England.

Fanny Taylor in 1846 had the great shock of hearing that Lady Georgina Fullerton, who wrote her favourite book, "Ellen Middleton", and whom she worshipped as "a great Anglican lady of exalted principles" (without ever having met her) had gone over to Rome, as had also Fanny's favourite curate, Mr. Gordon, who became a priest of the Birmingham Oratory. Two years later, in 1848, as a result of the Gorham judgment, Fanny's own director, Mr. Dodworth, together with many other devout and distinguished non-Catholics all over England, were received into the one true Fold.. * The blood of the martyrs had long pleaded to Heaven for redress. The Lord could not but remember the work of "Eleutherius, Celestine and Gregory." The Second Spring was dawning out of darkness, confusion and chaos, and many were the great and enlightened souls who were stepping out of darkness into the Light.

Yet Fanny Taylor gives no sign of real distress. More and more does she throws her whole self into her work for the poor, and has succeeded in getting many other friends interested in her cause. The movement of 1845 does not seem to have held

---

* In 1848 Dr. Phillpotts, the Protestant Bishop of Exeter, refused to sanction the appointment to a vicarage in his diocese of a certain Mr. George Gorham, whose views on Baptism the Bishop considered to be heretical. Mr. Gorham held that spiritual regeneration is not given or conferred in that Sacrament, and he denied that by Baptism infants are made members of Christ and children of God. Mr. Gorham appealed from his bishop to the Archbishop of Canterbury; but when the Court of Arches decided against him, he appealed boldly to the Crown, and received a judgment in his favour from the Judicial Committee of the Privy Council. The Archbishop, whose judgment had been reversed, loyally submitted to the Queen's authority; but Bishop Phillpotts continued the fight, appealing, in vain, first to the Court of Queen's Bench, then to the Court of Common Pleas, and lastly to the Court of the Exchequer. Mr. Gorham, having established his right, was inducted to his vicarage at Brampton Speke, North Devon, on August 6, 1850.

"Dr. Phillpotts had a final fling in the shape of a petition to the Queen, in which he refused to acknowledge her as head of the Church, but it was returned to him on the ground of informality. The outcome of the litigation was to establish that authority — even in matters of doctrine — resided in the Crown and not in the Church." The Times, April 16, 1925.

any special interest for them, though long after she had become a Catholic, Fanny related that she remembered her father discussing the Tractarians and saying: "They are good men, they will do much good." Her father had the famous Tractarian, Frederick Oakley, among his undergraduates. That distinguished convert, after his ordination, preached one of his first sermons at St. Joseph's, Portland Row, Dublin — a charitable institution which was later to come under the management of the youngest daughter of his Oxford Tutor.

And now in 1845-48 a disaster occurred in Ireland which was destined to have its influence on Church and State, not only in England but in many countries of the world. The Irish Potato Famine, coming at a time when an oppressed and island nation almost wholly depended on farming, was a crisis in the country's history — a crisis? yea, and a tragedy, but like Golgotha, it was destined to purchase whole colonies for God. Hundreds of hitherto prosperous families, not to count individuals, whose flocks and herds died of starvation, emigrated to America, to begin again in that vast and wealthy continent, which had progressed by leaps and bounds since its victory in the War of Independence. Hundreds of others, who did not hear the "call of the wild," or who could not arrive at paying what was then styled "the Passage," flocked to the British and Scottish ports and cities. London, Liverpool, Bristol, Portsmouth, Glasgow, Edinburgh, etc. saw sorry sights in the landings of whole families, victims of hunger, in search of work and a home. Others still made for Australia, that vast farming continent hitherto unknown to them except for its hearsay convict settlement of Botany Bay.

All three categories brought with them from Catholic Ireland a gift which money could not buy, and of which no oppressor could succeed in robbing them — their strong and lively Faith in God and in His Holy Virgin Mother. Missionaries in the true sense of the word were they, and from Canada to Peru, from Natal to Australia, and from the Hebrides to the London Docks, the Mac's and the O's of Erin and all who owned her for their motherland spread her spiritual empire under the banner of the Cross of their Lord. Great blood, great brains, great zeal and, best of all, hearts aflame with the Faith and with loyalty

14

to the Holy See were the precious gifts that the sons and daughters of Erin gave to the countries that accepted them, and of which they soon became an integral part.

Fanny Taylor, pursuing her great work in London right up to her twenty-first year, came into contact with many Irish emigrants during her daily rounds. It was really her first experience of the Catholic Faith in action. She saw resignation to God's permitted will in the lives of those to whom the Holy Mass and the "beads" meant their all. She saw and understood that they were children of God and His Blessed Mother, children of Nature's training, of the countryside, the woodland and of the sea that had encircled but not safeguarded their beloved land, children of all that keeps hearts in touch with Nature's God, yet a people not to be subdued by any injustice, for they knew that injustice and oppression are never from God.

Fanny Taylor had heard that a certain Viceroy of Ireland was brother of the famous Lord Spencer, who later, as Father Ignatius the Passionist, visited Ireland, with the permission of its Hierarchy, to solicit prayers for the conversion of England. The zealous Passionist was so favourably received that he came again and again. During one of these stays, which he called his "little missions," his brother, whom he was visiting, commissioned him that, on his return to England, he was to tell Gladstone for him that the Irish people would never submit to coercion, and that he, Gladstone, was to get them Home Rule. Years afterwards, Fanny was heard to say: "I never dreamt that I should ever meet the famous Passionist, and, to my joy, on November 13th, 1856, I met him at the Solemn Requiem in London for the Crimean soldiers. How I thanked God at that Mass for all He had done for Father Spencer and for me in our wonderful conversion, and for his sacred priesthood."

Fanny must also have heard of the Honourable Charles Reginald Packenham, nephew of Wellington, who had become a Catholic in August, 1850, and who had died a saintly death at Mount Argus Retreat, Dublin, in the March of 1856. "Much water had flowed under the bridge," as far as Fanny Taylor was concerned, from 1842 to 1856.

As has been told, on their arrival in London from Lincolnshire, the Taylors lived for a short time in Cumberland Place, until they moved to Brompton in 1844. Again, on George's marriage, the family moved to St. John's Wood. Before leaving Brompton, the richly spiritual sermons of a certain Dr. Irons, the daily prayers, the Church services and the frequent sermons at Holy Trinity Church had aroused in Fanny and Charlotte desires which the Church of England was never destined to fulfil. At St. John's Wood the work of spiritual growth developed, and many fervent Anglicans formed the congregation, which, Fanny tells us, included Lady Georgiana Fullerton until her "going over to Rome" in 1846. This "going over" of the lady she worshipped, without personal contact as yet, and of the many other "greats", as a result of both the Oxford Movement and the Gorham affair, did not seem to bother Fanny Taylor overmuch, although their repeated shocks followed upon one another, causing much confusion by their lack of logical precision.

Shane Leslie's "Life of Cardinal Manning" shows the confusion to have been immense. "Gladstone wrote of a famous Dean: 'I have seen Hook, he drivels,' while 'he of Exeter seems to have befooled himself.' Exeter's Chaplain, Maskell, wrote: 'Pusey says one thing, Robert Wilberforce another, Gladstone something else, and you (Manning) with an openness for which I give God thanks, speak plainly in contradiction of them all.' 'The truth seems to me that a Church takes a great deal of killing,' pleaded Gladstone."

Had Gladstone known the true history of the Church and the extent of "killing" it had undergone since its foundation, even to his day, most probably he too would have been convinced of the Holy Spirit's life-giving Light and Power in God's Church, and be among the famous converts of his time. Gladstone would have learned that from the days of the Catacombs to his day and to the end of Time, the Church has been and shall ever be on the Cross with her Divine Founder. The "In hoc signo vinces" of Constantine's victory becomes her own, as she knows she has Christ's promise that the "gates of Hell shall not prevail against her" and His Divine assurance ever holds good that He Himself will be with her "even to the end of the world." What a glorious Leader and Companion-in-arms! What a wonderful response! What King or Queen can number such a volunteer following down the years? Martyrs, hero-worshippers, lovers of both sexes have answered the call of the Victor of Calvary, Who died of sheer love for mankind, to purchase back what was lost through Adam's Fall, and thus show the worth-whileness of that Eternal Life which demanded such a price.

Gladstone had many friends among the eminent Catholics of his time, and was much admired for his breadth of vision and his understanding of national grievances during his long Premiership; and be it said to the credit of England that the exile, the emigrant and those persecuted for the Faith in other lands were always given shelter on her hospitable shores.

Another influence which somewhat enriched and helped to maintain the Christian and refined spirit of the period was that of the Pre-Raphaelite Brotherhood formed in 1848. Its leaders were Holman Hunt (1827-1910), John E. Millais (1829-1896) and the great Italian, Dante Gabriel Rosetti (1828-1882). Holman Hunt made the study of Sacred Scripture and especially of the Gospels live in his own life. Some visits to the Holy Land deepened this study, and imbued all he did with profound religious feeling. Who does not know his famous portrait of Christ, "The Light of the World," standing at the closed door with His lantern? Fanny Taylor, as Mother Magdalen, in later years, used to comment on the lesson from the study of the portrait, telling her Sisters the story of Holman Hunt's interview with his very honest but uninspired art critic. (The Pre-Raphaelites maintained that all inspiration in art ceased with Raphael, hence the title "Pre-Raphaelite.") The critic, having praised the colours, the lights and shades, and the dignified stand of the thorn-crowned Christ, objected that the door 'had neither handle nor knocker.' Hunt replied: "The door at which Christ knocks is the door of the human heart . . . Its only handle is inside." Only in Eternity shall we know and count the number of souls led to their Lord by means of the pleading, "seeking" appeal expressed in Holman Hunt's masterpiece. The artist himself, standing back to contemplate the work of his mind and heart, which, as was the case with Fra Angelico, caused him agony till his brush got it on canvas, is supposed to have said: "Lord, no one will refuse you entrance, for your Light is Love. You were born to love, You lived to love, You died of love, You rose to love, and for all Eternity You are Light and Love."

Some years before her death, and exactly during one of her stays in Rome, Mother Magdalen succeeded in procuring small prayer-book size coloured print pictures of the portrait for her Sisters, so quickly had its fame spread.

C h a p t e r   3.

THE CRIMEA AND CRISES

For all time, the year 1854 will be a landmark in Church History, as it will be in world history, and also in the story of the growth of the hospital system in England. The proclamation of the dogma of the Immaculate Conception on December 8th, 1854, followed on March 25th, 1858, by Our Lady's own re-assuring words: "Je suis l'Immaculée Conception" — "I am the Immaculate Conception" to the little shepherdess of Massabielle were words that set seal forever to the action of the Supreme Pontiff, and gradually also prepared minds and consciences for the further and willing acceptance of the dogma of Papal Infallibility in 1870. It was in 1858 also that the same saintly Pontiff declared the erection of the great statue of Notre Dame de Puy to be "a pious and national undertaking." The French captured at Sebastopol the guns that went to the making of this statue, which was for all time to be associated with Massabielle and Lourdes. Was it Our Lady's gratitude for this beautiful and magnanimous act that made her choose France for her world-healing miracle sanctuary for all time?

Fortunate years were these and those ahead for one whose life-work, yet unknown to herself, was to be one long and lovingly-sustained effort to promote devotion to Our Lady's Immaculate Conception and to the Most Sacred Heart of her Divine Son, Whose Good Friday cry: "Sitio" from the Cross she was destined to translate into the "Da mihi animas" of the saintly Cardinal Merry del Val, and work till death to assuage. The love of God was never idle in Fanny Taylor's family. Her father preached it in season and out, till his death, and when his daughter came to London from the innocent, honest country parish of Stoke Rochford, and more especially after her short stay in Miss Sellon's Sisterhood, she saw that this love must pour itself out and prove itself in action, even on those "who are one's enemies, or who differ from one in religion." He Who caused the manna to fall in the desert, Who had the happy surprise of "a broiled fish and a honeycomb" for His Apostles when they put ashore, is the same Who said: "As long as you did it to one of these My little ones, you did it unto me." And if a cup of cold water given in His Name will not pass without its reward, what a reward must be theirs who fulfil the corporal works of mercy for His love! How often is the capture of a soul for Christ due to the kindness shown in the distress of hunger, sickness, homelessness or in any of the many temporal or spiritual misfortunes of life? The exercise of practical and material charity for love of her God was to be Fanny Taylor's role in life, and that of the Congregation she was destined by God to found and to foster in the years to be.

The year 1854, as was said, marked the complete change in the hospital system in England. The country was plunging into the Crimean War, with France as her ally. Religious controversy, for the moment, gave place to the hurried mobilization of troops and to the battle-call which British patriotism had to respond to almost overnight. After the fierce battle of Alma, with its heavy list of casualties, very bitter and humiliating complaints were made to the British Government, showing up the lack of medical care of the wounded, the utter mismanagement in the hospitals, where many were dying from sheer neglect. Why were the British soldiers denied the care and comfort enjoyed by the French? At the first appearance of sickness at Varna, Sisters of Charity were sent out to minister to their French brothers. Were there no such nurses in England, it was asked, to do this dedicated and charitable work? English-women were not deaf to this call of mercy, and applied to the Secretary for War for information and permission. In Shane Leslie's "Life of Cardinal Manning" quoted by Father Devas, one learns what was being prepared behind the scenes. Manning knew that in the then British troops in the Crimea there were hundreds and hundreds of Irish and English Catholic soldiers. He was living quietly in

Rome and was a personal friend of Miss Nightingale and Miss Stanley. He saw his opportunity to increase the Catholic Chaplains at the Front, and kept Cardinal Wiseman and Archbishop Cullen of Dublin in touch with the War Office until he succeeded in raising the number from eleven to fifteen. He then wrote to Dr. Grant, Bishop of Southwark, with the hope of getting nuns for the East, since Mrs. Herbert and Miss Stanley were scouring London in vain for the right type of nurse. Manning immediately seized the opportunity of mobilizing the convents, and suggested Miss Nightingale as leader of the team. The War Office consented gladly, and at Dr. Grant's first call, five Sisters of Mercy from Bermondsey answered immediately, being as many as the Convent could spare. Having had permission for ten, the Reverend Mother of the Convent of the Faithful Virgin, Upper Norwood, supplied the other five, to Dr. Grant's unutterable joy. The Bishop had written to Ireland, but as there was no post on Sunday, and the departure was fixed for Monday, 24th October, and this being Saturday, any news from Ireland would be too late. "Sudden as lightning," wrote Dr. Manning to the Bishop, and so it was. On the morning of 24th October, the Sisters of Mercy from Bermondsey joined the Norwood Sisters at the Hotel Saxe-Coburg (Paris) under Miss Nightingale. After having braved a fierce storm between Marseilles and Malta (in which the vessel was nearly lost), and with the crew weary from their battle with the gales, and with the precious passengers mostly all sea-sick, they arrived at Scutari on 4th November.

When Miss Nightingale and her party had begun to operate in the Hospital, Manning saw he could do more with the War Office. Sydney Herbert, the Minister for War, was most agreeable, and Miss Stanley was asked to organize a second party and lead them to the East. It goes without saying that those in command at the Front had already witnessed and reported on the improvement in the work under Miss Nightingale and the devoted nuns, and on the spirit of dedication with which the latter faced an almost impossible uphill situation. With this second party, Fanny Taylor, after some indecision, and with the advice of her Anglican Director, determined to go. She often owned in after years that she fully believed this indecision was from the devil, especially as, after presenting herself, she found she was under the regulation age, being only twenty-two, and her heart sank at the thought of being rejected. Miss Stanley, however, rather than deny her party the services of such a valuable recruit, assumed the responsibility of over-riding the regulations. The ladies were ordered to do a course of some weeks' special training at St. George's Hospital, London, and the expedition was ready to start by the end of November. Fanny's description of the last night in England and the send-off the next morning is vividly written: "On the 1st December," she says, "the party of nurses and lady volunteers assembled at Mr. Sydney Herbert's house in Belgrave Square, and the rooms there presented an extraordinary sight; boxes of all sizes, galoshes, cloaks, bonnets, jackets, gowns, collars and caps lay in admired confusion in all directions. In one room a group were receiving their dresses, and of course the long ones fell to the short ones amid the hurried bustle, and vice-versa! Our costume consisted of a loose wrapping gown of dark grey tweed, a worsted jacket, plain linen collar and a thick white cap. Passing over the right shoulder was a broad strip of brown holland, embroidered in red worsted with the words: 'Scutari Hospital'; a short, grey worsted cloak, brown straw bonnet and veil completed the dress." The neat, khaki-clad, dignified nurses of World War II could not have imagined themselves moving about in 1854-55 in such surroundings and with such unimaginable inconveniences as were the lot of those brave and noble women of Crimean days, whose clumsy costume indeed was the least of their drawbacks.

Fanny Taylor goes on to describe the cab-drive to London Bridge, long before dawn, on that bleak December morning: "A long train of fifteen nuns, in their black serge dresses, white coifs and long black veils, awaited us, and all together formed a group such as was never seen before at London Bridge Station." The travellers were forbidden to take any luggage, except one box, which they were never to open from London to Constantinople; all else, cloaks, shawls, carpet-bags, etc., must be carried by hand. They started at 6.0 a.m. heartily cheered by the kind friends who had come to bid them good-bye, among whom was Mrs. Sydney Herbert, with gifts and encouraging words, and gentlemen perambulated the waiting-room with "Illustrated London News", "Punch", and — strange commodity! — tablespoons! There is no mention of 'beautiful soup' in "Eastern Hospitals and English Nurses", nor does the book give any hint of the serving up of her delicacy, "Turkish Delight" in fluid to the poor sick soldiers!

Though Sydney Herbert dare not appoint a military Chaplain officially, the War Office, equal to the occasion, and in league with Dr. Manning in Rome and with the Archbishops of Westminster and Dublin, chose Father Ronan, an Irish Jesuit, to travel with the party, who in the event received Miss Stanley into the Church at the Crimea.

The party was first billeted at Therapia on January 9th, and from there Fanny Taylor writes her first letter to her Mother. She tells her that Miss Stanley and Miss Talbot are off to Scutari and that Miss Stanley has to spend some days at the British Embassy at Pera (Constantinople). She has invited Fanny to come to Pera with them and return to Scutari with Miss Talbot. "We had a delightful steam down the Bosphorus," writes Fanny, and goes on to describe the beautiful palaces on its banks, houses over-hanging the sea, bright red and yellow, and then the bridge of Pera itself, what a scene! Greeks, Turks, French, English and many other nationalities mingled there. They then cross to Scutari Pier, and Fanny tells her Mother that it all resembles a scene from Fairyland. She says that if she is sent to work in Scutari, she will do her best, and will do the same in any other hospital to which she is assigned, but that for the moment nothing was final.

It was a joyous coincidence that in 1967, another "delightful steam down the Bosphorus" was the happy opportunity of two S.M.G.'s of the Mater Dei Convent, Rome, together with two nuns of the Society of the Sacred Heart, their near and dear neighbours of the Trinità dei Monti, with groups of their senior pupils from both schools. The Sisters wrote back to Roehampton, where Communities of both Orders are neighbours also (even from Mother Taylor's time) to say they had been right into Scutari. The "steam down the Bosphorus" had also an ecumenical touch, in that the Sisters met and conversed with Patriarch Athenagoras, who was photographed with them at Istanbul. Truly was it a happy and symbolic group — the venerable Patriarch with his bright smile and his long flowing beard, the

23

two Sisters in their blue scapulars, one on each side, and a little child in white "set in the midst".

Miss Taylor's first appointment was to Scutari. We quote from her book "Eastern Hospitals and English Nurses," written after the war. "Two days after my arrival, Miss Nightingale sent for me to accompany her round the hospital. (Miss Nightingale generally visited her cases by night). We went round the whole of the second storey, into many of the wards, and into one of the upper corridors. It seemed an endless walk, not easily forgotten. As we tip-toed along, the silence was profound; very seldom did a moan or a cry from those multitudes of deeply suffering ones fall on our ears. A dim light burned here and there. Miss Nightingale carried her lantern, which she would set down before bending over any of the patients. I much admired Miss Nightingale's manner to the men, it was tender and kind. All the corridors were thickly lined with beds, laid on low trestles a few inches from the ground. The whole building, which has since been reckoned to house 1,700 patients with a minimum of comfort, had to hold nearly 3,000."

"It seems" (to quote again from her book) "simply impossible to describe Scutari Hospital at this time. Far abler pens have tried, and all in some measure failed; for what an eye-witness saw was beyond description. Even those who read the harrowing accounts in 'The Times' could not have imagined the full horror of the reality. When we awoke in the morning, our hearts sank at the thought of the woe we must witness during the day, at night we lay down, wearied beyond measure, not so much from physical fatigue as from the heart-break occasioned by living amidst the mass of hopeless suffering. Among 1,500 sick committed to the care of three women, it was grievous to pass by so many on whom we longed to wait, cases of spotted fever in Corridor A, and see their poor hands grasping the sheets, and the poor sufferer, in his delirium, refusing the medicine on which his life hung."

After a make-shift stove had been invented out of a cocoa-canister, in an effort to provide beef-tea for those patients who could not swallow the food provided by Army Authority, the Inspector-General issued an order that no cooking was to be done in the wards. "It was heart-rendering then," Miss Taylor

Fanny Taylor as a lady volunteer Nurse with Florence Nightingale
in the Crimea, 1854-55.

Mother Magdalen Taylor years after.

tells us, "to hear those poor patients, accustomed to the beef-tea, cry out in their feverish voices: 'Give me a drink of water for the love of God!' Water we dare not give any. The Assistant Surgeons were very sorry, they said, but they had no power to help the situation — their duty was to obey."

After a short period at Scutari, Miss Taylor and two other volunteers went to the aid of Miss Stanley at Koulali, about five miles north of Scutari. The state of affairs here was not much different from there, but the affection and admiration inspired by Miss Stanley made hardship less intolerable. Although her health suffered for it, she refused absolutely to have any luxuries in which all those about her could not share. Her whole bearing and respect towards her fellow-workers recalls the poet's lines: "The little more, and how much it is, the little less and what worlds away!"

A Miss Smyth who had come to Koulali with Miss Taylor, and who was the stay of the nursing party, fell seriously ill. She almost lived in her fever ward, her whole thought seemed to be for her patients. Just at this time, news came from England that a third party of ladies and paid nurses had just sailed for the East and would arrive within a fortnight's or three weeks' time. What a joy for Miss Taylor to hear that her sister Charlotte was among the number. Poor Miss Smyth's last conscious words, before delirium set in, were to express her pleasure at the good news of the increase of staff so badly needed. On March 27th the Chaplain of the Church of England administered the Communion to her. Miss Smyth died on the 28th and was buried the following day. "The coffin," Miss Taylor writes, "covered with a white sheet, was carried up the hill by the orderlies of her ward, followed by the officers and ourselves. We laid her on the green hillside, far from the old church-yards of England; but we felt that the ground was sacred in some sense because of the noble and brave who were buried there. The sudden chill which comes at sunset in the East fell on us as we stood around the grave; the sun was sinking and lighting up Constantinople, the Bosphorus and the distant hills with its parting glow. A little wooden cross was planted on the grave, one of those so familiar in the great wars of our own day, but later a stone monument was erected, bearing her name and the date of her death."

25

"No word of praise follows," writes Miss Taylor, "and thus it is ever meet that a Christian should rest; he needs it not. For her the world's applause has passed away, as shadows flee before the sun. But we leave her in the humble hope that she will one day hear the words: 'Inasmuch as ye did it unto the least of these, ye did it unto Me'."

Chapter 4.

THE LIGHT THAT LED

"To seek is: 'to look for, to search for, to try to find out'," replied the Rector of Stoke Rochford, in answer to his child's question, on that now far-off Monday morning of 1838. There is no evidence that Fanny did much "seeking" for a Faith that was not hers, nor that she had made any contacts with Catholics prior to her volunteering for the Crimea. She acknowledges being shocked at hearing of Lady Georgiana Fullerton's conversion, and at the number of "goings over to Rome" as a result of the Oxford Movement and of the Gorham case; the greatest shock of all being that of her own 'spiritual director' — Mr. Dodsworth — whom she had considered the very essence of sincerity and loyalty to High Church principles. Fanny did not consider these changes as 'defections' or 'falls', but wondered how they could happen, as she reveals the effect on herself: "I never felt the same of the Church of England afterwards, vague doubts used to come into my mind, but I was too young to understand."

The fact also that Pusey or Keble did not succumb to the 'terrible spiritual epidemic' of Oxford was no small encouragement in her case, and Fanny, with her Mother and Charlotte, went on and clung to their High Church views. Yet by April 1855, Fanny Taylor had found, or rather must we say the Divine Hunter of souls, who found Paul in the street called Strait, and who sought and found Ignatius of Loyola in his hospital bed after the battle of Pampeluna, found Fanny in the Koulali hospital wards. How did it all come about? Miss Smyth's death had certainly no little part in the drama; then also, Fanny worked hand in hand with those whom she called: "My dear Sisters, my beloved Sisters," one of whom she worked immediately under. She became a very dear friend, and remained a special friend all her life — Mother Frances Bridgeman of Kinsale. Long years afterwards, as Mother Magdalen Taylor, and after having met many personalities in many lands, she was often heard to say: "Mother Bridgeman was the noblest soul I have ever met." In the wards, Fanny was fascinated by the relations existing between the nuns and the Irish Catholic soldiers. Often at night when the poor patient was dying, or unable to speak, she would see him look up into a Sister's face and seize the crucifix at her side with his dying gasp, to kiss the image of his crucified Saviour for perhaps the last time in life. She did not know as yet what these well-instructed, pure-minded men knew, that a Plenary Indulgence at the hour of death was attached to that loving, sorrowing kiss. These brave men were dying for a cause not theirs, and this latter fact evoked her pity and her reverence the more. Fanny contrasts the splendid order and management of the General Hospital at Koulali, under the Reverend Mother of Kinsale, to that of the Hospital of Scutari which she had left. In an old letter from one of the Sisters, Miss Taylor is said to have been too much in sympathy with the nuns. The suspicions of the Protestant chaplains were not only directed towards the nuns, but also towards any who were friendly with them. Mother Bridgeman was considered "a very dangerous person," and so was Miss Taylor because of her friendship with the Sisters. Again, it was said of Miss Taylor that to one of the ladies and to the parsons, "she was far more obnoxious for her Catholic tendencies than any of the hired nurses who had brought discredit on the work by their folly or misconduct." Even Florence Nightingale, so Catholic-minded at home, seemed to sacrifice her religious views for the sake of the great work she had undertaken in the Crimea. She gave the Protestant chaplains no cause for uneasiness. The case of Miss Stanley also, who had to return to England on hospital business before the arrival of Charlotte Taylor's party, and who had been received into the Church prior to her departure by Father Ronan, S.J., was another coal added to the fire of suspicion and prejudice, and brought forth a public enquiry as to who were the proselytizers; the Sisters and their High Church friends were completely exonerated.

The third party arrived on Easter Monday at 2.0 p.m. One can imagine Fanny Taylor's joy at welcoming her sister Charlotte, and vice-versa. With the group came a priest who had joined the party at Marseilles, and, as Miss Taylor thought it proper to suggest his dining with Father Ronan, S.J., "the whole party," she writes to her Mother, (all Protestants) "burst upon me in chorus: 'Oh, do let Father Woollett dine with us. He is our guardian angel, he is everything to us, we could never have got on without him'." So he stayed, and kept the whole party in roars of laughter. A parson and his wife and baby travelled with the passengers from Marseilles. The baby fell ill after putting to sea. The captain, on hearing that Father Woollett was a doctor as well as a priest, called him to the little patient, whom he cured, and the parents became the priest's greatest friends. The worried captain called Father Woollett a second time, saying: "Two of these ladies I have charge of have been sick ever since we left London, they say they are dying and must be put ashore at Malta. What can I do? They are in my charge, help me to bring them to Constantinople. Can't you help me?" Father Woollett went straight to the ladies, made them come with him on deck, gave each an arm, telling them they must obey, and, not heeding their protest, marched them along the deck to their accompanying cries of "We can't, we're dying!" Their cries were in vain, Father Woollett was obdurate; the spectacle was too ridiculous for words, and soon, amid shrieks of laughter from the onlookers, the sick ladies confessed themselves cured of their seasickness! The priest shared a cabin with an old Colonel, who was overheard saying: "Father Woollett, rather than manage those women as you have to do, I'd command a regiment of Bashi-Bazouks!"

And now comes the great event of her life for Fanny Taylor — "the touch of the Master's Hand," on her heart-strings, as sudden as it was certain. Father Sydney Woollett was the man destined by God as His delegate to receive her into the one true Fold. That very week, she had to confess to herself: "They are all right (the Irish Catholic soldiers) and I am all wrong." She would contact Father Woollett. He only arrived at Koulali on Easter Monday, and on the following Saturday, April 14th, he received her formal abjuration of heresy, heard her confession in the Camp Kitchen, the only available spot, and she was a Catholic! Father Woollett had to leave for the front next day, leaving his convert filled with holy peace, to make her First Communion at the hands of Father Ronan, S.J., on the Feast of the Good Shepherd, the second Sunday after Easter, April 22nd — a feast forever held memorable in the Congregation of the Poor Servants of the Mother of God.

Father Woollett, during his week's stay, examined Miss Taylor's case and saw that her reasons were solid, that Divine Grace had guided her and that external influences had played a salutary part. He found that Fanny Taylor was in love with her God, as she had ever been with His whole creation, that the daily lives of the nursing Sisters and of the Irish Catholic soldiers were living witnesses of the Faith they professed. Sitting by the bedside of those poor patients to write their letters home, such phrases as: "Tell my mother (father, sister, wife, fiancée, etc.) that I am dying happily, that God and His Mother will take my place in the home, and that I am well prepared," were dictated almost daily to Fanny in the wards. A Dublin boy, in particular, had told her to tell his young wife that he would watch over their baby from Heaven, that he had made a "general" to Father Ronan and was sure of the Lord's mercy. Fanny in all simplicity asked what a "general" was, thinking it to be a last will or testament that ought to have had witnesses! "Ah, Miss," he replied, "this is a grand confession of all you ever did in your life that pained God. God gives you pardon through the priest, and you are as light as a feather after it, as happy as a lark and as strong as Hercules." Another Wexford boy had taught Fanny the seven mysteries of the Dolour Rosary, and Mother Frances Bridgeman herself taught her how to meditate on the Magnificat. (Little did Fanny dream then of all she would owe Wexford in the years to be).

The following passage speaks for itself: "Father Woollett did not convert Fanny Taylor. The work of conversion had already been done by the sick and dying Irish soldiers, by the nuns and by the utter inadequacy of the Church of England to satisfy the spiritual needs of a woman who saw life, for the first time, stripped of its accustomed conventions, and who had the courage and the intelligence to face reality. God in His Providence sent her the right man at the right time. His shrewd knowledge of human nature enabled him to see the sterling qualities of this young woman. He did not hesitate; detailed instruction could follow later (which it did under Dr. Manning himself) if she lived to receive it. No time was to be lost, with shot and shell and death all around them. Father Woollett was determined that if she were to die, she should die a Catholic." (Life of Mother Magdalen Taylor by Father Devas, S.J., page 42).

Reaction was sure to set in after a week of such tension and strain. Charlotte writes to her Mother that Fanny needs some rest, and attributes her temporary indisposition to worry and work before the much-needed help came, with the arrival of her party. Charlotte will know the real cause when her own time comes; she is designed by God to follow her sister into the Church in two years' time. Mrs. Taylor is to know nothing of Fanny's change-over as yet, she herself must be the narrator of what she foresees to be a painful story.

After the Battle of Inkermann, and being attacked by fever, Father Woollett, after some months, was sent back to Koulali for a rest. To Fanny's great joy he continued her instructions, as she describes it, "walking by the Bosphorus." Some of these instructions she never forgot. He talked of prayer, vocation, etc., and gave her his confidence, wholly, doubtless, to strengthen her and to enable her to choose the better part. His story is so beautiful that she gives it all. "He told me of his own vocation — of his exceedingly happy married life in the world so soon cut short — of his nursing his wife day and night for a year — of his despair at her death — his rushing off to the Jesuits to be received — the stern refusal — he was told his motive was too human, and that he was unable as yet to judge rightly — if in earnest he was to come back in a year; that year of waiting was spent chiefly in converting his sister-in-law. Then at last he had entered the Society of Jesus, and he told me how completely his heart's wound had healed, how the love of God had filled his soul, and how religious life was far sweeter than any earthly joy. He told me also of the trials of the novitiate — how he was taught obedience. These were our grave talks. I was very young, and he told me all this that it might lead me to choose the better part.

"We still lived under the 'Reign of Terror,' but Father Woollett disapproved of this, and thought we ought "to take the bull by the horns." These were hard times for us Catholics. Mass was said in a sort of closet opening into the community-room. We had an orange coloured vestment which did duty alike for fast and feast. Confession were made at any moment, and in any spot where a priest could be safely found. It was fine training for a convert."

Father Woollett was full of zeal for God, reckless of his own life in the service of others, and a true and devoted friend of the nuns. He was always the same. There could not be a better type of the soldier of Christ than dear Father Sydney Woollett.

Fanny met him again in London after the War, on his way to the West Indies, and went to Stonyhurst in 1893 to see the old man, and found him as full of fun as ever. In the intervening years after the Battle of Balaclava, he had been appointed Vicar-General at Georgetown, Demerara, till 1862, when he was appointed Chaplain to the Forces and missionary in Jamaica till 1892, when he returned to England and died at Stonyhurst on 6th February, 1898.

As winter approached, it became evident that the services of the volunteer nurses were no longer necessary at the Crimea. They had done their work and done it well, and on 22nd November, 1855, Fanny Taylor, Charlotte and the other lady-volunteers on board the "Hydaspes", left the shore of the Crimea for ever, cheered, as they put to sea, by the hundreds of brave men they had served so well and with such kindly dignity and courtesy during their time in the East.

The journey home was uneventful, and nothing on record describes the arrival at London Bridge Station, but we do know that when Fanny and her sister returned, the family had taken up residence at Houghton Place, Somerstown. Nor have we any knowledge of what passed between Fanny and her Mother in that necessarily dramatic and awkward scene — the revelation of her conversion to the Catholic Faith. It may be assumed with certainty that Charlotte, who was so soon to follow her sister's example, helped out with the difficulty.

Fanny almost immediately put herself under the direction of Dr. Manning, who had returned from Rome and was Rector of St. Mary's, Bayswater. The future Cardinal, the advocate of the poor, the downtrodden and the lonely, was not slow to recognize the fine though yet unformed character of his spiritual pupil, and having completed her religious instruction, put her in the way of many charitable undertakings. He found in her an invaluable support for his work in the parish, as he will later, when, as Cardinal Archbishop of Westminster he, with Mother Magdalen, will establish the cradle of her infant congregation under his protection in the Archdiocese, and she will find in him a loyal and encouraging patron and father until his death.

The following letter, written by a Miss Gunning and quoted by Father Devas in his book, reveals much of what life was like at Houghton Place, until at least 1859:

"It was in 1858-9 that I had the happiness of spending a good deal of time with dear Fanny Taylor. We came to know each other through Dr. Manning and Father Dillon. How kind dear Fanny was to me, no one can tell — she so much older — so clever and so serious — I, all fun and laughter, knowing nothing in comparison. These years were for her a season of comparative rest, after the extraordinary fatigues consequent on her work during the Crimean War. They were also her first years as a Catholic, and were passed in retirement with her family. I often remarked that in her home life, although a recent convert, as was her sister Charlotte, they lived in the greatest harmony and affection with all the members of the family, particularly with their dear mother, who felt the change of religion, yet never showed it. All was love and perfect peace.

The sisters rose early and attended Mass daily. The morning hours were devoted to writing; in the after part of the day, hospitals and poor persons were visited. I never saw her without real work on hand.

It was at this time that "Tyburn" was written. I remember with what pleasure I listened to the manuscript, the chapters of the day's work being read in the evening, and how it consoled the dear writer to see my tears flow as the beautiful passages came forth, so humbly and yet so wonderfully read by her.

She used to come into our house, and we read French books together, as I was pretty well up in it; and then I went a good

33

deal to Houghton Place, and went everywhere about London with her, to sermons, to see people, to visit hospitals and work-houses.

It was a happy time, and her affection was mine, and I loved her more than any person I ever knew. It was an amusement to us to laugh about the odd quaint sayings of the poor. She used to enjoy and laugh to tears over their jokes, and the little journeys and mistakes we made in going about.

Marylebone and St. Pancras' Workhouses were visited frequently. They were in a very bad state at that time, and the poor inmates often ill-treated. These visits were the only bright spots in their miserable lives.

Dr. Manning helped her to find an outlet for her zeal, and in the Lent of 1859 she obtained permission for the use of a schoolroom at Bayswater, and there on Sunday afternoons assembled a number of poor girls — young servants chiefly — to help them to prepare for their Easter duty. After catechism and instruction on the Sacraments they had tea and bread and treacle, which Fanny had prepared — she sitting in the midst and taking it with them. They would then go all together to the evening service at St. Mary of the Angels.

She spent that Holy Week in retreat, rising very early on Good Friday morning, she was at the Sepulchre at 4.30."

In a letter of appreciation written from Rome to her niece, Mother Magdalen Aimée, His Eminence, Cardinal Gasquet wrote in 1926: "I fancy there are few now living that can remember her before God called her to be the Foundress of your Congregation, which under His Providence and protection has done so much good for the Church in many countries. I can say that I remember her at Bayswater, where, in company with the converts of the early sixties, she frequently came to see Dr. Manning; it was before her sister married Mr., or as we always called him, Dr. Dean. Though of course as a youngster, I had never anything to say to the Taylors personally, I used frequently to see her, and years afterwards I remember talking to her in Rome of my recollection of those days, and she was good enough to say that she recalled having seen me at St. Mary of the Angels, Bayswater."

Before the Benedictines of the English Province had their

foundation in Rome, the Fathers found a "pied-a-terre" in the extern quarters of the Convent of the Poor Servants of the Mother of God, and Abbot Gasquet was resident there for a time — a kind and helpful friend of the Foundress and her Community, and later, the venerated Cardinal Protector of their Institute.

Charlotte Taylor, who had been such a comfort to her sister at Koulali in the crisis of her religious life, had also answered the call of the Good Shepherd, and was received into the Church at Farm Street on August 8th, 1857, by Father T. Brownbill, S.J. She loved to attribute her final decision to a moment of grace in Southwark Cathedral, when, during the singing of "Hail, Queen of Heaven," the whole congregation bent the knee in reverence at the words: "Homage we pay on bended knee."

Two years after her conversion, Charlotte married Edward Dean, Fellow of All Souls, Oxford, and later Vicar of Lewknor in Somerset; he gave up all that life promised to become a soldier of Christ. Dean did not become a Catholic to marry Charlotte Taylor, nor did she to marry him. In fact, such was his fervour and the strength of his convictions that Manning and others thought the priesthood was his destiny. He himself, however, realized the difference between his Anglican orders as a profession, and the Catholic priesthood as a divine-given vocation, which was not his to choose. After much prayer and indecision, God sent Charlotte Taylor into his life, and he recognized God's Will in the event. One son and three daughters were born of this marriage. The son — Cyril Dean — was educated at Cardinal Newman's School, afterwards studied Law as a profession, and was in later years often consulted at the London offices of Randolf and Dean by his "Aunt Fanny", when as Mother Magdalen she needed legal advice on her purchases or other business problems. Cyril Dean was a fine type of the straightforward, down-to-earth Catholic layman, having had for his exemplar his saintly Father, whose holy life was crowned by long years of suffering, during which he became a helpless invalid. He was a personal friend of Father Faber, whose "Foot of the Cross" was a solace in his many years of resigned disability, and this holy resignation was evidenced by his inscription on the fly-leaf of this famous book:

"Juxta crucem tecum stare,
Et me tibi sociare,
In planctu desidero."

Of his three daughters, one, Lily Dean, married a Mr. Mason. Amy became a nun in the Congregation founded by her Aunt Fanny. She made her first Vows in the Roman House, as did some other Sisters in the early days of its foundation, and was received in private audience by His Holiness, Leo XIII. To her dying day the Pope's Blessing and his words in French: "Now you will be good, you will persevere, you will be faithful to the great grace God has given you," were an inspiration. As Mother Magdalen Aimée, she served God in the Congregation for seventy years, and died at St. Mary's Roehampton, in 1954, at the age of ninety. Her love for the poor and suffering was very great; her attention to the sick and wounded soldiers of World War I at Queen Mary's Hospital, Roehampton, was even outdone by her compassionate care and loving solicitude towards the victims there of World War II, more especially towards the poor exiled Polish soldiers, whose case was unspeakably sad.

Edward Dean's third daughter, who thought mistakenly for a time that the religious state was for her also, did great work for God as a most saintly lady in the world. Her devotedness and practical charity to the poor and lonely were proverbial, and her helpful aid towards Church funds at home and on the mission secured her many Masses at her death.

Chapter 5.

THE WOMAN AND THE WORKER

When Fanny Taylor found the treasure of the Catholic Faith on the shores of the Bosphorus, she thought, perhaps, that she had found a clear and easy path to her sanctification, and that once she had explained all to her mother, events would develop simply and sympathetically, especially as Charlotte also had now become a Catholic, and her husband was an excellent example of one. Allusion has already been made to the unfortunate financial condition of the family, caused by some imprudent investments of a brother. This brother, George, with his brother-in-law and with both their young families, had bravely made for Australia, and were doing well there. Charlotte on her marriage had left Houghton Place for her new home. Mortimer, the only brother at home, was a useless and improvident man for the management of affairs. "Spoiled by his mother" was the general accusation against him; a theorist who never put his theories into practice, at times he would be an extreme ritualist, then a pathetic agnostic, and up against every form of belief. By the end of 1859, it fell to Fanny to have to assume multiple responsibilities, if things were to right themselves at Houghton Place. With her ever invincible, unflagging energy and courage, and her great trust in God, she took on the role of manager and "Estate Agent" in the settling of two or three properties which involved much legal business at the time. Added to this were her constant care and anxiety for her mother, her work for the poor, her Sunday School, and her instruction of converts, with which Dr. Manning entrusted her, after her return from Paris. Miss Gunning's letter shed much light on Fanny's life in those days, and the "writing" alluded to would have been her famous book:

37

"Eastern Hospitals and English Nurses," which Miss Stanley, on their return from the Crimea, had begged her to write, to show up the desperate conditions under which that unfortunate campaign was carried through. The book served its purpose and ran into three editions, and was a best-seller for a time. Fanny's next book was "Tyburn", in which she does honour to her favourite among the English martyrs, whose name she will give later to one of her first and very accomplished English Sisters — Sister M. Campion, of the Roman House, to whom reference will be made in a later chapter.

"Tyburn" was the means used by God to bring its author into contact with Lady Georgiana Fullerton, who was destined by Him to become her lifelong friend and benefactress, until her death. "Tyburn" ran into many editions, and even as late as 1953 a further edition was requested, for which the Right Reverend Monsignor Duchemin, the then Rector of the Beda College, Rome, gladly and fittingly wrote the Preface.

All her work in London did not prevent Fanny from accompanying her dear friend, Miss Gunning, to her newly-chosen home, the Convent of the Sisters of Charity in the Rue de Bac, Paris, where she made her Novitiate, and became a holy and devoted Sister of Charity. Fanny knew Paris well, was fluent in the French Language, and was glad to renew her acquaintance with the daughters of St. Vincent de Paul, many of whom she had met during the Crimean War. Had Fanny, one wonders, a secret, secondary motive for this trip? The sequel will show, as on her return she must have had a talk with her mother, and gave vent fully to her own trend of thought, as a result of the visit. She was more and more inclined to think that God's choice for her was the religious state, the life in a convent, the Vows, the seclusion, the gift of her whole being to that God, the love and thirst of Whose Sacred Heart for mankind she longed to assuage with the total surrender of her life. Against this forceful attrait was the duty she owed to her all-too-sensitive, scrupulous mother, a quotation from one of whose letters at this time bears on the situation: "May God in His great Mercy comfort you when I am gone by the blessed reflection of how you tried to fondle and cheer your old Mother on her weary way, and would do anything in your power to give her pleasure and see

38

her look happy. Dear Fanny, it is so selfish of me to keep you from a devoted life, for I begin to see that you are more likely to be happy in a convent than at home; but it is such a struggle to say: 'Yes, go.' I think I can never say so, and death alone can set you free from me. Oh, why should it be so?"

In the autumn of the same year, a visit of some weeks to Boulogne was undertaken by Mrs. Taylor, accompanied by Lucy, Charlotte, and her husband, Fanny in her role of guide willingly accompanying them. Mrs. Taylor was much impressed by all the real Catholic life lived by the French, and especially was this evident in the Churches on the Feast of the Assumption. She had never been in a Catholic Church before, and contrasts the feeling of "a holy something" which she experienced, to the coldness and apathy of the Protestant Church. Many prejudices are evidently removed, in spite of her blaming herself for the momentary temptation of belittling her own church. So great were these impressions and her appreciation of all she saw, that she consents to accompany Fanny to the Rue de Bac, and there, at the Novitiate, they interview Père Etienne, the Superior-General, and the Sister Superior of the Convent. The conclusion reached was that Fanny should return early in the following year, 1861, and pay a prolonged visit, and see for herself if her vocation were to be a Sister of Charity. The strong attraction was there, but the peace of mind that should accompany it was not yet hers. Father Gallwey, S.J., who directed her spiritually, thought that Fanny's natural attraction to this Order, her great and tender love for Christ's Poor, her skill in dealing with the young, the suffering, the old and the lonely were, with her almost perfect knowledge of the language, sure signs of her vocation. So, in a spirit of humble submission and self-surrender, and with a will determined to follow whatever God's Will should indicate, Fanny set out for the Paris Novitiate on January 7th, 1861. After a period of weeks, however, and as she had become more and more attracted to the life, Père Etienne himself and the Sister Superior were convinced that her vocation was not for them. Fanny, ever in accord with the Divine Will, was puzzled and disappointed at the decision. She loved every moment she had spent there, she had thrown herself wholeheartedly into the work of splendid charity, she loved the Sisters and they loved her, she was ready

39

to sacrifice her Mother, her literary work — all. Yet God did not grant her desire. She packed up and returned to London, to the delight of Dr. Manning, who called at Houghton Place almost immediately, and gave her the contents of Père Etienne's letter to him: "Miss Taylor was not for the Rue de Bac, she would be wasted. Her personality, so strong, so sure of itself, so English, was needed for England. Even now Miss Taylor seems a finished product to work for God in your country, that so badly needs such women of faith and love of God." "Well said!" exclaimed Manning, pocketing the letter, and Fanny must have said her "Fiat voluntas Tua" simultaneously, as she resolves to take up her local apostolate anew, and pray for light. She would see Father Gallwey, who, Dr. Manning assured her, would agree also, for surely, with such a background as hers, and with such a history behind her, this decision of such a holy man as Père Etienne was no uncertain pointer.

Meanwhile Fanny hears that Lady Georgiana Fullerton wishes to see her. "Would a visit be possible, and when?" A real thrill this! She had known Lady Georgiana "by sight" for many years, and, as already stated, had read and re-read her book, "Ellen Middleton", written before Lady Georgiana's conversion and her own consequent shock in 1846.

Fanny's own account of this first meeting is best given here: " 'Tyburn' had just been published, and I heard she wished to see me. I called on her in Chapel Street with a beating heart; I could hardly believe I was to see her whom I had so long loved and revered. I can see her now welcoming me with the manner peculiar to herself — a mixture of childlike simplicity and high-bred courtesy — her eyes shone — her face lighted up with a smile. She praysed 'Tyburn'. She said: 'I could hardly lay it down when once I had begun, and as to the second part, I could not stop till I had finished it.'

No praise gave me such joy as this, and encouraged me to go on writing. Very soon we became intimate, and she becaame part of my life. The two interests we had in common were literary work and work among the poor.

She encouraged me to write as much as possible. She was always ready to help me in all my undertakings, giving me her own writings for nothing, though it was always a joy to her

The Church at Stoke Rochford and the pulpit where
little Fanny "did the lie".

Rev. Father Woollett, S.J., who received Fanny into the Catholic
Church, in the Camp kitchen at Koulali, April 14th, 1855.

when these writings were paid for by publishers, because then she had money to give away. This always struck me."

How wonderfully human, and, if one may say with reverence, even diplomatic and humorous the omnipotent God can be in His dealings with human souls, when His Will has marked them out for the accomplishment of His divine designs. He inspires them with desires and wishes that He Himself may fulfil them, and in this fulfilment His own divine plans are accomplished in their regard.

Lady Georgiana Fullerton (1812-1885), daughter of the first Earl Granville, wrote her first novel ("Ellen Middleton") in 1844, while still an Anglican. Fanny Taylor read the book while still in her early teens, and confesses having loved it for its singular beauty of style and its exaltation of High Church principles. She thought of the author as a most lovable and ideal lady, and enshrined her in her heart as a real heroine, hence her shock in 1846 at hearing that her "heroine" had "gone over to Rome," followed in 1848 by her own pastor and director — Mr. Dodsworth, and many others, as a result of the Gorham affair. Miss Sellon's Sisterhood was Fanny's next trial and failure; then there were the few years of her apostolate with her poor and her running of the Ragged School. The next call was the Crimea, and the grace of conversion, followed by a further course of religious instruction under Dr. Manning, and her renewed and fervent apostolate in the London slums, hospitals and workhouses of the period. Then there was her literary work, which took much of her time; added to all was the very necessary work with estate agents, legal advisers, etc., in the setting up of the family affairs which fell to her lot as the most competent, in fact the only competent one of the family left to deal with such business. Then there were her journeys to Paris and her stay at the Rue de Bac — another frustration, but which, as Dr. Manning interpreted it, "was a further pointer to the destined road."

Now her meeting with Lady Georgiana Fullerton, as the result of her first Catholic novel, "Tyburn", was a new event in her life, and one that was to have its influence on both their lives for many years to come. Dr. Manning, Fathers Gallwey and Clare, S.J., were the God-given supporters and spiritual

41

advisers in the new venture, in which Fanny was destined to play the chief part for the years ahead, years so full of spiritual fruit in general that one becomes breathless with amazement at the power of prayer and the work of the Holy Spirit in the latter half especially of nineteenth-century England.

When on September 29th, 1850, the saintly and sorely-tried Pontiff, Pius IX, issued his Papal Brief restoring the English Hierarchy and creating Dr. Wiseman its first Head, conferring on him the Cardinal's Hat a few days later, Manning was not yet a Catholic and Fanny Taylor was happy in her High Church practices and in her many social activities for the poor in London, while Lady Georgiana herself had been a Catholic for only four years — and yet these were they destined by God to blaze the trail in the years to be and sow the seeds of a Religious Congregation in that England of the Reformation, whose "Second Spring" had already budded forth with fair promise of a rich harvest.

Henry Edward Manning was in his 24th year when Fanny Taylor was born. He was educated at Harrow prior to his admission to Baliol in 1826, where he took a First in Greats. In 1832 he became a Fellow of Merton and received Anglican Orders within the year. He married the daughter of his Rector at Lavington, where he worked for seventeen years, and became eventually Archdeacon of Chichester. His wife died in the memorable year of Queen Victoria's accession, 1837, and, Tractarian as he was of no great colour, the Gorham affair having finally enlightened and disillusioned him, he was received into the Catholic Church, was ordained by Cardinal Wiseman, and said his first Mass at Farm Street, after which he set off for the Accademia in Rome, where he received a Roman Doctorate. While in Rome, as already stated, Manning, the great friend of both Florence Nightingale and Miss Stanley, was instrumental, with Dr. Wiseman, Dr. Grant of Southwark and Archbishop Cullen of Dublin, in getting chaplains and nursing nuns for the Crimea Campaign, that campaign which was destined to give England its great convert Foundress, in whom and in whose work the future "Poor Man's Cardinal" was to be paternally interested to the end of his life.

A painful and rather unusual event about the end of the

year 1866 brought Fanny into touch with Cardinal (as yet Father) Newman. As heretofore related, Emma Taylor had become a member of Miss Sellon's Sisterhood in 1848. Evidently, of late years all intercourse between her and her family had been forbidden, and poor Mrs. Taylor grew more and more worried about her daughter. Fanny, determined to put an end to what she considered "an outrageous lack of charity," set out with her Mother to Ascot to find out the real cause. What was their surprise to find that Emma had been sent to the Sandwich Islands, and this without a word to her Mother. Fanny wrote to Dr. Newman, and begged him to become intermediary with Dr. Pusey to get the prohibition removed. After some time Pusey answered Newman, saying that his office was not to be a channel, especially as the subject was a disagreeable one. There came a second letter to Fanny from the kind-hearted Newman himself, in which he says: "I cannot believe that Dr. Pusey knew, when he wrote, that your sister had left the country; it is all very cruel; and I will not allow myself to think that he has that power over his convents, which you think he has." The future Cardinal must have been instrumental himself in getting Mrs. Taylor in touch with the Bishop of Honolulu, who assured her of her daughter's happiness on her far-off mission-field, and saw to it that she was allowed to take on anew a reasonable correspondence with her Mother.

The result of Fanny's first meeting with Lady Georgiana Fullerton has been given in Fanny's own words a little earlier in this chapter, and the next very important event is her long-looked-forward-to visit to Ireland — that Ireland she had grown to love in the hospitals of the Crimea. The visit had a twofold purpose. In 1862 she had become proprietor of "The Lamp," in which she was now determined to insert a series of articles dealing with that country and its people, to whom she owed so much, in order that, understanding its national conditions and questions, and the character of its people better herself, she might be able to destroy those bitter prejudices against the nation which were so widespread in England at the time, and so detrimental to the cause of the Catholic religion. These articles were subsequently published by Longmans, Green & Co. in 1867 under the title "Irish Homes and Irish Hearts," and dedicated "To those who under strange skies, and amid the still stranger scenes of 'Eastern Hospitals' first taught me the worth of Irish character, the warmth of Irish hearts, and the depth of Irish faith."

The second and very important reason for her Irish visit was the result of further meetings with Dr. Manning, Fathers Gallwey and Clare, S.J., and Lady Georgiana Fullerton, who were unanimous in their decision that Fanny, while in Ireland, should visit Irish convents and study their many charitable institutions, and see the self-sacrificing work of priests and nuns and of the laity in every class of life, and also ascertain if any Orders of Sisters could be induced to take up work in England.

So Fanny, with a glad heart, and armed with introductory letters from Dr. Manning to the Irish Hierarchy, set out for Dublin at the end of February. She spends the greater part of Lent in research work for her book. She writes to her Mother from different places during her tour, and records having met Reverend Father Ronan, S.J., who gave her the 'Bread of Angels' for the first time at the Crimea. She goes to Drogheda and as far north as Newry, where she lodges close to the Convent of the Sisters of Mercy, "who are so kind," she tells her Mother. She will visit the Poor Clares also, whom she has grown to love. She writes next from Cork and says: "I hope that I have done a good deal for 'The Lamp' already." The next letter is from her beloved Kinsale. One can well imagine the mutual joy of those two great souls at this meeting. Working hand in hand amid indescribable difficulties as they did at Koulali, they will have much to recall. And now Mother Frances Bridgeman, labouring happily for God in the bosom of her beloved Community, listens to the post-Crimea story, with all its disappointments, as recounted by Fanny, who, still "seeking", will call at Kinsale again on many a later date, having "found" the unmistaken signpost that led to the Divine Will in her regard.

From Kinsale Fanny makes for Killarney and Kenmare. She is enchanted by the view of the Lakes, surrounded as they are by beautiful mountains and rich scenery. She is easily persuaded by a lady friend at the hotel to accompany her for a short row next morning on the Lower Lake. As they made out somewhat from the shore, the sky darkened, the wind rose and the waves threatened. Fanny, fearing some confusion, turned to the oarsman and asked: "Do you think we'll be drowned, Tom?" (She had heard him called "Tom" by her friend). "If you are not meant to be drowned, Miss, all the water in the Lake won't drown you," answered Tom, with his strong faith in Predestination, "and besides, Miss, I always wear the brown scapular." It was Fanny's first lesson on St. Simon Stock's gift from the Queen of Carmel, and of her care of all who wear it. Soon the tempest subsided. Fanny was the richer for the row, and loved to recount this experience in after years, and how it was the immediate cause of her enrolment in the brown scapular in Clarendon Street, on her return to Dublin, en route for London, in the autumn of 1867, just as "Irish Homes and Irish Hearts" had been published.

Chapter 6.

IDEAS AND ACTUATION

Fanny, on her return from her Irish tour, was more and more convinced that her life's work was to be the service of God in His Poor, but that He was demanding more than personal dedication to the work. Time was passing, and some decision had to be reached; she had worked for and served her beloved Poor before and since her Crimean days, and her love for them was something much greater than that kind-hearted pity which gets them many benefactors at times, but at times, no. To Fanny Taylor, all her life, the Poor were not merely people to be helped on occasions. They were, and should ever be, the social companions of Jesus, Mary and Joseph, living amid poverty, neglect and misery in the London and other city slums. Something more than mere occasional alms had to be thought out. The conditions for improvement had to be considered from many standpoints, and then also organized efficiently if the desired results in the uplifting of the spiritual and material lives of the people were to be achieved. Like St. Teresa, Fanny was never daunted at the prospect of poverty or an empty purse. When a great project lay ahead that would eventually lead souls to God, "The work is His," she would say, "we'll follow where He leads," and follow she did to her last gasp in her "seeking the Divine Will and its complete fulfilment in her life. During her absence in Ireland, a journey was being planned by Dr. Manning, Father Gallwey and Father Clare, in connection with a certain congregation of religious in Poland, of which Lady Georgiana had lately heard, and when Fanny returned to London, they were to discuss its work and spirit as it might be suitable for London. Full of the idea, Lady Georgiana had written to the Cardinal Archbishop of Posen, and from him had received a copy of their Rule, and much encouragement for their project. Fanny was also advised to visit a community at Saffron Hill, which did extensive charity among the working-classses. A Father Biemans, whom she had met, also encouraged her greatly, and when her visit to Poland was planned, gave her the address of Sisters at Antwerp, who became real friends and wise advisers in the first years of her work as Foundress, though they themselves had been founded only a few years before.

Prayers were redoubled for God's blessing on the planned journey, schemes were discussed, but nothing came to a head till January 1868. Some scrappy records, drawn up much later by Fanny (then Mother Magdalen) describe these earliest moves.

"In January 1868, I met with a person who, I thought, would be capable of beginning the work; and also with a priest (Father Biemans) who, I thought, would take an interest in the undertaking. During the course of the Spring I spoke to him on the subject, and he encouraged us to persevere.

On the 1st May, being also the First Friday of the month, Lady Georgiana, this priest and myself began a novena to the Sacred Heart of Jesus and the Immaculate Heart of Mary for the success of the undertaking.

In the course of the Summer a young woman named Mary Ward testified a desire to help in the project. We began to search for a house in the parish of Saffron Hill, but could not find one. Finally, on St. Raphael's Day, October 24th, we took possession of four small rooms in a little court leading out of Fleet Street."

Following on the occupation of the rooms off Fleet Street, the Annals continue:

"A few days afterwards, Lady Georgiana brought an image of Our Lady of the Immaculate Conception, and placed it on a little altar in one of these rooms. She, Father Biemans, the two postulants and myself said together the Litany of Our Lady, and put the work under her protection. A month passed and difficulties arose: the people of the house would not allow the poor to come to us... We could find no other abode suited to our purpose. The health of the elder postulant broke down completely, and I did not know what to do next.

We began the Novena of the Immaculate Conception on November 29th and before its close I was, in a very singular

47

manner, brought into communication with the Oblate Fathers of Mary Immaculate in Tower Hill. They encouraged our undertaking, and invited us to carry it on in their mission in connection with an industrial school for girls.

Mary Ward was willing to go to Tower Hill, and the work was accordingly transferred there on the Feast of Our Lady's Espousal, January 23rd, 1869."

Fanny began the New Year by making a Retreat under Father Clare, during which she had a letter from Father Porter, another S.J. friend of her Catholic life, encouraging her on her chosen way and advising her to put her whole trust in her God at her morning meeting with Him in His Sacramental Feast. He promises to offer Mass for her on the 20th January, "for what God sees is most to your eternal welfare," and adds: "I am not sure that some big trouble may not be the result." This prophetic forecast of some "big trouble" was to be shortly realized in the sudden death of Fanny's dear Mother, that Mother, who, while undoubtedly happy all her life in her own High Church beliefs, Fanny had hoped would ask before death to be received into the one true Fold. Mrs. Taylor, at the age of sixty, and as a result of the new meaning given by the Oxford Movement to the ceremony of Confirmation, "received the rite," she tells Fanny (who was away in the East) "at the hands of our Bishop, and heard his solemn address to the young."

For years her Mother's conversion had been the most ardent desire of her heart, and that she should have died without ever having partaken of the Blessed Sacrament was a deep grief. Mrs. Taylor never recovered after her first seizure, and so, though Fanny had sent in haste for a priest, nothing could be done. Of her Mother's good faith and consequent virtue she had no doubt, and she knew that whenever Mrs. Taylor felt drawn to Catholicism, she put the idea away as a temptation springing from her too great love for Fanny.

Sympathetic letters from Cardinal Newman, Father Gallway and her many Jesuit and other friends helped to soothe Fanny's sorrow. Lady Georgiana, who was away at the time, wrote her consoling sympathy, and said: "The strength of Catholicism lies, I think, in the power of rising again after a great sorrow — of feeling the *one* life is, as it were, over, and that God now calls us to begin another, without looking back save in prayer, and that is looking upward rather than back."

Fanny Taylor, with the strengthening grace of her January Retreat to urge her on hopefully in the way of obedience to the Divine Will, as her spiritual guides had sign-posted, did not stop by the wayside to fondle her grief for the Mother she had so cherished. She had already wounded that Mother's heart by her conversion, and as the years wore on, that wound did not heal, although it made no difference in her love for her youngest daughter, who as a consequence loved her the more.

Fanny was free now to join the little group — or "Community", as she liked to call it, with which she had hitherto worked by day. The following note from the early Annals describes the position: "On February 2nd, we took a small house in Chamber Street, Tower Hill. It was solemnly blessed by Father Ring, O.M.I., and Our Lady's image installed as Superior and Mistress of the work, or rather as representing Her who was thus chosen. The same day Frances McCarthy entered.

"The little Community was in great poverty; there was scarcely any furniture in the house. On February 11th, Teresa Byrne entered. Towards the end of the month I came to live with the Community and took charge of the house."

In spite of the fact that she was assured and re-assured by Dr. Manning and by all her spiritual guides of her great initiative and her vast capabilities for the organization of the great work anticipated for souls, the practical side also had to be considered. The responsibility and authority she was called upon to assume, and especially with regard to a new undertaking, which might in the event be a disappointment and a failure for many as well as for herself, loomed large to cloud her horizon and to discourage her. She was not entering a Religious Order that had its roots already soundly set in God's Church, and where she would find her natural place. She should herself be the sower who had to "sow the seed," tend the young plant in its growth, prune it, catch "the little foxes" that would destroy the vines. The harvest was yet but a hope, but a hope it was, and Fanny was not the one to yield to despair. She had completed her 37th year with her Retreat under Father Clare, and St. Ignatius' meditation on the "Three Classes of men" had gained her the grace of the third: "To give all to gain all." It was her Divine Donor who was giving the "all", as she was so often to convince young generous aspirants to her Congregation in after years.

The Annals give the state of affairs at Chamber Street. Fanny writes: "We had an Industrial School by day and also a night school. We had a great deal to do, but it was impossible to carry out the fundamental rule of the Congregation in Poland, i.e. self-support. We had no time to do so, but as the wants of the Mission were pressing, we felt it our duty to remain there for a time.

The Community was mainly supported by subscriptions from charitable persons, Lady Denbigh, Lady Georgiana Fullerton and others.

We received much kindness from the Oblate Fathers, and one special blessing was conferred on the Community in the friendship of the Rev. Father Healy, O.M.I., who was then attached to the Mission. He was a man of rare virtue, great calmness of judgment, warm powers of sympathy, and a perfect religious. He took the warmest interest in the enterprise, and in many an hour of discouragement and difficulty was at hand to aid and to advise; he was in every sense a true and faithful friend.

"In April, Mrs. Deverill, a widow, entered the community. We lived by a very simple rule, and our time was entirely taken up with the service of the poor. We had no time for the necessary training of a Novitiate, and moreover we felt very much in the dark about the Polish Rule and Customs."

Fanny's idea of a Religious Congregation devoted to work for the poor and, at the same time, self-supporting, deeply impressed Father Clare, her spiritual director. Lady Georgiana's idea of a few Sisters living in different localities and helping the poor was not conducive to a good, unified religious spirit, and, he decided, was impracticable for religious. He counselled that Fanny should go at once to Poland to examine the working of the Polish Order which might serve as a model, even if she and her group were not to be actually affiliated to it. Dr. Manning gave his encouraging blessing to the venture, and he and the Farm Street Rector gave the necessary letters of introduction. Fanny herself at this time could contribute a major sum to the travelling fund raised by willing friends, as the income from her various writings had become quite a substantial one from 1860 onwards, and from this she drew for her charities.

This great lover of Christ in His poor never wished to see alms abused, nor money wasted to encourage idleness. While she would insist on a good warm meal being served up for the poor who came to beg at the Convent door, and would also see that the visiting Sisters never found a poor family in want without providing help themselves as far as possible, or soliciting from friends even financial assistance if necessary, to bridge a deserving case over a difficult period, she would make a strong young lad earn his requested shilling and taste the happiness of work. For example, during a heavy snowfall in London, she got some of her poor night-school boys to clear door-steps and side-walks, and get paid for the job. Fanny provided the brushes and shovels, and when the thaw set in, her "snow-boys", as she styled them, had plenty to do. She would provide a tea-party at the end, when the lads would proudly count their weekly gain of shillings. Regular attendance at night-school was a condition of securing a job, and soon the First Communion group of teen-agers numbered twelve, all of whom had been employed in the vicinity of the Convent, which soon became a sort of "Labour Exchange" office, whenever businessmen needed assistants, messenger boys, or apprentices to any trade.

The week-ends were set aside for young girls' classes in religion, needlework, etc., and soon aspirants to St. Agnes' Guild in preparation for Children of Mary came into being, and the Industrial School went on apace. In April, as was said, a young widow, Mrs. Deverill, entered the Community. Being a young lady of a very kindly disposition, and a most promising and charming personality, Fanny, with Father Clare's advice, placed her at the head of the brave little band, who were really a consolation one to the other. Great and true priestly kindness was shown to the little Community by the Oblate Fathers, and especially by Father Healy, O.M.I., who was in charge of the Mission.

Bathia Deverill was greatly beloved by the poor and by all with whom she came in contact. She was ingenious in choosing the right boy or girl for the right post. Her protégés looked up to her as to a mother, and referred to her lovingly and familiarly as "herself". Even when she became "Sister M. Elizabeth" in religion, those whom she had trained and helped would still fondly allude to their benefactress as "herself".

And now Fanny saw that her very zealous and united little Community could well manage in her temporary absence. Lady Georgiana was to make frequent calls. Father Clare was to come every week for a conference, and Fanny was assured that all would be well. A few days before what she thought would be her day of departure, she had called on her faithful friend, Dr. Manning, who gave her his paternal blessing, and asking her "to come in to the Blessed Sacrament" with him, they both knelt in prayer for some moments. When they returned to the parlour, the future Cardinal said to Fanny: "Insist on their fidelity to their allotted prayer, and on their devotedness to the dear children while you are away." Having been assured of his Masses and prayers, she came away fortified, and gave his message when she arrived at Chamber Street. All clapped heartily, and especially as a beautiful fruit cake had been produced for what was to be called Fanny's "Good-bye tea." As she loved to relate in after years, the little group was already "Community-minded", even though none had as yet received the postulant status, nor did they observe any fixed order of the day. Father Clare had insisted that the first and chief step in the future programme must be the laying of the solid foundation of a healthy religious spirit. "The members of the little group were working themselves to death," he said, "but not getting any nearer to the religious state." However, Fanny's immediate journey to Poland had to be postponed by herself until July or August, as some hurried and unexpected order from her publishers had to be executed. This business done to her satisfaction and theirs, she set out early in August, 1869. After having assisted at Mass and received Holy Communion that morning, the "Veni Creator" was sung and the Litany of Our Blessed Lady recited, to implore the light of the Holy Spirit and the protection of God's Mother during the journey. After breakfast, Fanny's companions waved her out of sight, then returned indoors to recite Our Lady's Rosary in full, to ask Her protection on themselves, their house, and their work at Tower Hill during Fanny's sojourn abroad.

Chapter 7.

TRAVEL TRIAL AND DECISION

As Fanny Taylor, alone in her aloneness, made for Folkestone and Boulogne on that August day of 1869, one can easily divine her thoughts and fears. She herself had to construct each scene of the yet unknown drama in which she was to be the chief actress in the years ahead. From 1850 onwards, her experience of Church affairs in England had been vast. The Restoration of the Hierarchy, in the person of Cardinal Wiseman, and the undisciplined and wild uprisings consequent upon that glorious event and upon his first pastoral, "From the Flaminian Gate of Rome," the Cardinal's determined stand for the rights of Holy Church and the Papacy, as laid down and boldly stated in his letter to the Prime Minister, Lord John Russell, and the immediate and successful effect of his famous pamphlet, "Appeal to the English People," on the Press and the public, had all been known to Fanny before her great Crimean experience, and without doubt made her think deeply. On her return to London in 1855, God had so willed that she was to come under the influence of Dr. Manning, that great and practical lover of the Church, who was destined to finish her instruction and to be witness of her great worth and her dedicated work for so many years. Her own great love for the poor from her young years, her friendship with Lady Georgiana, and now, other souls with like intentions coming to join the great cause, were all signs, she believed, that God was asking her complete surrender. In full obedience to Dr. Manning and to her wise Jesuit guides this journey was being undertaken, and Fanny therefore assured herself that the Divine Will was being accomplished in her regard.

Her first letter to Lady Georgiana, dated August 8th, 1869,

is written from Liège; she informs her friend that she has had Holy Communion from a Jesuit Father at Ghent, all Masses being over at 8.0 a.m. The Rector there, to whom she had an introductory letter from Father Clare, was most kind, and gave her a note of introduction to the Grand Dame of the Béguinage. She saw at once that the life and work there were the very opposite to what she sought. Father Devas, in his "Life of Mother Magdalen", published in 1927, says that the letters on the journey to Poland are "so interesting that they are given almost 'in extenso'." In this present edition, however, a reproduction is considered unnecessary, if not also inconvenient. The haze of history has lifted in the past hundred years, and to-day tourism, the aeroplane, school journeys, television, the Press, the telephone, etc., have so eliminated distance that the most important events, problems and their solutions can be discussed across the world in a few moments. One wonders whether in another century the fountain-pen and even the biro will not have shared the fate of the all-important and time-honoured quill!

To summarise Fanny Taylor's very detailed and lengthy Victorian letters, then, it is sufficient to say that she visited and wrote from Liège, Ghent, St. Goar, Cologne, Coblenz, Mayence, Düsseldorf, Hanover, Brunswick, and finally Posen. She wrote what she thought of all the convents, cities and towns she had thus visited, but finally she concludes: "The more I see of foreign Institutes, the more certain I am that we must found our own. They have done it, and so must we." She spends many days at Posen and visits some of the branch houses of the Order as well. The Archbishop and his Vicar-General, and the nuns, were kindness itself, and the saintly Founder, M. Bojanowiski, of the Congregation of the Little Servants of the Mother of God (which she had gone especially to see), with the Archbishop's enthusiastic consent, gave Fanny full authority to establish a branch of that Congregation in England, with such modifications as should be needed to adapt it to the conditions of English life. The more she prayed, however, the more her mind seemed to harden against this idea. "They have some of our idea, but not all," she wrote, but she wisely withheld her personal opinion yet, lest it might influence her spiritual guides in their final decision. In the meantime, she received a letter from her London friend, Father Biemens, to say she will be expected at a given address at Antwerp on the way back. These nuns, to whom he had written on her account, were the Servants of the Sacred Hearts of Jesus and Mary, a Belgian Congregation to which the future Foundress and her spiritual children will have reasons to be prayerfully grateful for all time.

Fanny arrives at Antwerp on September 8th, and a letter to Lady Georgiana on the 9th says: "It will take all my space and strength to give you my impressions of this convent. It would not do, I fear, for us to copy or belong to. I say 'I fear,' because it would be so nice to have a Mother-house as near as Belgium, and the spirit of these nuns is so nice. Rev. Mother is a lady, rather old, I should think, but there are choir and lay sisters — Office of the Blessed Virgin said in choir — they don't visit the sick — they go out to give instructions — teach Sunday School — have a Patronage — and a large intern industrial school, no externs. I am glad I came; I shall learn a great deal, and Antwerp is very little out of my way home. I have ascertained all the above from the bright little novice who waits on me, and I am now expecting Rev. Mother to show me the house and to talk..."

In the Annals already referred to, this Antwerp visit is thus recalled: "I was most kindly received by the Community of the Servants of the Sacred Hearts of Jesus and Mary, in whose convent I remained till September 11th. I found it was mainly supported by a laundry, and the nuns urged me to choose that mode of support for mine. I was treated with the most generous kindness by these religious, and encouraged to persevere in my undertaking."

The following translation from their Antwerp Annals, so kindly placed at the disposal of the Poor Servants of the Mother of God for the 1926/27 edition of Mother Taylor's "Life" by Father Devas, shows the mutual friendship and esteem which the visit evoked on both sides:

"On August 4th, M. l'Abbé Biemans, a priest from London, called at our convent, simply to bring tidings to one of our novices of her brother, Rev. Brother Modeste of the Brothers of Charity in London. After a short interview, this good priest was just taking his leave, when it suddenly occurred to him to ask the Sister who accompanied the novice to the parlour about the object of our Institute. Having heard it, he seemed quite surprised, and told us that he had in his parish a lady, converted from Protestantism, who had the intention of beginning a similar work, with three companions, and that his design in coming to Antwerp was to look for a convent where one of them, Miss Taylor, could find hospitality, as she did not wish to go to a hotel.

Father Biemans came back in the afternoon, and after an interview with our Rev. Mother, it was arranged that this English lady should come to us. He showed satisfaction at this arrangement by saying that it was Divine Providence which had brought him to this house.

On September 8th following, Miss Taylor arrived. We could see at once that she was no ordinary person — a fervent Catholic, full of zeal for good works and love of the poor, making small account of herself, and engrossed in the work she was going to undertake for the glory of God.

The next day Miss Taylor took part in our mid-day recreation, and her conversation interested us very much. Knowing that, whilst a Protestant, Miss Taylor had nursed the wounded in the Crimean war, we begged her to tell us some particulars about it, which she did in a most charming way. She had already won the Sisters' sympathy, who were sorry that her departure was fixed for the next day. This day, and the next, she had long conversations with our Rev. Mother concerning religious life, which she wished to embrace, and works of charity which she wished to undertake with the three companions who had joined her."

Fanny travelled to London via Brussels and Tournai, and to her great amusement, and perhaps no little consternation, she was arrested at Boulogne as a Prussian, but released through the intervention of the British Consul after a short time. What a thrilling, if also a rather appalling experience to relate to the little group at Chamber Street, where she arrived on September 14th.

The time for a final and definite decision had now come, and Fanny begged to prepare for this by a retreat under Father Clare, during which she drew up notes, following the method of election of St. Ignatius, for and against the Polish idea. At the end of the Retreat, Father Gallwey, Father Clare, Father Healy, O.M.I., and Lady Georgiana were of one mind with Fanny, i.e. either to become affiliated to the Polish Order or begin a new Order on the Polish lines. Archbishop Manning stepped in, and absolutely ruled out any agreement that would make them in any way dependent on a foreign Order. Fanny's next appeal was that she might make her Novitiate in some existing Order, previous to becoming a Mistress of Novices herself. Against this appeal again, Fathers Gallwey, Clare and Healy set themselves absolutely, convincing Fanny that she would "spoil all by mixing the spirit of different Orders." The Archbishop agreed that Fanny had all she needed within herself, and was fully capable of guiding her subjects in the religious life. Her vast fund of experience, her ripe and mature womanhood, her strong trust in her Lord and in His Holy Mother, her spirit of self-effacement resulting from her sincere humility, and withal, her innate refinement and dignity of bearing, made authority at Westminster and Farm Street come to this final conclusion, and the sequel proved she was advised aright.

On September 24th, 1869, then being the Feast of Our Lady of Mercy, the first real beginning of the new Congregation was made. On that memorable day, Archbishop Manning authorized Father Clare to receive as postulants Fanny Taylor, Frances McCarthy and Mrs. Deverill. In October Anne Cooling entered the little Community. Being a tailoress by trade, and a most competent one, her former employers sent the work to the Convent to be done, where Fanny invited her mother to come and live with them for a while. Mrs. Cooling's three other daughters having also entered religion, she decided to break up the home, and accept the invitation. She too being an accomplished and trained seamstress, their united work helped much to increase the Community funds.

The Annals record at this point the wonderful success of the Children's Mission at Tower Hill. Six hundred went to Communion on December 17th and 1,200 to Confession — a great tribute to the efficiency and persevering work of the little Community, especially as Fanny herself had been away on her experimental journey until September. But another problem now

E

presented itself to the ever-active mind of her who was, when all was said, the person on whom the chief responsibility rested. The postulants were a fact; the beginning was made, but all this apostolic work was inconsistent with the quiet and seclusion necessary and proper to the life of the novitiate, which Fanny must needs found, and the postulants themselves realized this. Father Healy's regrets were great, but he was too much interested to put any barrier in the way.

The first move was made on All Saints' Day, when they rented a small cottage near Grosvenor Square, precisely at the back of Robert Street. It was a very quiet spot, and although Fanny had still to go with Anne Cooling and her mother to work at Tower Hill by day, they succeeded in getting the place ready for occupation by Christmas. For Christmas too, all prepared by making a novena to the Holy Child, which beautiful practice has continued now for over 100 years in the Congregation of the Poor Servants of the Mother of God. On Christmas Day itself, in that ever-memorable year 1869, they all united at Chamber Street and had twelve of the poorest and smallest of their school-children to dine with them — another custom which still continues in meals and other necessaries being provided for the poor on Christmas Day.

In January 1870, a retreat was given in the cottage at the back of Robert Street, at the end of which the ever-faithful Father Clare, S.J., was empowered by Archbishop Manning to give the Habit to Fanny Taylor and to her very faithful companions, Frances McCarthy, Bathia Deverill and Anne Cooling, who took respectively the names Sister M. Magdalen of the Sacred Heart, Sister M. Colette of the Immaculate Heart, Sister M. Elizabeth of the Infant Jesus, and Sister M. Joseph of the Immaculate Conception. The Annals describe the habit as "a uniform black dress, with a small rosary and black net cap," and continue: "We were poor but very happy. We had great spiritual blessings, being so near Farm Street, and we owed very much day by day to the pains Father Clare took with us. Hardly anyone knew we were religious novices, and yet, some who thought they knew dubbed us "New Poor Clares." Dr. Manning and Father Clare had a hearty laugh over the title; both knew what name the new novice — Sister M. Magdalen had already prepared in her heart, for her companions and herself, but the time was not yet.

On March 10th another postulant, Catherine Burrows, entered, to the great happiness of the little group, and this fact necessitated the speedy purchase of additional space near the Robert Street cottage. The Annals reveal the circumstances now. "On March 10th, Catherine Burrows came to join us. A few days afterwards, we took possession of two floors in 17 Robert Street, our cottage having become too small for us. We had always had a little Oratory with an image of Our Blessed Lady which Lady Georgiana had bought for us. This image has gone with us everywhere, as also the maternal protection of Her whom it represents. During March, we had a little altar to St. Joseph, for which we purchased an image of St. Joseph of the Sacred Heart, and had a great many devotions in honour of this dear Saint." A hundred years have passed, and "St. Joseph, Friend of the Sacred Heart" is still invoked daily wherever there is a convent of that little Robert Street infant Congregation, and many are the proofs of St. Joseph's aid in time of stress, and of his protection in dangerous situations.

More than ever now, with the increase of numbers, had Sister M. Magdalen to think out the problems of self-support and of the great and manifold pressing needs of the poor in the London of her day. With Charles Dickens' death in 1870, a great pen that had exposed poverty and its consequent results of misery and vice was laid down forever, but another force, a richly spiritual one, had been long active in the cause of justice, of religion and of social reform. From the coming of Cardinal Wiseman to Westminster, a new and hopeful era had dawned for the Catholic Church. The Restoration of the Hierarchy was the answer to the prayers and sacrifices of the Martyrs. The long night of darkness had passed, and the new Cardinal's "Appeal to the English People," in answer to the wild and outrageous reception which the Pope's Bull and his own first Pastoral evoked, showed his adversaries at once the man they had to deal with. Dr. Newman, commenting on the affair of Wiseman's reply to the Prime Minister's Durham letter, is supposed to have said: "Highly as I put his (Wiseman's) gifts, I was not prepared for such a display of vigour, power, judgment and sustained energy... In my own remembrance, there has been nothing like it."

Dr. Wiseman's preoccupation, once the tumult had subsided, was with converts. They flocked to him. The Irish refreshing enthusiasm of his personality made people love him, and it is said that even as late as 1850 he still corresponded with many who had been his classmates in a boarding-school at Waterford. He hoped too, that by blending the English element and the strong faith of the Irish in England, he would gradually but surely merge both sympathies and restore Our Lady's Dowry, as well as social order and understanding among the classes.

From 1858 to his death in 1865, Wiseman's chief confidant and support was Manning. Both men had the same great aim — England's conversion — and in God's Providence it was Manning who was destined to succeed Wiseman, and so Mother Magdalen Taylor (that was to be) rejoiced, as she could count on the Archbishop for every future help and support until her little Community "grew up" in Westminster. Pius IX knew only too well that the progress of the Church in England since 1850 was due not only to Cardinal Wiseman's wise and unbending attitude, but also to Manning's equally wise and zealous co-operation in those years. The interior inspiration felt by the Pope at Wiseman's death: "Put him there, put him there," was no uncertain risk to run; it was providential. Gifted with great learning and talents for administration, Manning was destined soon to bridge the gulf between Church and State. His burning faith in the holiness of that Church, born of the wounded Heart of the God-Man, gave him courage for the fray. His access to the rich, his farseeing diplomacy, his friendship with Gladstone and other statesmen of his day — all were of use to him who was to be remembered in history as the guardian of the poor, the founder of the Catholic elementary voluntary schools, the man whose influence was greatest in the settlement of London's great Dock Strike in 1889. He was ever the champion of the oppressed, and his constant sympathy for Catholic Ireland made him spare no pains to urge upon governments the necessity of solving its age-old problems. This, then, was the man who judged aright the balanced personality and the spiritual outlook of Fanny Taylor as a Foundress and a Mother. She too was

60

by birth and education an Englishwoman — an Englishwoman who loved her country with all the strength of her being; a woman who wrote of the Crimean nurse as "being there to represent the honour of England." She was, however, a woman destined by God to love with her whole heart and to understand another country — the country she had gone to the Crimea to find, the country that will be forever grateful to her name and coupled with her memory as long as her Congregation exists; the country whose destiny it was and shall ever be to gain mission Empire for God.

Among the many Crimean heroes whom Fanny had tended in the wards at Koulali, two boys especially stood out in her retentive memory. "Dublin boys," she styled them, but they were God-given angels of light to this "seeking" Anglican girl. She used to describe them as "holy, manly, pure." They dared wear their rosaries around their necks, and as Fanny held the teaspoonful of beef-tea to their parched lips, they taught her how to meditate on the sorrowful mysteries of the Rosary. They were true missionaries in their ward. All pain seemed slight to them when weighed against the agonies of the Son of God. Both boys died, and Mother Magdalen loved to relate how in their clasped fingers, before their crude burial on the lonely slopes above the Bosphorus, Mother Frances Bridgeman twined their blood-spotted beads.

Another incident of later date has its connection with Koulali days. A few years after Mother Magdalen had founded her Congregation and had made a foundation at Carrigtwohill, Co. Cork, a painful, if also a glad happening brought her mind and heart back to the Christmas of 1854. The Community Retreat was on at the Convent, and the Foundress herself had taken on the post of door-portress. The door-bell rang, and as she opened, a tall, noble-looking man of the country type, dressed in his Sunday best and returning from Mass, asked for his monthly "Messenger". (The Messenger of the Sacred Heart was distributed from the school or from the Convent hall). As he reached out a rather shapeless, gnarled hand, the nurse and the sympathetic mother combined in her great, tender heart, made Mother Taylor ask: "Poor man, what happened to your hand?" "Ah, Ma'am," he replied, "I all but lost it at the Crimea." Seeing her kindly eyes suddenly fill, he asked: "Were you there by any chance, we had nuns there?" "I was in Koulali, but I was not a nun then," replied Mother Magdalen. "Were you a Miss Taylor, by any chance?" he queried. Her affirmative thrilled him, he dropped his "Messenger", took her scapular in both hands and, kissing it, exclaimed: "Ah, I remember your face well, you were with Mother Frances (Bridgeman)." On Mother Magdalen's subsequent stays at Carrigtwohill, she made it a point to have Mr. Coffey and his wife for a visit, and was invited to see their home at nearby Hawlbowline. He had worked at the London Docks for some years after the Crimea, and "through the goodness of Dr. Manning got transferred to Hawlbowline in 1875, where his old widowed mother lived." "What a coincidence! What a connection! What a proof of God's care!" thought Mother Magdalen. And no wonder! The Crimean veteran, her conversion, Cardinal Manning, and now Ireland again, and the Poor Servants of the Mother of God.

Chapter 8.

THE FOUNDRESS AND FAITH

The increase of applicants to the new Congregation was phenomenal from 1870 onwards, and two fresh problems called for almost immediate solution — an established means of self-support and a larger house. Anne Cooling and her mother were trained hands at their work, but others of the new Community had to learn slowly and could not attempt much. Mother Magdalen immediately bethought her of the sound advice of the Antwerp nuns, and decided on a laundry. Catherine Burrows understood laundry work, and, say the Annals: "We consulted together... and though we had no idea how to begin, we prayed to Our Lady to help us. On May 1st we began the Novena. During its course I called on Baroness de Beaulieu and stated our needs. She took up our case warmly, and had many of her friends to do the same. By May 31st we had more work than we could do, and we were compelled to go house-hunting anew." By Whit Monday Mother Magdalen was directed to a large house in Cavendish Square, the finding and suitability of which were regarded as a direct answer to prayer. Transaction difficulties had still to be overcome; prayers to the Holy Spirit, to the Sacred Heart, to Our Lady and to St. Joseph were redoubled, and on Corpus Christi the house was theirs. The Annals record: "On June 26th we took possession of our new house, and great was the relief when we exchanged the heat and noise of Robert Street for the quiet and cool of Cavendish Square. It was half-past eleven p.m. before we had finished moving and were left alone. The room we intended for the chapel was filled with furniture of all kinds, but we placed the image of Our Lady on

63

the mantel-shelf, and kneeling before it, said her Litany before we went to bed. We had a great many crosses and difficulties in those first days, but were helped through them all...

On June 27, Father Healy, O.M.I., came to see us. He went all over the house, and was so pleased with it; he said we could not have found in all London one so well suited to us and so cheap. He took, as usual, the warmest interest in all our difficulties, trials and hopes. While standing in our oratory, and remarking, as everyone else has done, that this room seems built for a chapel, I asked him if he would say our first Mass, and he said he would."

The promise was never fulfilled. Father Healy was killed on the Feast of the Holy Cross, September 14th, on the railway between Holyhead and London. "He died with his rosary in his hands, prayer on his lips," wrote Mother Magdalen. "His poverty was so austere that nothing could be found to give to those who longed to have something that belonged to him."

On September 8th, Mother Magdalen had seen him at Inchicore. He renewed his promise of celebrating the first Mass at Cavendish Square on his return, and of giving catechetical instructions to the novices during the winter. She used to relate, at conferences to her Sisters in after years, how much he insisted, at their last meeting at Inchicore, on the great need for "properly trained nuns." "We want them very much; there are not nearly enough of these." It was his last advice on earth. Father Healy's death was an unspeakable loss to the infant Community, and many blessings after his death were attributed to his powerful intercession for the Sisters in spiritual and temporal needs.

Before the Irish tour, Mother Magdalen had paid a visit to her Antwerp friends, who received her, as she says, "with so much love and kindness," and she continues: "I stayed in their Community, followed the Rule with them, and learned all they could teach me. I cannot express in words the generous kindness of these Religious to our infant Community. They begged me to send for a Sister to whom they could teach many things in the laundry." Mother Magdalen sent to London for Sister M. Elizabeth, who arrived on August 22nd and remained till October 5th. She herself, after a fornight's stay, had gone on to Ireland after Sister M. Elizabeth's arrival, as already stated, and had met Father Healy in Inchicore.

In Ireland, she received the greatest kindness from the Jesuit Fathers, and especially from Father Ronan of Crimean days, who had given her her First Communion there on that ever-memorable Good Shepherd Sunday. She goes next to Wexford, to visit the Adoration Convent, where a very dear convert friend of early days is the Reverend Mother. They found time to give her the warmest welcome "and much wise counsel," she wrote in her diary. The Adoration nuns told another story — they were almost in despair for money for their new foundation; their London visitor cheered them up with her infectious gaiety, saw no difficulty that could not be surmounted, carried the Reverend Mother back to Dublin with her, and with characteristic gener-osity introduced her to a friend who was able to give her material aid that would otherwise had gone to Cavendish Square.

From 1870 onward and following upon her first visit to Wexford right on to her death in 1900 Mother Magdalen had proof of Our dear Lady's interest in her beloved Congregation. In the early years of the Congregation, Wexford was fruitful in solid, faithful vocations, and later they came from every county of that dear Ireland, to whose people she owed so much. As early as her 1870 visit, she had received no fewer than fifty applications, and of these she could receive only five, for want of room. In the June of that year, Catherine Healy and Mary McElligott entered. Mother Magdalen herself returned in September, and the new postulants were all in Cavendish Square by the middle of October.

The Annals give the account: "On October 24th, 1870, St. Raphael's Day, His Grace the Archbishop of Westminster visited the house with Lady Georgiana Fullerton. He approved of all we had done, gave an instruction to the Community, and treated us with much kindness.

"On October 31st, Feast of Bl. Margaret Mary, His Grace gave me the written permission for the following: to have Mass once a week, and the Blessed Sacrament reserved — Benediction once a week — to commence a retreat on November 3, and take the religious habit on the 8th.

"On November 3rd, Father Caradonna, S.J., gave us the

first instruction of a retreat. On November 4th, Feast of St. Charles, and being also the First Friday of the month, Father Caradonna said Mass in our chapel, and we all went to Holy Communion. After Mass the Blessed Sacrament was placed in the ciborium, and our dear and adorable Lord took up His abode amongst us..."

The Clothing ceremony at the end of the Retreat was performed by Father Clare, when Mother Magdalen and six of her companions received the then decided religious Habit.* Of these six, three had already begun, the other three were Mary McElligott, Catherine Burrows and Margaret Sweeney, who took the names, respectively, of Sister Mary Xavier of the Blessed Sacrament, Sister Mary Ignatius of the Precious Blood, and Sister Mary Teresa of St. Joseph. Anne Cooling had withdrawn from the Community some time after the regular Novitiate had begun, as her dear Mother needed her help and companionship in her ageing years. Mother Magdalen and her companions, happy in the Religious Habit and with the Blessed Sacrament dwelling in their midst, felt that first difficulties were overcome. If there were still greater problems ahead, He would be their strength Who had called them to His special service. More and more did Mother Magdalen see the wisdom of taking on a fully equipped laundry as a means of self-support, at least for the time being, and in this idea she was entirely encouraged by Sister M. Elizabeth, who had returned from Antwerp by now, fully trained in the use of laundry machinery. Sister M. Ignatius, too, was already an adept in the art, and although it was hard work, it was easy to learn, and soon became a precious boon to many young women and girls who would otherwise have to depend on odd jobs, or on a husband's or father's poor weekly wage for the family sustenance. One of the first Sisters who worked at Cavendish Square has left on record how, when letters of appreciation of the perfection of the work done came in, Mother Magdalen would be so glad and would ask Sister M. Elizabeth to tell the women

---

* The first uniform Habit was of black serge, with apron, girdle, large Rosary at the side and blue Scapular over which was worn a rather large crucifix. The head-dress and hood-veil entailed a lot of work. The present decided Habit is blue, with a neat Crucifix and a simpler head-dress.

responsible. When Sister went round on the appointed pay-day holding a tray with each one's little heap of silver, it was discovered that an extra shilling or maybe sixpence was the reward for the praise given! In Victorian times, it was generally the "lady of the house" herself who examined the linen as it came back from the laundry. Most of it had to be done by hand, either by reason of its rich embroidery or multiple frilling. House-linen bore the family crest or monogram richly wrought, and this had to be carefully ironed on the wrong side to make its perfection stand out. Then, too, it was the age when linen, lawn, cambric, muslin, cotton, etc., were in much demand and called for careful handling, as often with the "whirr-whirr" of laundry machinery in its first imperfect stages went the "tear, tear" of the precious work! It was still the age of the "frills and furbelows" mentioned in the "Vicar of Wakefield", and which needed all the perfection of the laundress' art, with her highly-heated gophering tongs, to make the frilled or gophered article a veritable triumph, showing neither scorch nor wrinkle.

Such was the work, with all its responsibility, which Mother Magdalen and her first members took on at Cavendish Square. Cardinal Manning admired her courageous venture and the humility which accompanied it. Her friends, Lady Georgiana Fullerton, Minna, Duchess of Norfolk, Lady Denbigh, Lady Newburgh and the Hon. Mrs. Pereira all helped with eager enthusiasm and financial aid in the purchase of machinery, etc. to make the undertaking a success, while it served its purpose at Cavendish Square. These friends of the early struggling days are chief among those whose names will always be held in grateful memory and be prayed for as benefactors by every generation of the Poor Servants of the Mother of God. As well as these real friends, Fanny Taylor had other well-wishers who considered she was wasting her time and talents when such a personality as hers was so much needed to do good in the world; her plans were all bound to be failures! To one such critic who pitied "poor dear Fanny", and wondered what she could do to help her desist from her course, Lady Georgiana replied with a touch of humorous malice: "Give her a good mangle, my dear, that will be the help she will value most!" Needless to say, the mangle never arrived. In addition to her pitying critics, "Poor dear Fanny Taylor" had to suffer from other so-called "constructive" criticism. "Who was this convert lady trying to improve the Church? What could she know of religious life? What was Church authority doing?" The "Church authorities" who could interfere were the Archbishop of Westminster, who had wished and authorized every step of her difficult road to God's Will, and her enlightened and God-given advisers and spiritual directors at Farm Street and Tower Hill, to which latter place and its work Mother Magdalen held on with dutiful and grateful fidelity until the Fathers were able to get their own O.M.I. Sisters to take it over. With regard to tea-table and armchair criticism of her doings, with St. Paul she counted it little "to be judged by man's day." She knew that her adorable Lord, who had "called her out of darkness into His marvellous light" would be with her and her faithful flock, who sought His Divine Will only in all the events of their days, every moment of which they had consecrated to His Sacred Heart.

No doubt the work was humble work, but so was that of the Divine Son of the Almighty, the Carpenter of Nazareth, whose words "Learn of Me, because I am meek and humble of Heart," were to be the challenge sentence for all time for those who would follow His Divine teaching, even to the folly of the Cross. Fanny Taylor's constant and regretful ejaculation was that of St. Augustine: "Oh Beauty, ever ancient, ever new, too late I have loved Thee!" Love of her Lord was to be her driving force and that of her little flock, to each one of whom she was tender and gentle as a mother. Such expressions as: "We consulted together," "We bethought us of a better plan," etc., show how the young and the more experienced of the little group lived in happy unity, all having a say in matters in order to be a help to her who bore the final responsibility for decisions. When Mother Magdalen Taylor died in 1900, her successor, Mother M. Lucy, who had been her assistant for many years, and who was unanimously elected Mother-General at her death, got the first Sisters who had known the Foundress from 1870 onwards to write their impressions of her. These "impressions" were later typed in book form for Community circulation, under the title: "Mother as we knew her," so that later generations of Poor Servants of the Mother of God might profit much by the example of those early years, and draw inspiration there-from. Perhaps the following short extract from the preface which introduces "Mother as we knew her" will not be out of place here:

"It will be seen throughout what a real Mother to her children our dear Mother Foundress was — how she loved them, appreciated them, worked for them, corrected and trained them for God. They in their turn loved her and were responsive to her great sincerity. We owe them much gratitude and love for the example they have left us in these pages. They were great women and great nuns; great in their sincere humility, great in their fortitude in laying the solid foundation of our beautiful Institute in prayer, obedience and hard work. All of this never interfered with their Community feasting, their fun, their love for their 'Mother' and our Congregation. May we all draw inspiration from their lives, and die rather than be un-faithful to the Lord and to the spirit that is our heritage: 'Life for Jesus Christ, labour for Jesus Christ, zeal for Jesus Christ, and all things through Mary, His most sweet Mother and our Mistress.' "

"One or two" (the preface says in another place) "who never saw Mother seem to be of the impression that she was hard, which we would not consider correct... Sisters who knew Mother could easily understand how this opinion arose, because Mother was so thorough, so practical and very exact."

A Sister who entered in 1871 writes of the Foundress: "I got the white veil on the 8th of October, and about three weeks afterwards, I was sent to Beaumont. This was a real act of kindness on Mother's part, for there lived a priest who had been my confessor in the world. Mother said: 'If anyone told you that Father Selby would be your confessor in religion, would you have believed it?' This was a great consolation to me. Like a real Mother, dear Mother Foundress was always doing little acts of kindness for us."

Another of the 1872 entrants wrote: "Once, when Mother went away for a time, she heard that the novices were lonely. She wrote: 'I don't know why the novices are lonely, I did not take away the key of the Tabernacle!' "

A Sister who entered in 1880 left the following: "During a

Retreat I was speaking to Mother, and after reproving me, like one who loved my soul more than my feelings, she said: 'How could you treat Him so? What has He done to you?' Although it is now eighteen years since this happened, her words are as fresh in my mind as when they were spoken."

Another Sister of an 1897 group wrote: "I was attending lectures at a day college in London on Saturdays, and as I failed to answer 'Yes' when my number was called, a postcard came to Brentford asking for an explanation of my absence. I don't think I shall ever forget the scolding I got, but it cured my indistinctness. About that time my own Mother was anxious to see me, but the journey being very long and expensive, she could not easily come. Dear Mother Foundress kindly allowed me to travel with a Sister who was going home, so that my Mother could see me."

Another Sister gives two examples of Mother's real motherliness to her children and of her sense of humour. "When I was a novice (1894) my brother came to see me while I was in Retreat and Mother said I could go to him and stay as long as he wished. Afterwards she sent for me, asked me how he was, and took the greatest interest in him and in his ship. She said she was very fond of soldiers and sailors, because they were so self-sacrificing. When Mother sent me to Ireland later on, she said: 'I am sending you over to convert the Irish!'"

The same Sister gives an example of Mother Foundress' dominant attitude when occasion called: "On one occasion, years later, a soldier came to Roehampton, and said he wanted to see his sister, who was in the Orphanage, and wished to take her out. The Superior refused, as she did not know the man, but he insisted and said he would not leave the house without the girl. The Superior went to Mother Foundress, who went at once to the parlour, taking another Sister with her. Speaking in a threatening tone, she said: 'I demand your regimental number and the name of your Commanding Officer,' whereupon the soldier made a grab for his cap, rushed out and was seen no more."

Another Sister of the early days wrote: "Mother, of course, had a great personality, and seemed fashioned by Heaven for great things... Whenever she gave anyone a scolding, one could

70

not help realizing that it was for one's good. She never said unkind or bitter things — she had too noble a nature and too much greatness of mind and heart to stoop to anything mean. Mother had a wonderful grasp of the meaning of religious life. To listen to her conferences, as I had the privilege of doing many times in Rome, seemed like listening to one inspired. Imbued as she was with the Ignatian spirit, she expected the best in obedience and charity from all her children."

Another Sister of the early Roman days, who became Mother-General years after, wrote: "When Mother Foundress came to Rome, she was our Novice-Mistress, gave us conferences and conducted our studies. She was never tired of inculcating obedience and charity, and in my private interviews with her, I remember how particular she was that I should cultivate an interior spirit of true charity, judging no one rashly, no matter how evident the reasons."

After having given these few "Impressions" from among many of the early days, a return to Cavendish Square and to life there presses itself at this very important stage. Numerous postulants applied for admission, many of whom were dismissed or departed after a period of trial, but many also received the religious habit and became spiritual pillars of support even to old age.

The apostleship for souls, nurtured by the growing fervour of the little band, was continued here such as it had been at Tower Hill. The Farm Street branch of the Children of Mary held their monthly meetings at the Convent, but as the number of applicants increased for the new Congregation, even the space at Cavendish Square became inadequate, and Fanny Taylor was house-hunting again. This time Roehampton offered an opening — a small house near St. Joseph's Church, into which a few of the Sisters moved in May, and then to a better and second house in the following August. Here they remained (with Cavendish Square still as headquarters) until a large and in every way finer house was offered at Beaumont College, Old Windsor.

In the April of 1871 died the Venerable M. Edward Bojanowiski, Founder of the Polish Congregation which had served Mother Magdalen as a model in some points. A Requiem Mass for the repose of his soul was offered, and with his decease, all connection between the two Congregations ceased.

In the autumn of 1871, the stability of the new Congregation was sufficiently ensured to justify its inclusion in the Catholic Directory as: "The Poor Servants of the Mother of God, 26 Cavendish Square," and in early September Mother Magdalen, accompanied by Sister M. Xavier, paid another visit to Antwerp for business reasons, and the New Year opened with a short visit to Paris, where she was again welcomed by the nuns of Marie Reparatrice. Glorious news awaited the traveller on her return: Archbishop Manning, who had never doubted her holiness, and especially its foundation — her true humility — had given permission for her to take the three Vows of religion for life!

On February 12th, 1872, accordingly, Father Clare said Mass in the Convent Chapel at Cavendish Square, and received in the name of Holy Church, her profession of the three Vows of Poverty, Chastity and Obedience for life. The simple statement in the Annals reads: "On February 12th, we kept the Feast of the Most Pure Heart of Mary. At 6.30 Rev. Father Clare, S.J., said Mass in our Chapel, and Sister Mary Magdalen of the Sacred Heart of Jesus (F. M. Taylor) made her Profession of the three vows of religion for life. Thus our Congregation may be said to be established."

Thus strengthened and consoled, Mother Magdalen was now encouraged to face other difficulties on her uphill path.

Chapter 9.

GOD-GIVEN GUIDES

On Good Shepherd Sunday, April 22nd, the happy anniversary of her own First Communion at the Crimea, Mother Magdalen had the joy of seeing two other of her first and most faithful companions take their vows, and on April 22nd she herself escorted to Beaumont the six S.M.G.'s who were to form the new Community there. They were to supervise the linen-room, take charge of the laundry and its staff, teach in the elementary school and visit the poor of the district. Charming as was the place, and despite the great attractions of the new country foundation, Beaumont was nevertheless a land of exile. Of the first departure it is recorded: "The day the Sisters were going to Beaumont, Mother sent all to the refectory, where we said 'Good-bye,' and some were crying as if they were never to meet again." Mother was charmed that her children, cooped up so long in London, could benefit by the beautiful Berkshire air, and Beaumont proved a real home; furthermore, the great spiritual "tonic" which they all prized so much awaited them — a Jesuit Father would give regular instructions to the Sisters, and so continue the religious training.

Mother remained at Beaumont all that week, sharing in the work as was her custom. Except for Sister M. Elizabeth and Sister M. Colette, the postulants of the first year were all young teenage children, looking to Mother for everything: a precious youthful charge for whose health, spiritual training etc., Mother was wholly responsible. To them she gave her whole heart's love, as they did to her, a love that exists between a mother and her children. She had infinite patience with them. As they grew older, she trusted and consulted them and was ever open to

73

their opinions, and so she mothered them in their lives for God, gave them positions of authority, and there is abundant proof of their competence and of their real religious spirit, even in the first decade of the life of the young Congregation.

Nor did their intensive spiritual aim, or the pressure of work, exclude all fun and healthy humour from their lives. Sister M. Xavier, the nominal Superior at Beaumont, has left on record two instances which taught her she was still an apprentice to the position, albeit a promising one. "A letter from Mother, from London to Beaumont, read: 'Send Sister M. Gertrude up to me to-morrow,' but I never thought that to-day *was* to-morrow. I did not look at the date, so of course Sister waited for *my* to-morrow, which was Sunday. I sent someone to the station with her, gazing sorrowfully after her as long as she remained in sight. It being Sunday, the usual train did not run, and consequently she got into town very late on Sunday afternoon. I had a letter from Mother telling me always to look at the date of a letter in future, and never to make the same mistake again; adding that now I was not to fret about it, but she hoped it would be a lesson to me."

The other is an instance of Sister M. Xavier's blind obedience, which in her humility she would relate against herself, adding: "God stepped in to save me!"

"When the date for the annual retreat drew near, one party of the Beaumont community left by an early train, Mother was to come for the remainder later. Those left, set to work to give the little convent an extra scrubbing and cleaning, so as to have all in apple-pie order before going to the retreat. The little band had just set merrily to work, turning out every room and corner, when the door-bell rang sharply, and a telegram from Mother was handed in. It ran thus: 'Move nothing; leave all as it is till I come.' Sr. M. Xavier went round to every room immediately, showed the astonished Sisters the telegram, and ordered all work to stop at once; brooms, dustpans, scrubbing-brushes, pails, all were to be left just as they were when the telegram was read. One or two demonstrated: 'Sister, please, may I put this back?' 'May I just clean up this?' No answer from the Sister in charge but to hold up the telegram before their eyes.

"After a few hours, Mother arrived with two strange nuns. As soon as she entered, she started back in surprise! Her consternation deepened as she went further, and found everything absolutely topsy-turvy to greet her guests, whom she had hoped, with a little innocent pride, to show over her spick-and-span convent. Sr. M. Xavier came out to meet her. 'What is the meaning of this, Sister?' Mother gasped. 'Your telegram, Mother,' Sister answered, handing it to her. Mother drew her aside: 'Did you not understand my letter?' 'I got no letter, Mother.' (The letters to the little convent arrived in the College post-bag, and were sent down daily by Father Rector).

"Two Sisters went up at once to enquire for it, and found that it had been put to one side and forgotten. The letter was to announce that two nuns were coming to stay for a week at Beaumont, and it gave minute directions as to how their room should be arranged, etc. When Mother Magdalen met the nuns, she found they had had other instructions, and could only come to Beaumont for a few hours — hence there was no need to prepare a room for them, and hence the telegram."

When the affairs at Beaumont were happily settled, and the new elementary school formally opened — to which opening Lady Georgiana Fullerton and many others of Mother Magdalen's London friends happily came — the Foundress was on her travels again to the North of England and her beloved Ireland, making known her new Congregation and her contemplated vast scope of work for God. During this journey, she and her companion made a digression and visited Holywell, which pilgrimage was a source of great joy to her, and resulted soon after in a record of her "Impressions" in "The Lamp", and later in her "Life of St. Winifred", wherein she also records that she has promised St. Winifred to have her name given in some form, always, to some Sister.

The November of 1872 marked the first death in the young Community. An Irish postulant, Mary Begley, from Enniscorthy, entered at Cavendish Square in January, and even though of not robust health, Mother Magdalen could not bear to send her away. She was of such a beautifully happy and simple disposition, and showed such signs of a good vocation, that it was hoped her health would improve. At her reception in June, she had been given the name of Sister Mary Antonia, and, strange to say, from then on her health deteriorated. In September she was anointed by Father Coleridge, and was visited on her sick-bed by Cardinal Manning himself, who gave permission for her to make her Perpetual Vows that same day. Sister lingered on till November, when she gave up her beautiful innocent soul to her Spouse. During her short life in religion, she was an example of extreme simplicity, humility and happiness in obedience, of which latter virtue she has left a quaint example, perhaps not to be imitated at a more intelligent and mature period by future postulants.

"Mother" (we are told) "gave them a half-hour glass (watches were rare among the community in those days), and told them to make their meditation in church, and that Father Caradonna would not come to hear their confessions till they had finished. They went into a bench near the confessional. Father Caradonna came very soon and waited for some time — then he coughed — made a noise — but the two postulants never stirred. At last the Father went to them and said he was waiting. Mary Begley only shook her glass, and said the sand was not down — that Mother had said they were to make their meditation first. He had to wait till they had finished."

Father Caradonna's sense of humour stood him in good stead, and what could be done but wait! Afterwards he told Mother Magdalen how delighted he was to see such simple obedience.

During the last months of Sister M. Antonia's illness, Mother Foundress reserved to herself the loving if painful duty of watching by her bedside all through the weary nights of her suffering. Some time before death, Sister M. Antonia had expressed a longing desire for a drink of fresh Irish buttermilk from her beloved farm house! Although Mother Magdalen knew it was a "delirium" wish, she wired to Ireland that very day, and the buttermilk was sent via Rosslare and Fishguard, and was at Paddington by the 11.30 a.m. train. The dear Sister was momentarily overjoyed, even though one sip was the sum total of her longed-for restorative.

Shortly after Sister's death, the Cavendish Square Convent, palatial though it seemed, in contrast to the Robert Street house, was again evacuated for a larger house at Mount Street. The number of applicants increased; evening catechetical, needlework and other groups needed rooms apart, and a house at 123 Mount Street, in the immediate vicinity of Farm Street, was secured. Here, on December 28th, 1873, after the usual blessing, the erection of the Way of the Cross on the previous afternoon, and with Cardinal Manning in their midst, the Poor Servants of the Mother of God solemnly dedicated themselves and their Congregation to the Sacred Heart of Jesus. From that day forward, the title "Of the Sacred Heart" was to be added to each Sister's name in Religion, e.g. "I, Sister Mary Agnes of the Sacred Heart" etc. His Eminence received the vows of four novices after the Mass, and the Annals record his beautiful talk on prayer, telling the Community "to knock at the Tabernacle door for daily bread." He begged special prayers for the persecuted Archbishop of Posen.

This consecration to the adorable Heart of Jesus was considered by Mother Magdalen as "the greatest event yet recorded in the Annals," and so her own account is here given:

"On December 21st, we began to work at decorations for the church (Farm Street), and finished on Christmas Eve. Christmas Day was bright and happy — the church beautiful. We then began our own decoration for the great event of the 28th, Feast of Holy Innocents, the greatest yet recorded in our Annals. His Grace the Archbishop came in full pontificals, and received the vows of four novices... His Grace gave a beautiful little sermon on prayer — told us to knock at the Tabernacle door for daily bread, and to pray for the persecuted Archbishop of Posen...

"After Benediction came the great event. The Community made their consecration to the Sacred Heart. The Archbishop standing by as witness — lights blazing before a picture of the Sacred Heart. Then followed the Magnificat and a hymn to the Sacred Heart. Fr. Wynne, S.J., assisted. Many friends were present — these took part in the Act of Consecration, and thus in the Heart of Jesus we end 1873."

A further account is added by a Sister of the Mount Street community of that day, which shows how fear and fun, border-

77

ing on the ridiculous, were never far apart in their early efforts to "polish up" their holy poverty for state occasions:

"When preparing the little chapel for the ceremony, we had to improvise a throne for the Archbishop out of two old rush-bottom chairs, tied together, and covered with a heavy curtain. The 'throne' was placed in what was thought to be the most advantageous position, and, to hide all discrepancies, the drapery pinned securely to the carpet. Unfortunately the unexpected happened. The Archbishop tried to move his throne, and found it rooted to the spot! The designers trembled for its fate, but fortunately it stood the test!"

A short time after these happy events at Mount Street, Mother Magdalen and her children at Beaumont, as well as the community at Mount Street, were to suffer, as they thought, another great spiritual trial, which at first the Foundress took very seriously, as something that might undermine all her plans for God's glory in the future. The Superior at Beaumont wrote to say that dear Father Selby, on whose direction and wise counsel so much depended, was about to be withdrawn, and "a Father Dignam" was coming in his stead. Within a period of days, Father Clare also, who had been everything to the Community since its very beginning, and to Mother Magdalen herself since her return from the Crimea, was being changed from Farm Street to Liverpool. Not only was Father Clare her confessor and director, but, being also the confidant and friend of the Cardinal, he had taken on himself, with the full authority of his Superiors, a large share of responsibility for the new Congregation. To Father Clare Mother Magdalen had turned in all her difficulties, and through him she had received the permission for the adaptation of the Rules of the Society of Jesus, which the Community had observed on a broad general scale up till now.

Oh! How "unsearchable" are the ways of God! Little did the anxious Foundress think at the time of this seeming crisis that it was Father Dignam, not Father Clare, devoted, encouraging and helpful though the latter was from the beginning, who was to help her right through in the work and sure guidance of the Congregation, even to its being fully approved and accepted by Rome. Had Father Dignam not been ready

78

and willing, with the full permission of his Superiors, to take up the work where Father Clare left off, the trial for the Foundress would have been great. Devoted as Father Digman was to the Sacred Heart of Our Lord, and to the spread of the Apostleship of Prayer in England, she and her Sisters attributed God's gift of him to them as the direct result of their Consecration to that ever adorable Heart. He had been introduced to Mother Magdalen some time before, and was interested in the new Congregation. He was a Jesuit of exemplary zeal and humility, and of their first meeting to arrange matters of primary importance, Mother Magdalen has left his advice on record:

"The one point he was anxious about was the religious formation of the first Superiors and Sisters, in order that the spirit of the Institute might be thoroughly grafted in them. 'It matters little what they *do*,' he would say, 'it matters a great deal what they *are*.' The development of the Congregation, its works of charity, its extension into different dioceses, might, he thought, all be safely left to develop in time. What he wanted was to make the Sisters *real Nuns*; they were to become true Religious; and moreover, he strongly held the view that it gives God more glory to bring one soul nearer perfection than to train many to a lower standard."

Father Dignam was now in his 41st year. It is evident from his advice, written above, that he was already acquainted with and fully acquiesced in her ideals, and was determined by God's grace to help in every possible way with the spiritual training of the nuns. He gave no fewer than fourteen of their annual retreats, and made himself responsible with Mother Magdalen for the framing of the Constitutions and the Custom Book of the Congregation.

Thus at peace about the spiritual formation of the early members of her precious Community, whose numbers were growing beyond all her expectations, Mother Magdalen set out for Ireland again in the January of 1874. To have a convent in the "Island of Saints", the dear country to whose people she had felt irresistibly drawn since Crimean days, was the ardent desire of her intrepid heart, and she was now determined to have a good try for its finding. An opening presented itself at

79

Clongowes Wood, Co. Kildare, and the work in connection with its large Jesuit College was to resemble that of Beaumont, more or less. A special asset, the Foundress considered, would be that this foundation would serve to make the Congregation better known in Ireland, as well as offering a testing-ground for aspirants to the Novitiate in England, so she accepted it, as she did also a foundation in Limerick, for a good "try-out," as she liked to say. Both communities, however, were withdrawn by 1876. The Congregation could not as yet supply the number of Sisters required for the work at Clongowes, and the house being very small and inconvenient offered many drawbacks for its intended purposes. After a period of great happiness and "spiritual fervour" enjoyed by the few Sisters who lived there, they saw their "dear Mother's point of view," but to their old age they would speak affectionately of the little Clongowes Convent. The Limerick house offered many anxieties, financial and otherwise, and could never be made self-supporting.

Meanwhile from Ireland came a welcome and pressing invitation from a Miss Fitzgerald, of Rockville, Carrigtwohill, Co. Cork, who wrote that "in no place in Ireland was a convent so much needed as in this village, and the people are earnestly praying to have the good Sisters come." This letter was followed by one from Father Seymour, the parish priest, saying what pleasure it would give him "to see one of your little convents established in this small town or village." He offered the site for the convent and a handsome subscription towards its erection, the remainder to be added by his friends and parishioners. "Friends and parishioners" indeed they proved to be, and on June 21st, 1875, when Mother Magdalen and two Sisters arrived at Carrigtwohill Station, what was their surprise to see Father Seymour and his faithful flock of "friends and parishioners", including the children, all in festive array to meet them. Their surnames were initialled many times by almost every letter of the alphabet, from "A" to "V" — spelling Aherns, Barrys, Careys, Coppingers, Collins, Cotters, Dalys, Egans, Fahys, Fitzgeralds, Foleys, Gearys, Harts, Ingrams, Joyces, Keans, Lawtons, Leahys, Mackeys, Meahans, McCarthys, McDonnels, Mulcahys, Murphys, Nagles, O'Gradys, O'Neills, Powers, Quirkes, Regans, Ryans, Ronans, Stauntons, Twomeys, Walshes. The Mc's and the O's were there in number, and, paradoxical as it may seem, the "U" was initialling an old man named "Ulrick", who was supposed to be of German origin, and his friend "Veriker" gave the "V" for both himself and his violin.

The platform and road from the station to the Church were strewn with flowers, while a triumphant ach bearing "Céad míle Fáilte" in flowers also was carried over the Sisters' heads, as the procession made towards the Church, where the Rosary was recited and hymns sung in a thankful, thundering chorus.

The nuns took rooms in the village while the Convent was being built, and with God's blessing their work developed rapidly. They took over the girls' school, the care of the Church and sacristy, the visitation of the poor and the sick and the supervision of the parish sodalities.

An apostolic boarding school was also begun, which was fruitful in splendid vocations to their own as well as to other Congregations. When Ireland set up its own fine system of education, the apostolic schools were replaced by secondary day and boarding schools, with even finer results for religion and education.

Our Lord's yearning prayer to His Father on the last evening of His life has ever been fruitful in Carrigtwohill: "That they may be one," He prayed. This "one-ness" in loyalty to the Faith of our Fathers, to the Holy See, to their shepherds, the Bishops, and to their priests, has ever been characteristic of the Irish nation since the days of St. Patrick. This altruistic and charitable bond, its oneness, was ever strengthened among themselves throughout the long centuries of persecution by their love for the Holy Mass and the "Beads". Mother Magdalen sensed this all-beautiful and strengthening spirit in the Crimean hospitals. She was now to see it fully in action and in unremitted practice in that Ireland to which she owes her "glorious Faith," and from whose nation she has still much to learn. But her great heart will pay back fully the debt she owes, and for almost a century now her spiritual children have given of their best, as they thank God and His Virgin Mother for the privilege of being able to do so. Mother Magdalen's verses "To Ireland" may be fittingly given here:

TO IRELAND

O Erin! — not my own, yet loved
   Almost with childlike heart —
In all thy joys and sorrows sore
   I'll ever bear my part.

To thee I owe my glorious faith,
   More precious far than life,
Which gives me courage to sustain
   The combat and the strife.

From Irish lips I first have heard
   Of Mary's spotless fame;
Found her, my Mother and my Queen,
   And glory in her name.

And then, oh, greatest gift of all! —
   By Irish hands was given
The Bread of Angels to my soul —
   The Lord of earth and heaven!

And, Erin, friends I owe to thee
   Whose worth I'll never know
Until I meet them all above
   Where joys eternal flow.

Then, kneeling at my Lord's dear Feet,
   I'll count them o'er like gold,
And thank Him for them every one,
   Until the sum be told.

And, Erin, I will ne'er forget
   The debt I owe to thee;
But strive to save thy children poor
   From sin's dread misery.

When e'er in London's streets so vast
   I meet sweet "Irish eyes",
I'll strive to save those little ones,
   And train them for the skies.

For love of thee, and oh, still more,
    Far more, for love of Him
Who shed His precious Blood to save
    The whole wide world from sin!

The time's at hand — 'twill soon be here —
    Finish'd earth's tears and moan;
The nations all shall be as one
    In our Eternal Home.

S.M.M.

Ireland, August 1872.

From that eventful day in 1875, when the arrival of "our wonderful English Irish woman" and her "holy nuns" (as Father Seymour loved to express himself) down to our own day in 1970, the S.M.G. Sisters have had nothing but the greatest kindness and happy co-operation from the successive Bishops and clergy of Cloyne.

Our present revered Bishop, Most Reverend Dr. Ahern, and by a happy co-incidence his Lordship's namesake — Canon Ahern with his curate, could not be more paternally interested in, and co-operative in every way with our Sisters and their children.

Loyalty to the Holy See and to its recent decrees is at once evidenced in the dignified and very rubrical adaptations in the grand old "Carrig" Church. More heartening still is it to see the crowds who receive Holy Communion so frequently.

Even the holy Dead in the nearby cemetery, seem part of the happy scene enacted daily in the Church of their Baptism.

Could Mother Magdalen in 1872 have looked into the future, even as far in as 1875, how much more lyrically rich might her verses be!

Chapter 10.

BLESSINGS AND BLOSSOMINGS

Two months after the Carrigtwohill Foundation, the Sisters from the three Irish houses were called on to join their Sisters in England for the first really united Annual Retreat which Father Dignam was to give. It was to be held at Margate, a temporary Retreat House. The voyage took four days, and the party numbered fourteen. The captain of the ship — the "Countess of Dublin" — was extremely kind, but the weather and the waves were not! The nuns consequently suffered sea-sickness all the time as the ship tossed and rolled its wild route to Plymouth. As there was to be a wait of five hours there, the kind Captain took the nuns to the Convent of Notre Dame, where they were cordially welcomed and feasted and made to rest for some hours — a kindness their Superiors never forgot for their dear Notre Dame Sisters. The retreatants landed at Margate at 7.0 a.m. next morning, and, in all, the crowd for retreat numbered fifty-two. What a joy! Naturally there were many lacks and inconveniences for such a number, but "Mother" was with them, and was not "Mother" home? They had come to their Mother to renew their spirit and learn more about the things of God. The Retreat was a splendid success and marked another encouraging epoch in the history of the Congregation, in that the Foundress and the Sisters themselves recognized the enormous graces and lessons that resulted from this grand re-union, so much so that the future Constitutions were to oblige the new Congregation "to spare no forethought, nor trouble, nor expense in gathering them (the Sisters) together in large numbers for this purpose... for by these gatherings our Sisters shall be preserved in unity of spirit and in the fervour of their vocation." To this Rule Superiors have been ever most faithful, and are rewarded at seeing the immense joy these meetings give the Sisters, especially when Sisters of the same family or other relatives are re-united.

When the Retreat was concluded, Mother Magdalen went to Ireland again, seeing to much business; she returned to London in late autumn (1875) and despite all her work on hand, including the difficulties of the Limerick house, which she was determined to close in the following spring, she consented to open another convent at Soho, one of the most miserable and neglected parts of the city. She named it "Convent of Our Lady of Pity." Three Sisters only formed the little community, but what a mission was theirs! From their tiny sanctum they visited the parishes of Warwick Street, St. Patrick's, Soho, Lincoln's Inn Fields, and the local workhouses, went once a week to Battersea for catechism and a large Mothers' Meeting — "a sure way of getting at negligent and careless parents," Mother Magdalen inculcated, "is to get their children to love you, as one whom they feel is interested in them and who wants to win them for God, and then work through them. Parents, except they be very bad, will do anything for their children." She always made much of First Communion breakfast, and did her best to make these days memorable for children and parents.

The spiritual results of the Sisters' mission work in London in those years were far-reaching. Underground travel was yet of the future, so of course were taxi-cabs, and even the horse-buses were often few and far between, and even when available, road fares were not always at hand — " a veritable remedy against arthritis and bad circulation" an old Sister used to say laughingly, and her health at 76 years was proof in her case, as she was still active in her zealous apostolate. The same Sister has left on record that "Mother could never listen to a tale of poverty or illness and not give some relief. Now it would be bread, tea, sugar and even coal." One evening (the Welfare State had yet to be born) a young workman came to Mother Magdalen, telling her that he was sent by the doctor to tell her "he must go to bed with pneumonia, and as he had no one to nurse him, he had better tell the Sisters." Mother Magdalen herself, taking with her some mustard poultices (the remedy in those days) went to his poor home and nursed him back to complete health.

Christmas Day, 1875, saw a beautiful re-union of all the London and Beaumont Sisters again at Mount Street. The tea-party for the poor children was the richer for each one's presence, for each house sent a present for the occasion. There was an impromptu concert with much singing, at which one little Irish girl insisted on producing "The Peeler and the Goat." Her small brother was the "Peeler", and wore Sir Robert Peel's cake-tin-shaped model cap worn by the Royal Irish Constabulary of those days. The little scene caused great laughter, and the pair were so happy that they asked to encore their masterpiece for the Holy Child in the crib! What was Mother Magdalen's joyful surprise, after the little party had gone, to find hidden in the straw of the crib the "Peeler's" cap and the "goat's" horny mask, left as gift offerings to the Divine Child. "Surely He was grateful for the sacrifice," she thought, and to the end of her days she loved to rehearse the scene.

The Annals for the end of 1875 read: "And thus ended the year 1875, a year full of graces from Our Lady and her Son to the Poor Servants — Deo Gratias for ever and ever."

Mother Magdalen's next move was to purchase three small houses in the village of Roehampton, Surrey, which she contemplated throwing into one, to serve as a temporary novitiate until such time as a properly equipped one could be built. It was an idea she had abandoned for the Beaumont house some few years back. Now Father Dignam also was all out to bring this idea to realization. "God sent him to the Congregation," thought Mother Magdalen, as now both Cardinal Manning and he rejoiced at the proposed change. Since Father Clare was no longer at Farm Street, there was no advantage to be gained by the novices staying there, and as the Jesuit novitiate itself had been established at Roehampton, "the spiritual training of the novices was secure," thought Mother Magdalen, uttering her usual "Deo Gratias."

The three houses were accordingly purchased on the 25th March, 1876, Feast of the Annunciation, and on June 23rd, Feast of the Sacred Heart, the first Mass was celebrated there by Father Dignam, who was authorized by the Bishop "to solemnize the opening of the new Novitiate, say the First Mass there and give the Habit to five postulants." As already stated, the Jesuit novitiate had also been established at Roehampton some time before, and the Sacred Heart Convent with its fine school was near, while the little parish church of St. Joseph served the small Catholic congregation of that day. Altogether Roehampton was the privileged little village of four tabernacles by 1876, and was humorously but reverently styled "the Holy City." The "city" too supplied mostly all its own material needs. It had its post-office, its bank, a police-station a mile away at Putney, its drapery, grocery, meat and fish-shops, its fine orphanage later when the Poor Servants came, and its public laundry, which gave steady employment to many poor women and girls from near-by Putney, Wandsworth, Mortlake, Barnes and Roehampton itself.

The Sisters, once settled in Roehampton, began their mission in the visitation of the poor and sick in the surroundings and in the town of Putney, where there was as yet only a small galvanized church and no Catholic school. As times improved and the number of Catholics increased, the present church was erected and dedicated to St. Simon Stock. By 1918, the Poor Servants opened a small school in their newly purchased house in Clarendon Road, and the Catholic children of the parish were given free education. The work was so encouraged that after a time another house was purchased in order to relieve the overflow — many of whom were the children of the well-to-do, and could consequently pay school fees, which greatly helped towards the maintenance of the poor school. Music, art, and French were taught by accomplished teachers, catechetical instruction had "pride of place" on the curriculum, and despite the fact that some of the paying school were non-Catholics, there was no watering-down of Catholic doctrine to suit them. If their parents wished them not to frequent the catechetical classes, well and good, but no such exception was requested.

Sister M. Thecla, who had been trained by the Foundress herself, and who was one of the first Sisters to work in the Roman school, was put in charge of Putney. "She had a great way with men," was Archbishop Amigo's description of his

87

lifelong friend; and "with the Lord in prayer" might be added by those Sisters who knew her best.

After about a year of activity at Putney, Sister M. Thecla bethought her of a great plan, and with the full consent of the Mother-General (then Mother M. Stanislaus) and full authority from the Bishop (Dr. Amigo), she set out to take, with the kindly co-operation of Father Livesey, parish priest of Putney, a census of all the Catholic children of the town. In this work she was helped much by a Mr. Comerford, a fine type of the Catholic layman of his time. He visited Whitehall with Sister, and put the question: "If the necessary number of Catholic children going to State schools could be listed, and the number of Catholic rate-payers (urged thereto by their Bishop) signed an appeal for a public enquiry at Putney Convent, would Lord Eustace Percy (then Secretary of the Board of Education) honour the meeting with his presence? This his Lordship consented to do, when the date was fixed.

In the meantime, earnest prayer was doing its great work, as it always does. A Catholic benefactor came "out of the blue" as it were, and offered to build the school and hand it over to the Poor Servants as an act of gratitude to God for His goodness to him. He wished to remain anonymous for a time, but his great gift of Putney Catholic School for the children of the parish, without any expense to the parishioners, has caused his name to be inserted in the archives of the Poor Servants and to have the Sisters' prayers as long as the Congregation lasts.

In due time the meeting was arranged, and a goodly crowd of the "fors" and "againsts" greeted Lord Percy on his arrival. As the minutes went by, dialogue became very free and friendly, and even non-Catholics were brought to see the justice of the question at issue — the recognition of the school at Putney by the Board of Education. One mother in particular was determined to "have her say," and spoke up fearlessly thus: "I want all my children at the Sisters' school, and nowhere else, Your Honour." "Are you a Catholic?" asked Lord Eustace. "No, I'se a 'nostic', but my husband is, and he would not marry me if I did not promise to bring up the children Catholics. And sir," she continued, "Sister told my boy you were comin' and that you were one of the Percys of Northumberland who

88

fought in the Wars of the Roses, and ye were all Catholics then." She was clapped by the crowd as they roared with laughter, and Lord Eustace laughingly replied: "I'm glad your boy is learning history."

A high tea brought the meeting to a happy conclusion. Soon the new school began to rise, to be staffed by fully trained experienced teachers, and recognized by the Board of Education in 1925.

As well as this mission work at Putney, Mother Magdalen also introduced the custom of sending small companies of Sisters, at the weekends, to keep up night adoration at the Soho convent, "to offer continuous supplicating prayer for the prevention of, and in reparation for, the many sins committed against Our Divine Lord and His Virgin Mother in the great city of London, and especially in that quarter of it, by night."

Meanwhile, in the midst of her efforts for the glory of God everywhere, and the straightening out of her plans for the laying of a solid foundation for the future, and the encouragement of seeing the number of promising applicants increase, another heavy cross was being prepared for the Foundress, towards the end of 1876. In 1875 she had appointed one of her most faithful and promising Sisters Novice-Mistress in her stead. Sister M. Gertrude was a novice in the early days in London, and both Dr. Manning and Father Clare saw in her a woman of great promise for the future. It was she who offered "to go out to beg" when in desperation the Foundress assembled the postulants (who were many) one day, and told them they were free to leave, as her funds were absolutely spent and she saw no way of providing the immediate necessities of life. Some suggested "writing home" for help. This was not permitted, neither was Sister M. Gertrude allowed to go to beg, and not one postulant consented to leave. As ever in her needs, Providence provided, and next day most generous help came to Mother Magdalen from an unexpected quarter. Sister M. Gertrude had come to Roehampton with the novices in 1876, but her health soon broke down fatally, and by October death claimed her — its second victim from among the Poor Servants. In the loving letter written to the Communities by Mother Magdalen we have the details: "I was called in haste, and I have never forgotten the picture I saw of Sister

M. Clare, in her white veil, with an expression of pitying love, such as an angel might have worn, clasping Sister M. Gertrude's dying form... All who knew Sister M. Gertrude revered her as a saint. In her short life she had known almost every form of suffering, yet her sweetness and cheerfulness were unalterable, as were her self-devotion, loyal love of the Institute, and deep humility."

During the lingering weeks of dear Sister M. Gertrude's illness a bazaar was being planned in aid of Carrigtwohill convent. The whole parish was interested, as were the Foundress and the communities in London. Lady Georgiana was soliciting among her London friends, and wrote to her great friend, Monsignor Talbot, at the Vatican "to ask the Pope for some little gift" for the bazaar. Pope Pius IX, to whom Monsignor Talbot was Private Chamberlain, gave him four precious cameos chosen from a number on his table, and bade him send them with his blessing. His Holiness showed much interest in the story of the Crimean convert Foundress on whose behalf Lady Georgiana had solicited "some little gift." Especially was the Pontiff interested in the Foundress' connection with Dr. Manning, whom the Pope knew well in his Roman days, and who, he also knew, was wholly instrumental, with Cardinal Wiseman, in obtaining and transmitting His Holiness' permission to Dr. Grant of Southwark and Dr. Cullen of Dublin for the increase of Catholic chaplains for the Crimean Campaign, when Sydney Herbert, Minister of War, gave the "yes" of the British Government to his request. Manning, the Pope knew, was the man behind the scenes, who, encouraged by the success of his first project, went further, and soon the Catholic nuns were with the dear wounded in the Crimean hospitals, where Miss Taylor and Miss Stanley had 'defected' to the Catholic Church! Yet in God's designs it was not the saintly, sorely-tried Pius IX, but his successor, Leo XIII whose memory was destined to be forever held in affectionate reverence and benediction by the Poor Servants of the Mother of God. It was Leo, "Mother's Pope," as the Sisters loved to name him, who first received her in audience, who approved and signed the "Lauda" or first Brief of Praise of the Constitutions and the first recognition of the Congregation on July 18th, 1879, the second in the summer of 1892, and the final on 19th July, 1900, exactly twenty-one years after the first Brief, and some six weeks after Mother Magdalen's death. It was Pope Leo, also, with his Cardinal Vicar, who from the first had wished Mother Magdalen to open a school in Rome, and precisely in the English quarter, which she did in 1887. A magnificent church was added later, and dedicated to St. George and the English Saints. The full history of the Roman Foundation will be of interest in a later chapter.

Chapter 11.

THE BRIEF OF PRAISE

The first General Chapter of the Congregation was held at St. Mary's, Roehampton, on September 2nd, 1877, at that time the Feast of the Guardian Angels. At the wish of Dr. Danell, Bishop of Southwark, Father Dignam presided, with the consent of his Provincial. This Chapter marked another definite stage in the development of the Congregation.

Before an Order or Congregation is approved and officially recognised by the Holy See, it must have passed through a time of trial, of probation, as it were, or experiment, to the satisfaction of the Bishops in whose dioceses its members work. Its chief aim must be the holiness of its members, who are to be witnesses to Christ in their apostolate in His Church; it must show good prospect of stability, and it must have its Constitutions, Rules and Customs carefully and clearly drawn up to undergo a very detailed and rigorous examination.

In the period now passed for the Congregation, Mother Magdalen's motto had been "Festina lente" in the training of the spiritual life of the young aspirants God had sent her. She knew, for example, and only too well, that a youthful postulant on entering religion would find the new life strange for some time, and entirely different from that lived in her parental home. She therefore insisted on a spirit of motherliness in those Sisters appointed to teach them in the various departments. Sincerity and openness, born of simplicity, were the traits the Foundress liked to find in one who wished to consecrate her life to God. The over-zealous, the fussy, the self-confident, the close or the diplomatic character she would treat otherwise, while also showing a real motherly interest and spirit of sweet forbearance that spelled encouragement. "You are not leaving a margin wide enough for Our Lady to stamp her image on you," she would say, or "You must root up the weeds, if you want Our Lord to sow the seeds," and the postulant or novice in question would confess to feeling as if "Mother" read her soul.

Mother Magdalen moved slowly in this all-important work of training the young. She never acted hastily in imposing spiritual obligations on her children, but worked on a few broad principles, and experience proved the holy wisdom of her plan.

Father Dignam was now set free, as far as possible, by his kind Provincial, Father Jones, to give himself to this work of drawing up the Rules and Constitutions, and to be the Foundress' unfailing ally to bring the project to a happy conclusion. At the end of 1876, he was sent to St. Helens, Lancashire, to take on light parish work, where it fell to his lot also, a few years later, to initiate the great and holy work of the establishment of the Apostleship of Prayer in England. Throughout 1878 he gave himself wholeheartedly to the assistance of the new Congregation, and brought his many spiritual and literary gifts and his knowledge of religious life to its development. He was ever ready in his priestly humility to seek advice from others; he will advise the Foundress "to consult Father Porter on such and such a matter, as his advice is better than mine,' and again: "You will have many alterations to suggest when the MS. is submitted to Father Morris or any other Canonist. There will be suggestions and corrections from another point of view. Even if you don't send me a word of what you write, writing will clarify your ideas more than you can imagine. If you have a question to ask, write it down, if a suggestion to make, write it first." His final advice reveals much of the man that he was: "Any and every change (in his manuscript) by which you judge the Congregation will be made more acceptable to Our Lady, I shall wish it as much as you."

The draft was so near completion by Christmas 1878 that Father Dignam was able to announce his coming to Roehampton some days after the feast for final consultations, and the date of Mother Magdalen's departure for Rome was settled for January 4th, 1879. His letter ended: "Tell them all I prayed for them in my Midnight Mass. If they ever mean to serve Our

Lady generously, *now is the time.* Their lives during your absence will make a most important foundation-stone in the Congregation's life. God bless you, my dear child."

Mother Magdalen was accompanied by Sister M. Clare, whose health had not been to the Foundress' satisfaction for some months before. This Sister was a native of Wexford, and had been recommended to the Congregation by the Reverend James Cullen, a priest of the Community called "Missionaries of the Blessed Sacrament," and afterwards the well-known Father Cullen, S.J. In her very young days, this child had shown evident signs of a true vocation. She was possessed of rare intelligence, and even then would always find a way out of difficulties. She showed a talent for art also, and early in life scraped some colour off the walls to colour some drawings she had copied. Her parents were persuaded by friends to send her to a School of Art in Dublin, for which she went to prepare by attending a preparatory class recently opened by the Loreto nuns in her neighbourhood. Her one aim was to give glory to God by perfecting herself as much as possible. At the end of two years at the preparatory school, she heard of the Poor Servants of the Mother of God. All intentions of the Art School were abandoned, she applied to Mother Magdalen, was accepted, and received the Habit on September 22nd, 1874. After First Vows in 1876, Sister M. Clare was sent to Louvain with another Sister to study hospital nursing under the Augustinian nuns, who worked the Grand Hospital in the city. When the year had finished, the Sisters returned to London, but dear Sister M. Clare, in the midst of her hospital work, had cared too little for her own health. After sufficient change and rest, however, she improved much, but she never regained her former strength. After an attack of rheumatic fever had seriously impaired her health, she was sent to Ireland for a complete change, then to Hastings. Her bright and cheerful disposition helped her much, and as Mother Magdalen hoped that a long period of change would fully restore her, and especially a visit to the Eternal City, she thought well to have her as companion, so the dear young Sister was overjoyed.

The travellers reached Lyons on January 16th, and had hospitality from the Sacred Heart nuns. Next day they left Lyons for Turin, spending only one night there, and made for Florence next day, to fulfil an appointment with the Very Reverend Father Beckz, General of the Society of Jesus. They were met at Florence station by the English Father Alfred Weld, S.J., who had provided hospitality for them with the Sister Oblates of St. Francis de Sales. Next morning they visited "San Marco", the great Dominican Monastery which gives the square its name, and whose museum (until confiscated by the Government and given the designation "museum") was the part occupied by the monks, whose every cell boasts of the inspired religious art of the famous Fra Angelico. Much as Mother Magdalen wished to let Sister M. Clare feast her eyes and her youthful mind and heart on the artistic treasures of Florence, and its beautiful Renaissance history, they had to move on to Fiesole to keep their appointment. "We took an open carriage," writes Mother Magdalen, "and drove up the long hill to Fiesole." "Long hill" is the true description for the road that leads to this wondrous town, from whose top one looks down on Florence, with its historic river, the Arno, meandering along in the glorious sunshine, and like a silver ribbon, dividing the city in two, only to have its loveliness still more enhanced by the architectural beauty of its medieval bridges.

"We were both like children that day," wrote Mother Magdalen, who, in the midst of most serious business and even in periods of disappointment and frustration, could relax and enter into and enjoy the joys of others. She was so happy that day at seeing her faithful and very promising Sister M. Clare enjoy all this beauty after her long months of illness, and she hoped this joy would hasten her complete cure.

Reverend Father Weld, on their arrival at the Jesuit House at Fiesole, ushered them into the Father General's room. His Paternity showed great interest in the story of the new Congregation. He conversed with Mother Magdalen in French, and gave her his blessing and the motto: "Priez, Espérez, Travaillez," which Father Dignam often reminded her of in later disappointments. After the Fiesole visit, they moved on to Rome and to the Convent of Marie Reparatrice, near the Pincio, where they were to have hospitality, and where Mother Magdalen had a nun friend. Little did she dream that January day in 1879 that the spot on which she stood by the Pincio was in God's mind, that very spot where her beloved first foundation in Rome was to be situated, and that, by the express invitation of Christ's own Vicar, Leo XIII; and that by 1885 His Holiness' wish and kindly invitation were to be realized completely.

From Rome too she wrote to Lady Georgiana that she had been to the Trinità and had been cordially welcomed by the Superior, to whom she delivered a packet from their convent at Rue de Varennes. A few days after their arrival, Cardinal Howard had obtained a private audience for them, and on January 29th, His Eminence ushered them into the presence of the Holy Father.

"We fell at his feet," she writes, "and he laid his hands on our heads, saying in French to me, 'You are English,' and to Sister M. Clare, 'You are Irish.' Then he read the letter I had brought from Cardinal Manning, and asked many questions about England and the poor, and said the foundation of our Congregation was a good inspiration from God. He spoke so beautifully, I could not keep back my tears. He asked how many we were, and when I answered: 'Tres Saint Père, nous sommes quatre-vingt et trois,' he replied: 'Mais bientôt vous serez quatre-vingt cent et trois.' His Holiness went on to speak to us of his interest in England and Ireland, of the work for souls it was given us to do, how much we might do for God, how ready we should be to sacrifice ourselves for souls. He asked if we had brought our Constitutions to Rome, and finding that we had, he said: 'They will be examined, and I do not doubt you will receive the approval of the Church, and that approval will make your work grow and fructify and bring forth fruit.' Then he deigned to bless the rosaries and crucifixes we had brought, and lastly our Profession rings, which we boldly laid in the palm of his hand. Then we were dismissed, and went home full of joy."

This joy, with an earnest request for fervent prayer, was communicated to the Sisters in England and Ireland, and Lady Georgiana was also informed of the course of events. Luckily, too, Cardinal Manning was in Rome, and Cardinal Simeoni, head of Propaganda, told Mother Magdalen he would confer with His Eminence. Cardinal Manning told her afterwards at the English College that he would get the Cardinal to let the Rules be examined by Father Armellini, S.J., who understood English, and that "we should certainly get the Lauda."

Having got through so much, Mother Magdalen's cup of joy was full when she and her companion were admitted to the Holy Father's Mass in his private chapel. She loved all her life to recall the indescribable sense of nearness to Our Blessed Lord experienced when receiving the Blessed Sacrament at the hands of His Vicar. How she must have thanked her Divine Guest for this privilege! How she must have resolved at that moment to set up as many tabernacles as she could (for this was her "craze") and to draw ever more and more souls to love and to work for the consolation of that Divine Heart so athirst for the souls for whom He died!

At length Mother Magdalen was told that she had only to wait now for the decision of the Consultor, the Right Reverend Abbot Smith, O.S.B., who had been appointed to report on the whole matter to Propaganda (the Congregation governing the affairs of Religious Orders and Congregations at that time, as the Sacred Congregation for Religious does in our day). Needless to say, Mother Magdalen's further days of waiting were spent in visits to the sacred and special shrines in Rome. She invoked the intercession of Our Blessed Lady with almost every step as she visited the shrines and tombs of countless saints and martyrs, and nowhere with greater fervour, perhaps, than in the rooms of St. Ignatius of Loyola.

At last Holy Week brought the Foundress the news that on the Wednesday, Abbot Smith was to give her his judgment on the Constitutions. Of the venerable Abbot himself, Mother Magdalen wrote: "He had the reputation of great severity in his judgments, which was more than confirmed by his appearance. He was extremely tall and portly, of a severe cast of countenance, and his manner at first most repelling and eccentric. Under this was hidden a truly kind and faithful heart." The two nuns, with beating hearts, set out for St. Paul's-outside -the-Walls, and were shown into the parlour, where the Abbot met them. After the first introductory words, he became most cordial, and said: "I have read a great many Rules and Constitutions in my lifetime, but I never read any which pleased me so much as yours. The man who wrote these must have drunk in the spirit of St. Ignatius for at least twenty years." (Father Dignam had been just 23 years a member of the Society at this time). Abbot Smith had not the slightest clue as to who had written the Constitutions... The Abbot then went with the nuns into the Basilica. "Have you seen," said he, "the place where St. Ignatius made his last vows?" The Sisters replied that they had supposed this act had taken place in the ancient Basilica, which had been destroyed by fire in 1823. "No," said Abbot Smith, "it is not generally known that a small portion of the ancient Basilica escaped destruction, and is now incorporated into the present building. It was in the chapel of Our Lady, which was also that of the Blessed Sacrament, that St. Ignatius said Mass, made his own final vows, and received those of his companions on Easter Friday, April 22nd, 1541." He led them to the spot where a tablet on the wall records the great event. He then took leave of them, saying: "You may be at rest, you are sure of your Brief."

Another audience with the Holy Father, who was encouragement personified, and a promise from Cardinal Howard to look after their interests, brought Mother Taylor's business to an end for that time. As she prepared to leave the Eternal City, she regretted that though so many English-speaking Catholics came to Rome for Holy Week and Easter, nowhere could they hear the "Three Hours" or any special service in their own tongue. In God's good time she was destined to supply that want in a church dedicated to St George and the English Saints, attached to the convent which she was to found.

The return journey was also a series of pilgrimages which took in Assisi with its wonderful shrines of St. Francis and St. Clare (we can imagine Sister M. Clare's joy here!). From Assisi they went on to Loreto and the shrine of St. Zita, where the incorrupt body of the little servant saint has lain for nearly seven centuries. After this, Lourdes, and Paray-le-Monial were visited. "At Lourdes," Mother Magdalen wrote, "the grace of a cure was not vouchsafed for Sister M. Clare, whose resignation was continually voiced by 'Our Lady knows best'." At Paray, the travellers had an interview with the saintly Père Ginhac, S.J., who afterwards wrote Mother Magdalen the following letter:

" Paray-le-Monial,
Maison La Colombière,
24 juillet, 1879.

Ma Révérende et Bonne Mère en N.S.

Que Dieu, N.S. soit béni de cette douce paix qu'il vous a commu-inquée ici, et qui dure encore.

Le retraite que vous ferez plus tard aura pour résultat, je l'éspère, de confirmer cette divine paix.

Vous pourrer venir quand vous serez libre.

J'ai fait deposé sur le tombeau du V. Claude de la Colombière l'écrit que vous m'avez envoyé dans votre lettre. Comme il contient les prières que vous vous proposez de faire, ce sera comme une supplica-tion qui du tombeau du bon Vénérable montera vers Dieu. Je vous envoie de ses reliques.

Que le divin Coeur par l'intercession de son fidèle serviteur rende la santé à votre chère malade.

Je me recommande à vos prières, en union desquelles je suis, Ma Revérénde Mère,

Votre tout dévoué serviteur en N.S.,

P. Ginhac, S.J. "

England was reached on May 21st. In August a large number of Sisters had assembled at St. Mary's, Roehampton, for their annual Retreat, which was to begin on August 18th. What was Father Dignam's and Mother Magdalen's joy to hear from Cardinal Manning that he was to visit the Community that afternoon! The Sisters all assembled to welcome His Eminence, when in a most fatherly manner he asked all to be seated, and then produced the much-longed-for and much-prayed-for Lauda, or Brief of Praise, signed by His Holiness Leo XIII and dated July 18th, 1879 — a date the memory of which was forever to be kept holy by the Congregation, and each year on July 18th a general Communion of Thanksgiving is offered up by all the Sisters. Naturally, Father Dignam, who was there to meet the Cardinal, was overjoyed beyond words, and said afterwards to Mother Magdalen: "The moment I saw the Cardinal's face, I knew he had the Brief in his pocket."

Mother Magdalen's diary, referring to the glad event, reads only: "It was indeed a happy day for all . . . the first recognition by the Holy See of the value of Father Dignam's work." And later: "This was one of the greatest joys of Lady Georgiana's life." Of her own large share in the work there is never a mention. The "I" was never a characteristic of her writing or of her strenuous work — God's glory and consolation were her sole aim in life, and to His Divine Grace and to the helps He sent her in others she attributed all her blessings.

Congratulations poured in from the heads of Religious Orders, from the Bishops and priests who helped her, or whom she had helped since Crimean days. A special "Express" arrived from her dear Mother Frances Bridgeman, while Father Dignam took on himself the joyful task of notifying his brother-priests, Father Woollett, Father Clare and Father Ronan, whom God had sent to Fanny Taylor in her first "seekings."

The increasing illness of dear Sister M. Clare clouded Mother Magdalen's joy at this time, and as the months wore on, it became evident that the dear Sister's life on earth was fast drawing to its close. While in Rome, she had obtained permission to copy in oils the only likeness of St. Ignatius taken in his lifetime, and the work was excellent, according to competent artist judges. Sister was very wrapped up in what she termed "my St. Ignatius," but while the colours were still not quite dry in parts, the portrait met with an accident which the Sister Artist considered to be irreparable at first, and the Foundress was astonished at her calm and unperturbed acceptation of what she called "Our Lord's little way of treating us." The injury to the picture was made good, however, and it now hangs in the Sisters' community room in Brentford — a treasured heirloom of the blessed past.

On April 4th, 1880, the transferred Feast of the Annunciation, twelve postulants were clothed in the religious habit at Roehampton; though very weak, Sister M. Clare begged to see each one in her white veil, so that, as she put it, "I may know all my Sisters in Heaven." Death came in the afternoon of April 15th, after she had received the Last Sacraments, and on the anniversary of her having received Holy Communion at Assisi. Surely St. Clare was mindful of her faithful client, whose death was a great and personal loss to each Sister of the Congregation. Every act of her all-too-brief life was said to be an act of inspiring sisterly love for her Sisters, and even after the sun of her life had set forever, its beautiful afterglow seemed to remain on that dead face, as if to assure all who prayed by

100

her lifeless corpse that "Eye hath not seen, nor ear heard, nor hath it entered into the heart of man to conceive what things God hath prepared for those who love Him." (I Cor. 2:9)

Business called the Foundress to Paris after Sister M. Clare's funeral, and she took advantage, with her companion, of a few days at Paray-le-Monial — an oasis surely in her life of labour and now of present sorrow. They were there for the Feast of the Sacred Heart, and one can well imagine the intensity of her loving prayer to that Heart, for Whom alone she lived and suffered, and His Divine Heart must surely have been her supreme solace and the fount of many and special graces for her soul and those of her Sisters. She had a special permission from Rome to be admitted into the Visitation enclosure, and visited with intense devotion the scene of each apparition of Our Lord to St. Margaret Mary. After this privilege to their Mother, the Poor Servants at her request made it a daily practice to pray for the beatification of the then Venerable Claude de la Colombière, St. Margaret Mary's confessor, who had first preached in England devotion to the Sacred Heart.

A very important step in the progress of the Congregation was taken by the Foundress in 1880, when with the usual indomitable courage and trust in God, she took possession of a magnificent old-fashioned house, standing in its own beautiful grounds, at Brentford, Middlesex. This was the first freehold property bought over by the Congregation. When its purchase was finally decided upon, the Foundress heard that the proprietor would never agree to its sale to Papist nuns! The woman of quick decisions bethought her of a plan: she dressed in Victorian high-class style, as did also her companion, Mother M. Dismas, to whose beautiful, fashionable Bond Street hat was attached a pretty net face-veil of late 19th century dotted design. On the 21st June, Feast of St. Aloysius, both "ladies" with their legal adviser met the proprietor, inspected the house and grounds, and on the Feast of St. Anne the transaction was completed. The nuns were in possession in the first week of August, and on the Feast of St. Clare, August 12th, the first Mass was celebrated by Father John Morris, S.J., and the first convent since the Reformation, with its beautiful tabernacle housing their Divine Guest, was entered in the Catholic Directory for the New

Year 1881 as: "Poor Servants of the Mother of God, The Convent, The Butts, Brentford, Middlesex."

Mother Magdalen loved to connect all the important steps she took for God with the saints whose feasts occurred at the time, and wished such dates to be remembered by the Sisters. The founding of a new house, which meant another tabernacle for Him who had "come to cast fire on the earth" was her joy. The work in Brentford was most visibly blessed from the beginning. A large public up-to-date laundry helped to employ many poor women in the town itself, as well as being a means of support to the rented "houses of mission" in London. Visitation of the poor, catechism classes, instruction of converts, sodalities, the great work of the Apostleship of Prayer, so dear to the heart of the Foundress — all that could possibly be done by the new Community to help on the Reign of Christ was undertaken in happy and full co-operation with the priests of the parish.

A large orphanage was soon added to the existing house, and an apostolic boarding school was started, for which a further house was purchased. To this school (dedicated to St. Stanislaus) came some very promising aspirants to the religious life, many of whom eventually became Poor Servants of the Mother of God, or joined other congregations. One of the Foundress' joys in Brentford was to watch these dear teenage aspirants at their lively games or rounders or other sports on the convent lawn. Another very satisfying pleasure was to see the poor women from London parishes of Seven Dials, St. Patrick's, etc., coming for a day's feasting and recreation in the grounds, the expenses of which, including transport, were paid by Lady Georgiana and her friend, Lady Newburgh, until Lady Georgiana's death in 1885, but even after Mother Magdalen's death in 1900, the "Garden Party" was an annual event until 1908. The Apostolic School was closed before World War I, at which period also the Sisters began to teach in the Parish School of St. John's, where they had already taught catechism since the Foundress' day. In her day also, and to her great joy, the first Corpus Christi Procession for the parish took place on Brentford lawn, and has had its glorious recurrence for almost a century now. A magnificent new chapel at the lawn level was built in the 1950's, as was also a fine and modern infirmary for the aged and infirm Sisters, who gladly come to Brentford after having lived out their lives for God. Their loving work now, apart from their particular hobbies such as knitting, needlework, etc., is to pray for the Holy Father, the Church's many needs, the Congregation and its many forms of apostolate undertaken by the various communities. Their infirmary is connected with the Chapel by a gallery, which looks on to the Laundry from one side and on to the beautiful lawn from the other.

The happy atmosphere belonging to Brentford since the Foundress' days can still be sensed in that lovely spot. Her room, her stall, the first statue of Our Lady, of the early hard days in London, are all treasured there as well as her lovely motherly photograph and those of Father Dignam, Father Clare and Father Scoles.

At the other end of the original house, a beautiful home for poor handicapped girls and those in need of care and protection was built also in the 1950's, as an improvement on that which already existed. The girls (or "dear children", as the Foundress loved to call them) are truly happy in their home and proud of it. They are trained (when capable of being taught) in cookery, needlework, knitting, laundry, poultry-keeping, infirmary and sacristy work. They have beautiful concerts, happy outings to seaside resorts, and the grounds of Hampton Court, Kew Gardens and Syon Park offer glorious opportunities for walks and picnics. On all such outings they are of course accompanied by Sisters. An annual spiritual retreat is the high-light of their year, and frequent visits from and to their relatives are welcome.

The Convent was also from its beginning, as it still is, the happy meeting-place of many Sisters for their 8-days' Retreats, of which there are two annually. Until the Roman House claimed her, the Foundress spent much time at Brentford, and especially at Retreat times, when each dear Sister had the joy of a long tête-à-tête with the Mother she revered and loved.

The spirit of the Brentford of yesterday vibrates happily in that of to-day, and trusting ever in the vivifying grace of a benevolent God and in the intercession of Our Lady, Mediatrix of All Graces, the spirit of its holy Foundress shall live on in the Brentford of to-morrow. The late lamented Cardinal Valeri, their one-time pupil and later their Cardinal-Protector, told the Poor Servants of the Mother of God, shortly before his death, that their Foundress was "born for now." If that "NOW" was more than two decades ago when Vatican II and its norms concerning Religious were still in the offing, the Poor Servants of the Mother of God ask themselves: "What would their Foundress do were she living in 1970? Surely her first prayer, as in her life, would be 'Thy Kingdom come' and her next yearning aspiration would be also our Lord's own, 'That they may be one.' "

From the interior power-house of this zeal for God's Kingdom and from the burning spirit of charity and "oneness" which ever feeds fervent souls, she would undertake any and every apostolate to console and assuage the longings — the "Sitio" of that Divine Heart ever pleading for the souls for whom He died.

Rev. Fr. Clare, S.J., Fanny's first God-given guide in London.

The Rev. Fr. Dignam, S.J., who, with Mother Magdalen,
wrote the Constitutions and guided the young Congregation
for well nigh two decades.

C h a p t e r   12.

HARDSHAW HALL,
ST. HELENS AND THE SACRED HEART

Mother Magdalen could not rest on her oars for long in the happy haven of Brentford. She had to launch out again into the deep, to obey the call of her Divine Captain, but obey she would, this time to "pastures new" certainly, but not to velvety lawns, rippling waters nor to a land of beautiful sunsets. Father Dignam had often reminded her to "Remember Jesus is never separated from His Cross. Never think you love Him truly till you love His Cross, for it is planted in His Heart." In the year 1876, it will be recalled, Father Dignam was appointed to the Jesuit parish of Holy Cross at St. Helens, Lancashire. His description of the town at that time is interesting. He writes thus to his nun sister at Bruges: "I have none but poor, and they are as thick as bees. We are six in number, and as jolly as you could wish. Out of doors the first aspect of St. Helens would give you the horrors. The town is spotted over with great wastes and cinder heaps and the refuse of chemicals. The air is charged with sulphur and other strange things, so that often when you get up on a wet morning, you find the streets coated with blue slime. Clean hands are a thing you give up. The children burrow for cinders while they are still smoking, and look very like imps, but they are very good boys and girls for all that. My labours are confined to a very small field, but it took some little time to tell one row of huts from another. The houses are much worse than they need be, for there is very little real destitution, but the work is so dirty that they settle down in it, and give up the idea of appearances..."

A widespread coal strike and a cruel snowy winter in 1880 increased the misery and increased also in Father Dignam's mind the growing conviction that a convent of nuns who would visit the poor and teach them how to live was greatly needed, and naturally he thought of Mother Magdalen and those whom he called "his own children." The Notre Dame nuns were already in St. Helens doing great work in the schools, but more was needed. Father Dignam had already approached the Bishop, who was rather obdurate, fearing that small communities at such work would fail in religious discipline. Father Dignam now begged Mother Magdalen to see the Bishop herself, while he wrote to Monsignor Talbot and to Lady Fullerton for testimonials of work done and blessed, as the result of full fervour and of spiritual discipline maintained. The brave Foundress was in Liverpool by the end of January 1882, and on February 1st she and her companion, Sister M. Sebastian, heard Mass, went to the Bishop, were received most kindly by His Lordship, and returned on the following day, as he bade them, for the written permission to commence their foundation at St. Helens! In her buoyant spirit of joy that yet another Tabernacle was to be erected and that her Sisters were called to work among the poor and the suffering, Mother Magdalen set to work at once. A telegram called Sisters M. Emmanuel, M. de Sales, M. Leonard and M. Benedict from London. An offer of a small house at No. 18 George Street was accepted joyfully, and that very afternoon some necessary furniture was purchased. From the Convent of Notre Dame, where they had been guests during the negotiations, Mother Magdalen and her companion moved to George Street and welcomed their London Sisters on the following day, when a beautifully cooked dinner was sent to the little community by their gracious friends of Notre Dame. Tables and chairs had not yet arrived. A dinner service was supplied by kind neighbours, and, seated on the floor, with Mother "in the place of honour on the first step of the staircase," the first meals at St. Helens were thankfully partaken of. The Sisters set to work immediately, and with the generous help of kind friends, unwrapped the bedsteads, made the beds, preparing one room for a little oratory, and the whole process, we are told, was watched by little grimy, curious faces and noses flattened against the window-panes, so that in order to have the minimum (or maximum!) of privacy for a few days, the Sisters curtained the windows temporarily with the canvas wrappings in which the new furniture had been packed. The Sisters had carried with them from London the small statue of Our Lady around which they had first gathered as aspirants to ask her maternal blessing and help. A small statue of the Sacred Heart was also brought, and St. Joseph was not forgotten. Father Dignam came with a large crucifix, saying: "I have brought you the Cross, because it is dearest to my heart."

Work in the town was begun by the Sisters in the very first week, the Annals tell us, Father Cardwell sending two Children of Mary to show the Sisters the different parts of the town, and Father Egger provided a map of the districts they were to visit. The first poor patients visited by the Sisters made them realize what the Lord expected of them at St. Helens. The Annals tell the tale: "The first two patients we visited were going to receive Holy Communion, and Father Cardwell wished us to prepare the room for him — he got one of the Children of Mary to show us the house. She had a basket containing linen cloths, candles, candle-sticks etc. to use when the Fathers went to give Holy Communion to the poor in their own homes.

"The Sisters found one poor woman in a miserable state of poverty, and no one in the house but an old man. It was hard to know what to do first. She was so dreadfully dirty that the priest could scarcely give her Holy Communion in that state. So one Sister prepared the table, and another tried to wash her face and make her a little tidy. After a great effort they got a little water, but only in a cup. It seemed impossible to get anything like a towel — it was something like a piece of an old shawl they got to wipe her face with. At last they had her a little tidy, Father Cardwell remained looking on — his face beaming with joy...

"One afternoon the Sisters met with a man who had hurt his hand very badly. He asked them to undo the bandage and make it more comfortable, as the hand was very painful. They went to see him next day and found him no better. On the third day he was much worse. He asked them to send for a priest, and a Father went to him — he had scarcely left when the man died. The poor fellow had neglected his religious duties for more than 30 years."

A Mothers' Meeting was started soon, and a laundry, to give poor women and girls work. An Instruction Class was begun both for grown-ups and for children, and several were received into the Church or received back after years of neglect. In those days it was a usual sight in the early morning, as the Sisters made their way to Holy Cross for Mass, or went down town shopping, to see poor young urchins with chilblained hands searching through large cinder heaps and dustbins for bits of half-burnt coal, dry crusts of bread, or part of an orange thrown away in its rind. To Mother Magdalen and to her Sisters, their own poverty and very many inconveniences weighed lightly when compared with the needs of the poor, ere yet the great chemical works of St. Helens were in full working order to give employment to many. For the men in the mines, her sympathy was great. Businesslike ever and methodical as she was, she got the Sisters, while on their visitation, to register the names and addresses, and occupations of the various fathers of families, and especially of the younger men who worked in the coal-mines. For these she opened a night school and held regular classes, as she discovered that many could neither read nor write. The dear "pupils" got really enthusiastic, and wonders were wrought. Catechism classes were started, prayers were learned by heart, general talks on morals and ethics were given by a Jesuit Father, and the three "R's" classes were attended by many non-Catholics as well.

The daughter of a non-Catholic herself — and of a staunch clergyman at that, Mother Magdalen knew from personal experience that conviction must precede conversion, and that the grace of the true Faith is God's free gift to the seeking soul of the adult, who is often called upon to pay a great price for the "precious pearl." When Catholic men or boys brought their non-Catholic friends to the night school, Mother Magdalen never watered down Catholic doctrine for their convenience, or for fear of their interrupting questions — in fact, these helped to emphasize her teaching all the more, and there were many conversions as a result. But it was for neglectful, careless, half-hearted Catholics she was most concerned, and during the Sisters' visitation of the parish, many such were hunted up, many lapsed Catholics, too, on the verge of eternity were helped back to God before death.

This constant visiting in the homes, the frequent contacts with the sick, the aged and the dying, as well as with the fairly well-to-do and the fine old Lancashire type of gentlemen, made Mother Magdalen ponder and resolve. The fruit of her prayerful pondering was to see that the one very great and pressing need for St. Helens was a Catholic Free Hospital, and her prompt and determined resolution was to see to its realization. She voiced her idea to Father Dignam and to the Father Rector of Holy Cross, came to London herself to talk matters over with her Council, and in a short time went back and laid her plans before His Lordship the Bishop. Time, and the knowledge of all the good accomplished since the Sisters' coming to St. Helens had fully quieted his Lordship's qualms, and he gave his permission.

In January 1882, the Beaumont Foundation had to be given up, much to the regret of the Foundress, who could no longer supply the number of Sisters required, as the St. Helens Foundation opened up a large field of labour. Assured as she was that St. Helens and its future hospital were God's Will, and having had the necessary authorization, Mother Magdalen determined to make a small beginning on the Feast of St. Francis Xavier, December 3rd, 1882, when she took a few sick women and children into her little house. If, as the poet says, "The child is father to the man," one may rightly add also that "The child is mother to the woman," in Mother Magdalen's case, when one thinks how, back in her childhood, she constructed a little "ark" after her first Bible lesson on Noah's preparation for the Flood, and gathered into it for protection all the slugs and snails, ladybirds, a poor desolate robin, a fly released from the spider's web, and even the wounded mouse released stealthily from her father's trap in the stable.

She soon saw the immense value of the little she and her Sisters were doing, but all were anxious to have things on a much larger scale, and more efficiently done. The difficulties were enormous, the poverty and inconveniences in the way were reasons for depression, but the great lover of the Sacred Heart had long since proved the truth of the Divine Promise: "Where two or three are gathered together in My Name, there am I in the midst of you," and again: "If you ask the Father anything in My Name, He will give it to you." Nothing daunted, therefore, she sought the help of those influential friends whom she knew would understand. The first and most necessary step was to get the Sisters trained. To this end she wrote to Mr. Wegg Prosser in December, 1882, to say how anxious she was to have her Sisters trained at St. George's Hospital, telling him that "Mr. Charles Hawkins has kindly undertaken to plead this cause at the Board, and H.E. the Cardinal has promised to write to the Board." She goes on to say that "her heart is bent on succeeding at St. George's," and that she is acting with the full sanction and co-operation of the Bishop, the clergy and of various Catholic doctors of the town. The reply was a full-hearted "Yes." The next pressing need was a larger house, and a much more adapted one, if doctors were to send patients, so house-hunting began immediately, as Mother Magdalen realized the necessity of taking in men. Father Egger, S.J., of Holy Cross, set out each morning on the search, as did also two Sisters, and in December 1883 a second house was taken at 34 George Street. This house was secured through the great kindness of another friend of the Foundress, Mr. J. B. Leach, afterwards, and until his death the loyal Chairman of the Hospital Committee. This house was rented for six months only, as Mother Magdalen had her prayerful eye on the one house in St. Helens that would lend itself for what she sought, and, as ever, put the matter in the Hands of the Divine Physician of souls and bodies. The house was Hardshaw Hall, which in God's Providence was destined to grow with the years into the fine Catholic Hospital we see to-day. The Annals give the account of the take-over in 1884: "One evening Mother went to visit the Convent of Notre Dame, and there unexpectedly met Mrs. Walmesley, the owner of Hardshaw Hall, with whom we had been negotiating for some time. The difficulties in the way of getting it seemed insurmountable — amongst them that of meeting Mrs. Walmesley. Sister Marie Anne, our dear friend at Notre Dame, managed this meeting for us at last. All was settled that evening, and Mother came home with the joyful news that Hardshaw Hall was to be ours in six months.

"Great obstacles still stood in the way, as the tenants would not give up the keys at the end of the term, though they had promised to leave a week before the time, to allow the Sisters to begin on July 2nd. On July 1st, some of the tenant's furniture was still at Hardshaw Hall, and the Sisters were told they must buy it in order to get possession. Mother asked to see it, and went with two Sisters to the Hall. When they got in, she told the tenant they did not mean to leave, but would keep possession. He departed, very ill-pleased, locking the door and taking the keys with him. But they were able to get out by a back window. In a few hours the bill of the furniture came, and though some of the things were of little use to us, Mother sat down and wrote a cheque for the amount at once. The keys were sent up a little later. Next day, the Feast of the Visitation, we went to live in Hardshaw Hall, and soon after made our Retreat."

From 1880 onwards, and Father Dignam's call on Mother Magdalen, and her own later idea of a free Catholic Hospital in St. Helens, her courage, her magnanimity and her absolute trust in God were enormous. Even her staunch friend and admirer, Lady Georgiana, gasped at the speed of her astonishing attempts at St. Helens. In the height of the all-absorbing attention needed for her London houses, she resolved on a bazaar for help to meet the Sisters' fees at St. George's Hospital, and this in St. Helens itself. At the same time, the night-school "boys" became enthusiastic, and a "Penny Fund" was organized, and all sorts of original ways and means adopted, so that soon the enlargement of the already "large" Hardshaw Hall was contemplated. Even her great sympathizer and helper, Lady Georgiana, threw cold water on her go-aheadness, but the "valiant woman" and her Sisters had had ample proof already of the great-heartedness of the One in whom they trusted. The "scio cui" of St. Paul led them on, and what they did next astounds one. They had the Bishop's permission for the building of annexes at Hardshaw Hall, but where was the money to come from? A crusade of prayer was organized, and the Foundress made up her mind immediately, and sent one of her Assistants, Mother Aloysius Austin, and Sister M. Dismas to a well-known Catholic builder to ask him to build the additions to Hardshaw

Hall and wait for payment until the money was found. The builder asked for a day's delay to give the reply to this unusual order from a group of poor nuns "but a few years in the town," as he must have thought! What was Mother Magdalen's almost unbelievable surprise and joy when a letter next day informed her that the builder in question had consulted his wife, and both agreed to have the necessary wards built at their own expense! These benefactors were Mr. and Mrs. Peter Middlehurst, whose names will ever be held in benediction by the Poor Servants of the Mother of God, and are inscribed in the archives, to be prayed for as long as the Congregation lasts.

Work began at once to clean up Hardshaw Hall, and it was decided that the new hospital should be called "Providence Free Hospital," to prevent any misunderstanding, as the Church and parish were both named "Holy Cross." Although the brave Foundress never made the slightest detour from the path she had chosen to follow, many were the obstacles to be overcome. Just when Hardshaw Hall was being contemplated and the Sisters in the two small houses in George Street were bravely holding the fort, Sister M. Winifred fell seriously ill. Despite all the doctors' efforts to save her precious life — "a life hidden with Christ in God" as Father Dignam described it, — she died at St. Helens on November 24th, 1883, with a happy, expectant look on her face. All her life her devotion to the Holy Souls was great, and she died in their month, her eyes fixed smilingly on a picture of Our Lady appearing to the Holy Souls and lifting them, as it were, from the flames. Her loss to Mother Magdalen and to the brave little Community was part of the price to be paid for the great work begun for God's glory in the North. The following is an extract from the sermon by Father Dignam at St. Helens on the occasion of Sister M. Winifred's funeral:

"When we look at the remains of our dear little Sister, who has passed away from us in the flower of her womanhood, we see the necessity and the wisdom of despising the world, of turning our backs on what it offers to us and keeping our hearts detached from all. It seems to me such a short time since I saw Sister M. Winifred, then almost a child, enter the Novitiate. Once admitted, she only longed for the day on which she might pronounce her Vows and see the black veil cover her head, which would mark her as the consecrated spouse of Jesus Christ. That hour came, and as a formed Sister of the Institute, she has left this world for Heaven. We might have thought that a life so humble, so simple, so devoted, would have been spared longer, but God was watching Sister M. Winifred, and when He saw her ripe for Heaven, the fatal malady set in which terminated her earthly life. When we see her in her coffin, her Sisters kneeling round her, bound to her, not only by super-natural but also natural affection, her relatives and friends, who feel her loss so deeply, we cannot but grieve with them. Still we have consolation, and that lies in the faith Sister M. Winifred herself possessed. Her death was calm, happy and resigned; her desire was to do 'whatever God wishes.'

"When we look at that coffin with its white pall, does not our heart rejoice? What does it say? Her dying life is over. Now at last she has begun to live, received as the Spouse of the Lamb. She has been admitted to sing the song unknown to others than virgins, and 'to follow the Lamb whithersoever He goeth.' But let us not forget to pray for her soul. Pure and de-voted as she was, she has passed and been judged by the light of Eternal Truth, and we know that the least degree of defile-ment unfits the soul for entering Heaven. She has done us good! Let us in our turn repay her by prayer — the only thing it is in our power to do. But while we pray, and pray much for her, let us profit by her lessons of virtue, and let her example teach us to despise this world and all it contains. May she rest in peace. Amen."

It was about this period also that the Foundress was to have another cross to carry in London itself. Some time before, Charlotte Anne, Duchess of Buccleuch, called on Father Gall-wey, who in turn called on Cardinal Manning, to discuss the possibility of rescuing poor victims of the so-called "social evil," and who, many of them very young, having once fallen, were unable to help themselves.

The Foundress had already purchased a house in Green Court, and had gathered there many poor Catholic girls in her pitiful endeavour to win them back to good living. Not only had this house become too small for their numbers, but worse still, it had been molested by those who had been robbed of their prey, and who boldly and barefacedly threatened to send the nuns away. Fearless ever in face of a threat to her children, she determined to take her stand as Green Court was attacked one evening. Having already had five names on her list, she threatened publicly to expose these and "the others" as she appeared before them in the doorway. Tall and dignified, her blue eyes flashed angrily and fearlessly on the group as she spoke, finishing with: "Stay on, please, yet a minute." She never moved, and they, thinking the police were on the way, made off, to watch, no doubt, from some hidden corner, when, as luck had it, two policemen did actually come along, and Mother Magdalen beckoned them into the Convent. Whether her culprits witnessed the scene and took to their heels she never knew, but she and her poor inmates were no longer molested.

Later on the Refuge was moved to Percy Street, and afterwards to 31, Soho Square, and finally to Streatham in 1888. In this great work of mercy and pity, the kind Duchess of Buccleuch was all out to help the Foundress, and she also had the full support and co-operation of Cardinal Manning, who preached on behalf of the great work from the pulpit in Farm Street, and gave it his heartfelt blessing.

Meanwhile, business was brisk at St. Helens. What joy for the Congregation, and for the Providence Community, when it was made public that Cardinal Manning himself was coming North to open the Hospital on September 14th, 1884. His Eminence fully expected his welcome. He was "the people's Cardinal," the future go-between and peace-maker in the great London Dock Strike of 1889, with which his name will be forever linked in the social history of London. He was a great Churchman, with a Roman Doctorate, the friend of Gladstone and of the wealthy and learned, whom he justly and diplomatically got on his side in his fight for the workers, the poor, the Catholic schools, and homes of all types. The people of St. Helens of every creed and class got wildly enthusiastic about his coming there, and the whole town was en fête for the event. His Eminence was received on his arrival by the municipal authorities, by Father Rector of Holy Cross, and by Father

Dignam and Father Clare, whom he knew well. Lady Georgiana from her sick-bed wrote: "Really, to have the Cardinal and Father Clare surpasses all one's hopes. 'Vou n'êtes pas dégourdie,' as the French say, and lose nothing from want of asking." She sent her old friend a cheque of £10 to help towards the cost of the luncheon which she supposes Mother Magdalen will have in the new Hospital for His Eminence and the municipal authorities.

The Cardinal, preaching at Holy Cross on the Sunday evening, said: "You may perhaps ask me why I should call upon you for this work. Well, my dear children in Jesus Christ, my first answer might be to plead this — there is no good work in the Province of Westminster to which I ought to be a stranger, or where, in a long experience of 20 years, I have ever found myself accounted as such. But that is not my reason, and if that had been the only motive, I should not have been here to-night.

"I am bound to tell you that the Rev. Mother under whom this Hospital is founded and opened has been intimately known to me for the last 30 years. My knowledge of her commenced at the time when that terrible war in the Crimea had reached its utmost point of suffering, and when my illustrious predecessor, the late Cardinal, laid upon me the office of seeing that there should be nurses sent out for the care of our Catholic soldiers. It was at that time I first knew the Rev. Mother. She went into the hospitals where every form of death, disease and suffering existed in a degree which perhaps the history of no war could parallel. It was indeed a training for any work she can do in this place, and I will say it is a claim on the help, support and sympathy of the people of St. Helens. I am confident, too, that her name will draw to this place the aid of a multitude in England."

On the day of the actual opening, His Eminence told the people of St. Helens what he thought of the Poor Servants of the Mother of God. He spoke of their great apostolic work in the worst slums of London; how they would go distances of an evening to prepare the poor invalids' rooms and tables for the reception of their Lord in the morning; how they taught poor women and girls that "soap was cheap and water plenti-

115

ful," and made them take a pride in keeping their homes clean and tidy. He told them how he had transferred 700 boys from the district school at North Hyde, for the sake of their Faith. These nuns came to his help and took over the management of the house until other provision was made. During an epidemic, the Cardinal went on, he had been able to provide two isolation hospital tents for the worst cases. In the height of the tragedy, the Sisters' cottage was completely burned down; they had to take rooms on the same floor as the poor sick boys whom they were nursing, with the natural result that some became affected by the disease and died. Yet the Sisters continued at their work of extreme though dangerous charity for five years.

Thus, with Cardinal Manning's enthusiastic attitude and heartfelt blessing, the Providence Free Hospital began its wonderful career. Its night-school grew apace, and so did its Penny Fund. One worker actually gave £10 for the improvement of the Guild Hall (schoolroom) "in gratitude for all the benefits received there." Later, a certain "Tom" of the night-school was found outside the Hospital teaching his little son the mystery of the Blessed Trinity by its three gables!

The foundation stone of the new annexe to Hardshaw Hall was laid in 1887 by Lord Stanley, afterwards 16th Earl of Derby, and the building was ready for use by 1888. It would be almost impossible to keep pace with the growth of the "Providence" from then on. During the Foundress' life her Lord, in Whom she trusted completely, opened every door through which she sought entrance, as she in her turn never failed Him in her efforts to spread His Kingdom and to assuage His thirst for souls. This was the spirit with which her Divine Bridegroom inspired her, and which she tried and prayed to instil, with the help of his grace, into the heart and soul of every Sister whom He sent her. The onward, ever-hastening tempo of our modern age would find this wonderful woman alive and alert to Holy Church's every call on to-day's Religious of the Aggiornamento. A fine business sense and a tactful handling of matters gained her the trustful respect of Bishops and men of affairs, but it was in her dealings with, and in the training of the spiritual lives of her Sisters that her real self and her aims were best reflected. While, with the poet, she knew from experience that

116

"A little learning is a dangerous thing," she also agreed with that axiom of philosophy which says that "one cannot give what one has not got," and therefore, while she inserted in the Constitutions of the Congregation that "Every talent which may be discovered in the Sisters must be carefully trained to perfection," she ever insisted on that first and greatest essential — "A life of closest union with Our Lord in His Eucharistic Life and with His Holy Mother, Spouse of the Holy Spirit, whose seven gifts they so need in their apostolic life, if the walls of the Interior Castle are to resist the onslaughts of the enemy of mankind, whose pretended power is ever vanquished by the joyful humility of the trustful and prayerful soul, who, thus shielded, may safely seek after all knowledge relative to her state as a woman and a nun; ever dedicated to the salvation of other souls and to the diffusion of the 'good odour of Christ,' wherever she goes."

With the purchase of Hardshaw Hall, and its transformation from the "Hall" to the Providence Free Hospital, much had been accomplished. The Sisters at St. George's Hospital, London, had been accepted and had done well. Cardinal Manning's gracious presence at St. Helens, and His Eminence's introduction of the Foundress and her Sisters to non-Catholics and Catholics alike, scattered, as chaff before the wind, any fears the people might have had of these strange women, whom some considered as foreigners coming to implant a Roman religion. Mother Magdalen paid no heed to idle comment, but having obtained the rightful authority for her work, she and her Sisters went on with their apostolate without distinction of creed or class. The dear people of St. Helens rallied to the great work of their hospital, the night-school, and the Apostleship of Prayer, which Father Dignam was zealous in propagating in the North. The League of the Apostleship of Prayer had been founded near Le Puy in France in 1884, and Father Maher, S.J., introduced it into England and Ireland in 1865. After his death, and until Father Dignam's transfer to St. Helens and his having been appointed Central Director, the League had almost died off, only to get new impetus from Holy Cross, in which Mother Magdalen and her Sisters took an active share. Now came his happy chance, and a "Penny Messenger of the Sacred Heart"

117

was published by Manresa Press, Roehampton, in the circulation of which the S.M.G. Sisters took an active part.

A fit ending to this chapter on the Providence Hospital is Father Devas' quotation of the words of an invalid protégé of Mother Magdalen, who had been a patient in the early and very difficult days:

"Providence Hospital is simply an embodiment of Mother Magdalen's childlike confidence in God. Its early beginnings, its struggles, its developments, tell their own story of that living faith in the Providence to which she dedicated it. The great and many obstacles which she encountered, and which would have caused many other holy souls to turn away wistfully, but disheartened, and lay down the proposed work as impracticable, seemed to melt away in face of that strong trust which, while sparing herself neither toil nor pain, was the rock on which she rested all."

The Blessed Mother of her Lord had long ago taught Mother Magdalen that the secret of all strength lay in complete trust in Him who had wrought His first miracle out of time, as it were, rather than refuse her who had never refused Him anything. Towards the end of 1884 and during her Retreat, the Foundress wrote:

"My lady and my Mother Mary, in the presence of God and His Holy Angels, I choose thee this day, the fifth day of my Retreat, in a special way as my Superior. Thou art indeed by every right the first Superior of this Institute — thou art the Lady and Mistress — I am only thy head servant.

"Lady and Mother, I want this choice of mine, this obedience to the be *real*, and thus I bind myself as follows:

1. Every morning to kiss thy hand and ask thy blessing, to recognize thy authority.
2. Never to act without asking permission inwardly — and when it is important, outwardly.
3. Never to give a reproof or correction without asking thy leave.
4. To have thy image ever before my eyes.
5. To say my beads devoutly.
6. To go to thee when sad, tempted or troubled.

7. Never to dispense myself from rule or custom without thy general or particular permission.
8. To renew my general permission every month.
9. Every night to ask thy pardon and thy blessing — kissing thy feet and thy hand.
10. Once every week to give thee an account of conscience.
11. Once a month to spend a day alone with thee.
12. To hold tight my beads when tempted.

Finally — to remember it is to *thee* not me, respect should be paid. By thy wish only I should correct or punish. And by keeping these points I shall keep my great resolution for this Retreat, i.e.
> To have constant recourse to Mary.
> To live in dependence on Mary.
> To strive to imitate Mary.

Mother, I know I shall often fail — but I will be sorry, not hard, and I will always remember thou art my *Mother*.
> Thy unworthy child,
> Mary Magdalen of the Sacred Heart,
> Poor Servant of the Mother of God Incarnate.

Nov. 21st, 1884."

Such is the story of the Providence Free Hospital until 1884, and when it was well under way, Sister M. Dismas (her of the Brentford Property and the Bond Street hat and veil!) was nominated local Superior — a post she fulfilled loyally and competently for eleven years, sharing in all the work with her beloved Community as well as seeing to the needy and poor of the town.

God in His Divine Providence, Who inspired the Foundress and Father Dignam to bring this great work in St. Helens into being, and Who sent to her aid not only the Jesuits but the chief authorities of the town, has provided equally for His Providence Hospital down the years. During the Boer War, the Foundress, who from experience knew what the wounded soldier suffers, ordered the Providence to open its wards to as many as possible of "the returning brave." Again in World War I, her daughters, mindful of her example, did the same, for which authorities at the War Office were most grateful, and supplied a new piano for their entertainment.

Spiritually also, if the Providence walls could speak, one would hear of the many miracles of grace wrought within their compass, for which it thanks the Divine Source of all grace, and His devoted and loyal clergy. Furthermore, down the years it has been blessed in its Chairmen, Councillors, Committees and Secretaries, its medical and nursing staff, as well as in the success of its training, its domestic staff, its guilds of every type, who work for its well-being. In a word, Mother Magdalen Taylor's daughters to-day thank the people of St. Helens of every profession and calling, of every creed and class, who have made the Providence what their Mother meant it to be, a haven of peace and hope for the sufferer, where the sweet charity of Christ is administered all day and all night long by those who serve the poor patient in His Name Who said: "As long as you did it to one of these, My least brethren, you did it unto Me."

Lady Georgiana Fullerton

Mother Magdalen Aimée,
niece of the Foundress.

The Patriarch Athenagoras with two of
our Roman Sisters at Istambul (Constantinople) in 1967. The Sisters were
actually in Scutari!

Received from the Trustees
of the British Museum
for the original MS.
of Cardinal Newman's
Dream of Gerontius
the sum of thirty
pounds. £30. 0. 0.

Fanny Margaret Taylor

(By kind courtesy of the Executors
of the British Museum)

C h a p t e r   13.

FATHER SEYMOUR, THE HOLY SEE
AND SURPRISES

The winter of the year 1884, that had made Providence Hospital an accomplished fact, given it a great woman as Superior, a little band of trained efficient nursing Sisters to care for its patients, men, women and children, had given it now an efficient Committee and a Medical Staff, second to none. Accordingly Mother Magdalen, thanking God for His bounty, could leave the Hospital to His care, and so Ireland beckoned her again. This was to be her last visit to dear Father Seymour of Carrigtwohill, who was now preparing to meet his Divine Master. The Carrigtwohill Sisters, whom he delighted to call his "holy nuns," tended him to the last, and to this day there hangs in the Convent parlour a photograph of the holy old priest, showing the grand, dignified patriarchal figure that he was.

This time there was a great change evident in the dear old man. A Sister who was in Carrigtwohill at the time leaves on record the following very interesting account of the meeting:

"In the summer of 1884, Mother was busily engaged at St. Helens, making arrangements for the Hospital, and from there she came to Carrigtwohill. Father Seymour had just bought a new cab, and was delighted to put it at Mother's disposal. As soon as she arrived, he came to see her. When she heard his voice in the hall, she started to come downstairs to save him the trouble of going up. As he came to the foot of the flight, he caught sight of Mother at the top, and called out in a loud voice: 'Céad míle fáilte, Reverend Mother! Oh, what a glorious work you have been doing for God, what a glorious work!'

Mother told him about St. Helens. He said he was thanking God with all his heart for letting him have something to do with her Institute, that he might have a share in its good works. He told her of his new cab, how much it cost, asked how she liked it, and said it was at her disposal during her stay. She saw at his Mass next morning that his health had failed much, and the nurse, in the big-hearted Mother that she was, immediately instructed Sister Superior to get special medical advice for the dear old man, and mentioned a number of little comforts which were to be provided at once."

Another little interesting item from the same pen is recorded in the same letter, and is worthy of note here. During this visit to Carrigtwohill in the summer of 1884, an old soldier who had served in the Crimea called to ask if she were Miss Nightingale, as he heard she was at the Convent. She received him in the kindest manner. He told her of the different engagements in which he had taken part and the names of his commanding officers, most of whom she remembered. The good old man was delighted. He told her that his wife was English and that he himself, under God, had been the means of her conversion. He asked if his wife might come to visit her. Mrs. Fitzgerald came next day, and said to the Sister who answered the knock at the door (electric bells were not yet the fashion) that her husband made her come without delay, and that Mother Magdalen was the noblest soul he had ever met.

The year 1884 was drawing to its close, and the new year had two great sorrows in store for that noble-hearted woman, who for a good thirty years now had braved so many set-backs in her up-hill climb to God. Love for her Lord was her driving force. He was her All, the source of her strength and her trust in her every crisis. This was the spirit she ever strove to instil into her Sisters — that strong trustful interior life of union with God, Whose grace was to give strength for every difficulty and enable them to rise superior to every adverse criticism, every tinge of bigotry, which she knew only too well they would have to confront in their work.

Hidden in that seemingly strong personality, that could so check and quell at times when danger loomed, a woman born to love souls and work for every creed and class, there was, however, a deeply personal need for sincerity and sympathetic understanding. Over this sensitive characteristic of her nature she had complete control, but now and again in her life we get a peep. For instance, writing to her very dear friend, Lady Georgiana, whose aims all through her life were so akin to Mother Magdalen's own, and who now alluded to her approaching death, she says: "Dearest Lady Georgiana, do not say you will not be long after her (Lady Londonderry, who had just died). I feel as if I *could* not go on without you. Even though I cannot see you, I know you are there, praying, suffering for us. No, God will keep you alive, though your life is a sort of martyrdom — I was going to say 'I fear,' but I will not grudge you the joy of suffering, if it be God's Will."

Lady Georgiana died on January 19th, 1885. Her death was most holy and peaceful. To her friend the loss was great; she had been such a buttress of strength, so staunch, so wise, so like-minded, so loving, that her death left a deep void in Mother Magdalen's life. Of the death and funeral, there is only a simple statement of facts: "Lady Georgiana, of blessed memories, was laid in her grave (in the cemetery of the Sacred Heart Convent in Roehampton)." Father Dignam wrote to sympathise with the Foundress, knowing that Lady Georgiana's death was "a deep pain boring down to the quick. Indeed I grieve with you, for she is a loss to the whole Church."

When Mrs. Craven was writing the "Life of Lady Georgiana Fullerton" she hopes "to be assisted by all her best and dearest friends — and by *you* in particular, dear Mother Magdalen, who were certainly one of the dearest of all." Many years afterwards, Mother Magdalen supplemented Mrs. Craven's "Life" by her own "Inner Life of Lady Georgiana Fullerton."

Mother Magdalen's second cross in 1885 came with the death of dear Father Seymour — a cross, because it was a cross and loss to her dear community at Carrigtwohill Convent, which she loved to call the "Irish Mother House." She loved her visits to Ireland, and Father Seymour once confessed to Sister M. Thecla that he always came away the better for his spiritual chats and business dealings with "that very understanding, Irish Englishwoman."

In the summer of 1885, after having had the consolation of

receiving her niece, Charlotte's daughter, into the Congregation, and seeing her clothed, with others, on her feast, July 22nd, at the hands of Father Porter, S.J. (afterwards Archbishop of Bombay), Mother Magdalen set out for Rome again, this time for the approbation of the Rule (the necessary period having passed since the "Lauda" or Brief of Praise had been given).

On her way with her two companions (Mother Aloysius Austin, who was her Assistant-General, is mentioned as one), they visited Loreto, Venice, Bologna. She writes on October 30th:

"I thank God indeed that He has allowed me the great grace of another visit to the Holy House, every stone of which speaks to one of Our Lady. All is so much improved here, and so much more devotional than seven years ago. I think there has been some sort of reform; there is more life in everything, and really praise and prayer are incessant, from five in the morning until four in the afternoon.

"We saw Venice by moonlight; at our leisure, I may say, for the mosquitoes made all sleep impossible; and in the morning we went in a gondola to a little desolate church dipping its steps into the water. There we venerated the body of St. Lucy. She rests above the altar, dressed in silver.

"At Bologna, we were still more impressed; we saw the body of St. Catherine, which is very wonderful. She is sitting up in a chair, calm and stately in death. We kissed her very hands and feet! I cannot tell you the extraordinary sight it is, as you kneel before her. Then we venerated the tomb of St. Dominic, dear to all our Associates. It is gorgeous in beautiful carvings and marble."

From Rome, on November 1st, in the same envelope, is another note:

"We arrived last night, and what a joy to be here! We lost no time in going to St. Peter's as my two Sisters were eager to see it on this feast; and certainly, it is a type of a 'great mutitude which no man can number, of all nations, and tribes and peoples and tongues,' Wonderful are the thoughts which St. Peter's brings; the untold happiness of being a Catholic, and the longing desire to bring others into the fold. Heart of Jesus, hear our prayers!"

And on November 12th, to one of the Mothers in England:

"I have seen Cardinal Jacobini — the one Cardinal Manning wrote to — the Pope's Prime Minister. He was so good to us. He said, 'You have brought a most excellent recommendation, I shall speak to the Pope to-morrow about you.' As he left he said, 'Pray to Our Lady for me; I need it so much.'

"We also saw Cardinal Howard, who was very kind and nice. These visits over are a great relief. I waited over two hours for Cardinal Jacobini, and mounted five flights of marble stairs.

"I am sending you the 'Plan' (of the Institute) in French — it has cost time and labour. Mère St. Anne translates for me, but insists on going over everything five times *at least*..."

On the 27th they visited the General of the Jesuits, Father Beckz, at the Novitiate of St. Andrea, where the body of St. Stanislaus rests. His Paternity told Mother they had still ten months to pray yet, against the threat of being turned out of their house, which was to be pulled down to make place for a new street. He was anxious that Mother Magdalen should see the tomb of Charles Emmanuel, who was a Jesuit and a relative of the reigning Italian King. His Paternity proposed that his attendant, Père Lavigne, should accompany the Sisters, but Mother Magdalen said that the sacristan could easily show them to the tomb. He gave the visitors his paternal blessing, and, says the account of the visit, "Mother A. Austin cried with joy."

The nuns of Marie Réparatrice had again given kind hospitality to the Poor Servants of the Mother of God, and in a familiar chat with her old friend, Mother Madeleine, one day, the latter suggested: "Why don't you come for good, and make a foundation?" Poor Mother Magdalen in her humility exclaimed: "We! What could we do here?" A convent in the Eternal City far exceeded her dreams, and yet by Christmas Day, the usual greeting-letter from Rome to her beloved Brentford had a footnote from Mother-General: "We are to have a house in Rome by the special desire of the Holy Father. It is only just settled. I scrawled this off for the post, and beg you to pray well. I will write fully by the next post."

The "next post" was watched for eagerly by the Brentford community, and brought full particulars. When her friend at

Marie Réparatrice mentioned "a foundation in Rome," Mother Magdalen had "a perfect horror" of it. She and Mother Aloysius Austin talked it over, but she confesses, "we felt afraid, and the subject dropped." However, they put the intention into the Novena of Grace, and also that of the Immaculate Conception, and one day while praying in the Church of the Gesù, the brave Foundress felt an inner conviction that Our Lady wanted it. She writes: "So I said to her that she must give me a sign." A few days later, she mentioned the subject to a lady who had never seemed favourable to the Institute of the Poor Servants of the Mother of God. "I thought she would surely say there were too many convents in Rome already." However, she warmly encouraged the idea, and even offered herself to interview the Cardinal Vicar (Cardinal Parocchi) as soon as possible. This was Our Lady's sign to her ever trustful Poor Servant.

"The Cardinal sent for us, was most favourably impressed by what he heard of the new Congregation and its work in England and Ireland, said he would like to have us, he would speak to the Pope and I was to come again on Monday."

On Monday she went again, and after having had to wait her turn for a long time — "Many priests," she writes, "went in and out, and gradually the room was half filled with nuns, at last we got in, and he said: 'Yes, you are accepted, you are blessed. You may begin at once, you will do a great deal of good. Begin in a modest way, because you are Poor Servants. Look out for some place, but be sure you keep in the English quarter. I want you there among the English.' "

Mother Magdalen's letter ends with: "Now we have to look for a place, which is very hard work, as rooms are very scarce in the English quarter. So you must pray much for us. It is so plainly the will of God, when the Holy Father really wishes for us, that I cannot doubt, and Our Lady will take care of us."

Our Lady did take care of them. Mother Magdalen had asked her for a sign that the Divine Will was being accomplished in this question of a Roman foundation. Sign after sign was given, each one more significant than the preceding one. The lady whom the Sisters had hitherto misjudged as prejudiced was found the most enthusiastic; the Cardinal Vicar went to the Holy Father, who gave not merely a permission, but a command. They were to "look out for some place and to begin in a modest way." They were to keep in the English quarter.

Mother Magdalen's first act on her arrival in Rome on that momentous day of November, 1885, was to seek out an artist who could be recommended as "very efficient" in order to put on canvas her beautiful idea of the Incarnation, when the great Archangel had explained away Our Lady's virgin fears, and had left her in adoration of her Omnipotent God, now having come to partake of her substance and become man within her to redeem the world. Father Armellini, S.J., who knew almost every artist in Rome, put her in touch with Aristide Dies, who could converse with her in French. When the work was almost finished, and after all her instructions, Mother Magdalen found he was still leaving room for the Angel, and could not be reconciled to the idea of a picture of the Annunciation without the Divine Messenger. Mother Magdalen came back that same day with a New Testament in French, and read St. Luke, I, v. 38, after which he begged to fill the space with his vase and lilies. They seem out of place in their particular corner at that historical moment, nevertheless are of interest for their story. On December 19th the work on the picture was completed, and on that very day, their house-hunting succeeded, and they found a flat in via San Sebastianello, leading off the Piazza di Spagna — the Pope's desired spot for the Poor Servants of the Mother of God, in the English quarter. The final "sign" for Mother Magdalen was the receipt of a substantial cheque from Mr. Alexander George Fullerton.

In writing to the Sisters in England to tell of the finding of the house and their visit to the Cardinal Vicar to acquaint him of the find, the Mother Assistant wrote:

"Your hearts would have been moved to deep gratitude to God and Our Lady, if you had been present when the Cardinal Vicar was speaking to Mother. He is an Italian Father Dignam! He arranged our designation, etc., as it is to be on our circulars, himself. We could not help feeling quite at home with him, and when Mother gave him the bound copy of the "Messenger of the Sacred Heart," as Father Dignam had asked, he read from it, and said many nice things in French, and then in English: 'I thank you.' He reads a bit of the 'Imitation of Christ' every day, and read us a passage in seven different languages, to amuse us, and let us hear him read English! He is the fourth Cardinal we have been to see on business, and all are so kind to Mother."

On the last day of 1885, the following entry is found in Mother Magdalen's diary:

"Till half-past one in Chapel, and so ended 1885, a year full of great events — Miserere mei, Deus — after Thy great goodness! Deo gratias more times than I can speak . . . I end this year at the feet of Jesus and Mary.

"1886. I begin this year in Rome, in the Heart of Jesus — in the arms of Mary, and under the protection of the Holy Apostles Peter and Paul — St. Thomas of Canterbury — and all the Saints of Rome."

On January 2nd, 1886, she wrote to Father Dignam, who was already up-to-date in his knowledge of her experiences with the Pope and his Cardinal Vicar, and in the foundation of the Roman house.

"I must tell you of the great thanksgiving service at the Gesù on the last night of the year, at which, before the Jesuits were driven from their church, the Pope always used to be present. During the long ornate Vespers, which lasted an hour and a quarter, English folk are surprised to see that everyone walks and talks; they might think the Romans irreverent, but manners are different here, and when the Te Deum begins, they would soon change their minds. The great hymn of praise is sung to a simple tune, the whole of the people answering the choir, the church is crowded and the effect grand; then the Tantum Ergo sung by an angel voice, and the Benediction according to Roman use: soft music plays, while the great bells ring, and Gesù bells have a kind of muffled sound, very sweet.

"At the Ara Coeli yesterday, the sight was one not to be forgotten. The Crib is immense, the figures being as large as life and very beautiful. Opposite to this, little children preach by turns, not dressed up, but coming in their poor clothes. It was charming — the little things talking away, one showing how Our Lady nursed the Bambino, and how cold He was. The love of the Roman poor for Our Lady is beautiful; Madonna is a mother indeed!"

On this date also, one of her companions writes:

"On January 2nd, we began to live by day in our own little flat, via S. Sebastiano, at the foot of Monte Pincio, returning in the evening to Marie Réparatrice. One of us went in a cab with most of our belongings, Mother and companion followed on foot. The nuns had found us a good Italian woman to help us with the cleaning etc. We managed fairly well, with many signs, and the few Italian words at our command, interspersed with French. Our first visitor was the picture of our Blessed Lady, Mother's own. The artist himself brought it."

Far from the Foundress' mind on that day in November 1885, when she ordered the picture of the Annunciation (or of the Incarnation, as she loved to call it) was the thought that Our Lady meant it to stay in Rome, in the spot which she was to choose, and later to be the altar-piece of Our Lady's special altar in the Mater Dei Church of St. George and the English Saints, where so many Masses were to be celebrated in her honour and where the Community of her Poor Servants was to visit her in a singing procession, as was and still is the Community custom in all houses to this day.

On January 7th, the Community took leave of their very kind nuns of Marie Réparatrice, and took up their abode in Via S. Sebastianello, 16.

"The floor was the safest place for bedsteads," writes a Sister, "and our first meal was an enormous dish of macaroni, sent by kindly Italians who run a public 'Cucina' in the large quadrangle courtyard outside, and who were delighted at our coming. Night prayers were said and points of meditation given by Mother before our own picture of our dear Lady."

To offer a means of livelihood to some poor women and in order to get in touch with some younger girls who needed shepherding and help to support themselves, the practical, humble organiser began a small hand-laundry, as she was advised that the Italian women were careful and splendid laundresses, and that the Church linen in some churches badly needed overhauling. Between these women and girls who knew no English, and the Sisters, who were as yet ignorant of "la bella lingua italiana," there were many causes for mirth and patient charity.

From the beginning both Leo XIII and his Cardinal Vicar wished the Sisters to open a school in Rome, where catechetical

129

teaching and moral training could go hand in hand with English. Schools in the city where the language was taught had hitherto excluded religion altogether, or made little account of Christian doctrine.

Mother Magdalen had already had some Sisters in England specially trained for school work. Two of these, Sister M Thecla and Sister M. Rodriguez, were called to Rome immediately, and the Bank of Divine Providence came to her assistance again in the person of Mr. Fullerton, who at this stage had seen the result of Mother Magdalen's prudent and far-seeing vision in carrying out successfully the Holy Father's idea for her Roman house. The following letter to the Congregation explains what the Cardinal-Vicar called 'il miracolo' and shows how the very loving Mother shares all her joys with her now rather large family:

"Rome, April 20, 1886. May our dear Lord give you all Paschal gifts and graces, and may we all keep Easter week in a good spirit of preparation for our dear Lady's month of May, which comes to us so quickly. Please God, ere its close, I shall have seen you all, or nearly all. If you would only pray me home quickly, I should be so glad. I thought you would have done so by now, but here I am still, stuck fast!

"Now, my dear children, I have a great deal of news to tell you: Mr. Fullerton has bought us a house in Rome, the very house in which we are now lodgers! What do you say? What can we all say to this wonderful mercy of God and favour of Our Lady? Will you help me in thanking Them for all? Will you pray with all the might of grateful hearts for Mr. Fullerton, and will you recognize with me what a proof this is of the sanctity of our dear Lady Georgiana? Be sure her prayers have brought it about. Much as I have longed to see her since she died, I never did till I was praying about this foundation, and then for one instant she beamed on me, full of joy and love. And I doubt not the prayers of our dear Sisters who have gone before us, especially our dearest Sister M. Clare, have had much to do with it.

"You may be sure this has not been brought about without much trouble and anxiety. The last month has been a very trying time, and so will it be till I can get away. The Cardinal Vicar is ever so pleased, and told me it would be a great consolation to the Holy Father . . . Now do pray well and be faithful to Our Lady."

Before leaving Rome for England at the end of May, Mother Magdalen had another private audience of Leo XIII, this time to get a special blessing for Father Dignam, for whom and for his special shrine of the Apostleship of Prayer at St. Helens, she had got painted in Rome a picture of the Sacred Heart pleading. This was to be a special thank-offering to Our Lord for all His blessings to the new Congregation, and to Father Dignam for all he had done for it. Mother Magdalen's own account of this historic meeting is given 'in extenso' and is dated:

"Rome, May 4, 1886.

We had private audience yesterday of our Holy Father, and I asked his blessing for the work, and for you, and for the new office; so on the very day of the opening (of the 'Messenger' Office, St. Helens), it had the special blessing which you most prize on earth.

That is not all. I took with me the new picture of the Sacred Heart Pleading. 'Holy Father, this is for the Apostleship of Prayer in England!' He took it on his knee, with his wonderful eyes fixed on it: 'Que c'est gracieux! It is indeed beautiful! Was it painted in Rome?' 'Yes, Holy Father.' 'When do you leave?' 'To-morrow, Holy Father.' 'Could you lend it to me? I want to have a copy.' 'Oh, Holy Father, accept it, pray, from us.' 'No, no, I do not want to deprive you of it.' The Sisters, (forgetful, I fear, of strict Pontifical etiquette) raised a sort of little chorus of: 'Oh, Holy Father, do grant us this happiness!' At last, he accepted the gift, with evident pleasure. *So your picture is gone,* and I think you will not be sorry to have lost it in that way.

Now to tell you about that audience, I scarce know how. The Pope was simply as a tender father amongst his children; patted our heads, and asked about all our houses, spoke of our work in Rome, and the good we should do, blessed all we had brought, and asked which of the Sisters were English and which Irish. 'I love Ireland,' he said.

I lost all fear, and was courageous enough to say: "Holy

Father, grant us a favour.' 'What is it?' he asked. 'Some good people outside want to have your Holiness' blessing.' 'Ah,' he said, 'now you make me walk.' He got up, leant on the novice's shoulder, and walked with her through the rooms. He said to her: 'Now you will be good, you will persevere, you will be faithful to the great grace God has given you.'

He rang a bell and sat down. Enter a Monsignore. 'Bring those people in.' 'Yes, Holy Father, they are M. Fullerton's servants.' Then he said to me: 'Le bon M. Fullerton, il a été très généreux?' 'Yes, Holy Father, he has bought us a house.' Then he asked the Monsignore if he knew the house, and was told: Yes, and where it was. The servants came in, and fell at His Holiness' feet. We all kissed those dear feet again and again, and he gave us a solemn benediction...

We may be at Paray on the 8th (Father Dignam's birthday). I wanted to have the picture there, but now can only take a photograph, and the first volume of the 'Messenger'.

The artist is greatly pleased at the Holy Father's approbation of the picture and will begin another at once. It must be exactly the same.

P.S. I cannot tell you what an unearthly figure the Holy Father is now. As he sat there, all in white, it seemed so like going to Our Lord Himself, and surely, after the Blessed Sacrament, *it is*."

The artist, Professor Gagliardi, was so pleased with the Pope's praise of his work that he immediately set to work to execute two replicas — one of which travelled to its English destination, and the other formed the altar-piece of the Sacred Heart Altar in the temporary convent chapel. "Temporary?" Another surprise! Mr. Fullerton, seeing the successful progress of the spiritual and temporal apostolate of the nuns, was not satisfied with the size of the little chapel, but there and then resolved upon an actual Church. The temporary chapel was blessed and opened by Bishop Brownrigg of Ossory, who on October 27th said Mass and reserved the Blessed Sacrament. "Deo Gratias, a thousandfold!" writes Mother Magdalen in her diary. "How good Thou art, my Jesus!"

The work on the new Church then resolved upon, to be built in memory of Lady Georgiana, began immediately, and was sufficiently advanced to be opened for occasional use on January 19th — the second anniversary of Lady Georgiana's death. His Grace, Archbishop Kirby of saintly memory, the then Rector of the Irish College, gave the first Benediction, and for the first time in history the "Three Hours" was preached on Good Friday in the Lent of 1887 in English, by Father Herbert Lucas, S.J. This Good Friday service, preached by Father Peter Paul Mackay, O.P., for thirty consecutive years, has never been omitted since.

On October 6th, 1887, after Mass had been celebrated, the Blessed Sacrament was reserved for the first time, and Mother Magdalen, rejoicing over yet another tabernacle, wrote in her diary: "Our Lord took up His abode in the Tabernacle, obedient to my wish!"

The new Church was dedicated to "St. George and the English Saints," and on January 19th, 1888, the third anniversary of Lady Georgiana's death, Mother Magdalen had the joy of seeing the Cardinal Vicar (still Cardinal Parocchi, her great friend) receive the first vows of her niece, Sister Magdalen Aimée — whose vocation she attributed to Lady Georgiana's prayers. Addressing the newly-professed Sister, His Eminence said that the Mother of God was speaking to her from Heaven, saying: "Daughter, I charge you with the care of the children of your fatherland even in Rome, and do you, after my example, answer: 'Behold the handmaid of the Lord, be it done unto me according to Thy word.' " He further advised the newly-vowed nun to strive after the highest perfection, and more particularly the virtue of deep humility.

His Eminence wished the Sisters to help the Italians also in Rome, and in particular the "spiritually poor," who stood in such great danger of infidelity on the one hand, and the snares of proselytism on the other. Bishop Hedley of Newport preached in the evening.

Whenever Mr. Fullerton came to Rome, he loved to hear Mass in the Church built by himself, and would call to consult Mother Magdalen about her various charities, in which he liked to participate. He outlived the Foundress by seven years, and was made a Knight of Malta by Pope Pius X, in recognition of his various services to the Church.

133

The school was opened on the Feast of Our Lady's Presentation, November 21st, 1887, with Sister M. Thecla in charge. English-speaking children came in numbers, and Italian parents begged that theirs also might share in the advantages of an English Institute. Mother Magdalen, however, "to make assurance doubly sure," after securing a note of introduction, went straight off to the Ministry of Education and laid her cards on the table, in order that no tinge of illegality could bring discredit on the good work afterwards. The Minister received her and Sister M. Thecla in a most gracious manner, so that they felt quite at their ease as the matter was duly discussed. Not only did he give full permission for any Italian parents who wished to send their children to the new school, but he encouraged such action by entering his own little son. He also advised Sister M. Thecla to take on the full Italian syllabus after a period of experimentation, having English as the modern language, but of course stipulated that the examinations had to be external and in open competition with those in the State schools.

Work for her dear poor had always had first place in Mother Magdalen's heart. The teaching Sisters devoted their half-holiday weekly to an ever-increasing group of poor girls, who were taught religion, needlework and housecraft. Their catechism classes were presided over by an Italian Jesuit. Although naturally these classes were in Italian, Mother Magdalen saw to it that they also learned English, and were thus competent to work in English and American families, of which there were many in Rome at the time. The sick and the indigent in the worst hovels of Trastevere were visited and helped, and even from outside the walls of Rome, priests, having heard of the Sisters' apostolate, called at the convent with names and addresses of people in great spiritual and temporal need to be visited by the Sisters. God's great gift to the Community in those years was Sister M. Prassedes, an Italian Sister to whom Mother Magdalen gave over the charge of the poor because of her native language. She loved them, and was happiest when the large quadrangle courtyard was filled for a hot meal every Monday during the winter months. Parcels of food and clothing were sent in by well-to-do friends to be distributed by the Sisters, who gradually got to know and distinguish between the needy and well-deserving and the lazy and good-for-nothing. Mother Foundress insisted, however, that such were to be contacted, because the devil "had always work for idle hands to do."

Mr. Fullerton was charmed when he saw the magnitude of the Sisters' many-sided apostolate and the success of their social activities in the Roman house, and, as ever, his charity-cheque preceded his every visit.

Facsimile of the Foundress' hand-writing.

Chapter 14.

HISTORY IN HASTE FROM 1888 TO 1967

The story of the Roman house must claim another chapter, if God's beneficence to Mother Magdalen and to her first heroic Sisters is to be fully understood. The year 1888, being the Jubilee Year of His Holiness, Leo XIII, brought crowds of visitors to Rome, and the new Church was just ready in time to be of great service to English-speaking pilgrims. From all five continents, visitors came, including, of course, Church dignitaries and priests of every rank, Superiors of religious orders of both sexes who, as the year offered, coupled the joys of the Jubilee with business relating to their Congregations and other affairs. Added to these were crowds of Catholic laymen and women, Press representatives and biographers of almost every nation. The Italy of Napoleonic times, of Mazzini, Cavour, Garibaldi, and of the Papal Zuaves had much to offer: the Italy whose every city spoke volumes of Christianity's trials and her triumphs over paganism, heresy, schism and defections within herself, and which saw her Pope (Pio Nono, as he was affectionately called) deprived of the Papal States and of the Church lands everywhere, except those of the Vatican itself. Later, when the French had to withdraw their Roman troops for the Franco-Prussian War, Rome fell to Victor Emmanuel II, and Pius IX and his successors became prisoners in the Vatican until Mussolini's Concordat of 1929, which, by the Lateran Treaty restored long-denied rights to the Pope and the Church.

To return to 1888 and to Mother Magdalen's happy share in the Jubilee is to see her busy beforehand with her Sisters in providing suitable accommodation for as many as she could in the extern parts of her now large convent. Many nuns especially were her guests, as they also sought her wise counsel in their difficulties. "We can never be kind enough to nuns who are away from their convents," she used to say to her Sisters. This teaching of their Foundress has never been forgotten by the communities of her Congregation even to this day.

Innocently proud to show visitors round the new Church, she explained the altar-piece of the High Altar, depicting the well-known scene — "Not Angles but Angels," which led to the conversion of England by St. Augustine in 597, that of the Sacred Heart Pleading, which backs the Sacred Heart altar even to this day, and Our Lady's altar, with its beautiful altar-piece showing Christ's Mother lost in adoration and wonder at the thought that the Omnipotent God had taken flesh in her womb — Mother Magdalen's own idea.

Pope Leo's Jubilee over, the new Church and school in perfect functioning order, the rules for the treatment of the poor of Rome happily drawn up and Sister M. Prassedes entrusted with their full observance, to her own immense delight — her relatives were chemists in Rome, and whenever anything in the medicinal line was needed by any of her poor "cugini", she knew where to apply! — Mother Magdalen, sure of approval, was free now to leave, and entrusted the Superiorship of the Roman house to Sister M. Veronica, who was a nun after God's own Heart, a fervent religious ever, a loving and understanding Mother to her community and a wise counsellor and guide to all who sought her help in Rome. She was tall of stature and dignified in her every movement, while her countenance gave the assurance of the utter sincerity and sympathy of her heart. The present writer remembers the then Bishop Amigo of Southwark visiting St. Mary's, Roehampton, one evening in the 1920's. To the community assembled in the noviceship to welcome His Lordship, he said: "I wanted to pay you this short visit after my stay in Rome, and when I give you my blessing at the end, I will ask God for you all, that you may be as humble, as holy, as motherly and as queenly withal, as Sister M. Veronica of the Roman house. It lifts my heart to God each time I meet her in Rome."

Canon Law had not then specified the duration of the office of local superiors, so "Madre Veronica", as she was affectionately called by the Italians, headed her happy community long after the Foundress' death in 1900.

Forming that community for many years were Sisters whom necessity had compelled the Foundress to draft to Rome while still second-year novices. She herself was their Novice-Mistress until she confided their training to Sister M. Veronica. Happy and privileged were they, and they had their Mother's unalterable love. As she shared their poverty as well as their every hardship, and especially their first difficulties with the language, so could she be as a novice herself with them, and enjoy to the full their every little narration of the happenings of a school-day. She taught them by word and example how to "put on Christ" in dealing with one another, with the school-children and the poor. Those far-off days knew neither typewriters, dishwashers, vacuum cleaners nor central heating. The Sisters themselves did the work, with the aid of their first faithful Italian helper, Judita, whose name lives still in the Roman house. The Sisters of those early days, whose names will ever be held in benediction, were: — Sisters M. Thecla, Rodriguez, Agnes (Manderin), Bernard, Brigida, Campion, Odilia, Raphael, Stanislaus, Quirinus, Faber, Augustina, Prassedes, Julian, Anne Xavier, Francesca and Evangelist.

Later, too, of course, as things advanced and numbers grew, the community employed the necessary help, but their little allotted portion of housework did, and must ever belong to the Sisters themselves, as his Excellency, Bishop Hodges of Virginia, could testify, when, at one of his visits during Vatican II, he came in one Saturday unannounced, and found the Sisters in blue working aprons, active at their charges, and, to his Excellency's delight, he was warned by Sister Margaret Gertrude jokingly: "Be sure, your Excellency, when you see our Sisters in Virginia, tell them you found us all working!"

Later, after the Foundress death, a long-cherished wish of hers was fulfilled when a second foundation in her beautiful Italy was requested. Reverend Father Strickland, S.J., who had known the success of the Roman foundation and the dire need for such an apostolate in Florence, worked with the then Scallopian Cardinal Mistrangelo to entice the Mother General of the Poor Servants of the Mother of God to send "even a small community" to Florence, where there were so many English and American Catholic children attending non-Catholic private schools whose curricula of course included no religious education for Catholic children. The acceptance of this offer, with all the apostolic work its future would entail, was looked upon by the Head Superiors of the time as a sure sign of God's Will and a direct answer to their Foundress' prayer. Ever since the Roman foundation, she had longed for a sister-convent away from the city, where the Sisters could go in turns for a change during the great and overpowering heat of the Roman summer. It was not, however, until 1907 — seven years after the Foundress' decease — that a foundation came into being in the beautiful city of Florence, the history of which shall have its place in a later chapter.

Even though Mother Magdalen was busy in Rome in 1886, it will be remembered that she returned to England at the end of May, and from then to the following October did her visitation of the London houses, after which Rome again claimed her and other Sisters whose names have already been given. During her stay in England, incredible as it may seem, she negotiated for and planned another foundation, which meant, to her overflowing joy, another Tabernacle and another great work of charity. She had long looked for a house that would serve as a real home and a refuge for poor outcast London girls who, after serving, as it were, a short probation at the London Refuge, could then be removed far from their familiar and miserable slum environment and live their lives over again in a happy contrasting atmosphere. Such a haven was now brought to her notice in Streatham, through the kind offices of the Bishop of Southwark. The property belonged to Mr. R. H. Measures, and was adjacent to Tooting Bec Gardens on the one side and to Streatham Common, North Side, on the other. The building was named "Russell House", and had been hitherto used as a women's reformatory, with public laundry attached. Mr. Measures, though not yet a Catholic, was delighted to hear of Mother Magdalen's aim, and was most co-operative during the negotiations. The Poor Servants of the Mother of God became his tenants and his neighbours in March, 1888. One of her Mother Assistants in Brentford and a companion, Sister M.

Regis, saw to the fitting up and furnishing, and, as the Foundress had wished ever, the best room on the ground floor was chosen for the Chapel, and was opened to the public. The new Mission was started on May 4th, Feast of the English Martyrs, and Mass was said in Streatham for the first time since the Reformation. The zealous pastor was the Reverend Father William Lloyd, who was parish priest of Streatham till his death in 1912. He had the great joy of seeing the foundation stone of the present fine Church, the gift of Mr. Measures, being laid by the Bishop of Southwark (Bishop Butt) in 1892, and consecrated the following year by Cardinal Vaughan. Knowing it to be Mother Magdalen's desire, the donor himself, though not yet a Catholic, asked that it be dedicated to the English Martyrs on their feast.

On July 22nd, 1888, Mother Magdalen was home from Rome and came to Russell House to spend her feast. Kneeling in the little Chapel during the Mass of the great penitent saint, and surrounded by the crowd of poor girls rescued from sin, and singing so fervently, her Mother's heart rejoiced, and all the more as she saw them approach the altar-rail to receive their Eucharistic Saviour. Surely the words of Our Lord to Simon the Pharisee: "Many sins are forgiven her, because she hath loved much," came to the Foundress' mind on that memorable morning, with regard to these poor girls. She had indeed helped Our Lord to "pitch His tent in the midst of them," and she knew that "His Heart would never grow weary of them." She saw her own dear children, to whom she had given her whole-hearted love and the fulness of her spirit, there to care for and train these girls. Nor was this all; she had already heard of the results of their visitation of the Parish, the return of many long-lapsed Catholics to their duties, many of whom had not got their children baptized. Catechism for adults and children began, and many marriages had been set right. Soon, too, it became the usual proceeding for the nuns to give up their places in Chapel to the ever-increasing crowd, as they thanked God that they could kneel on the large oak staircase outside! The Catholic congregation so increased that within two years, a second and even a third Mass had to be provided, and still the accommodation was not adequate, until God inspired Mr.

Measures' gift of the Church, which was completed in 1893, and the gift of the True Faith some years later was his rich reward and Mother Magdalen's crowning joy.

That 22nd of July was never to be forgotten by the Foundress. Her dream and that of Father Gallwey, S.J., of Lady Georgiana, of Charlotte Anne, Duchess of Buccleuch, had come true. She was in the midst of a crowd of poor girls rescued from sin and evil surroundings. The effect of Christ's healing love was already visible in their happy countenances — but for poor Mother Magdalen the cross was to conclude the day's rejoicings: a letter was handed to her on the evening of the Feast, from one of her dear and much-trusted S.M.G.'s to say she was leaving the Congregation. Her example was followed by another, and, naturally, Mother Magdalen dreaded further defections, but luckily such was not the case. The reasons? They are as old as Religious Life itself: the realization that one is not used as one ought to be, that one is called rather to govern than be governed, that one's personality is not appreciated as it should be, etc. It spells ever a neglect of prayer, a certain self-esteem which can be disastrous if Our Lord's great lesson, "Learn of Me, for I am meek and humble of Heart," be not hearkened to and practised. However, the broken-hearted Mother advised and sought advice and did all in her power to save the two victims from themselves, but no confidence whatever was placed in her who had loved them and trusted them so much; and the "unkindest cut of all," as Shakespeare has it, was to have handed her the letter on her feast night — which night she spent entirely alone in the little Chapel, with Him Who understood.

Father Dignam wrote from St. Helens:

"Certainly there is no exaggeration. Your troubles are indeed terrible, and, God apart, unendurable; but neither the one nor the other, if you trust in Him and are seeking His Will, and that alone. Shall not my soul be *subject* to God? *There* is strength enough to carry ten times as many crosses as He wills to heap on you; but don't hope to carry them of your own strength. The present time of agony may bring much light, but I do not think it is a time to act. Let your strength be in the thought that what God has given you to do, He Himself will accomplish... God

141

wants you to do *His* work, not yours, by *His* means, not yours. He will baffle every plan, take away every consolation, till you are like wax in His hands...

"Don't be surprised at this universal crash of misfortunes all at once; it is no bad sign; and if you can but maintain your courage, you will look back on it afterwards with consolation. You must act for the best, and you need not fear my disapproving; it is a time of moral trial for them all. You must not expect them *all* to be capable of realizing your troubles; this is always the case in communities under trials of this kind. But God sees it all, and will not withdraw His hand if you call on Him and keep (I say it again) your head as calm as you can...

"You would be very, very wrong to let your present immense difficulties abate your confidence. It is so, exactly so, that God tries the work which He blesses, and where are you to get your merits from, if it be not from fortitude and constancy at such times as these? God knows all about it. He can do all things. The work is His. What have you to fear? Suffer, then, but hope unchangeably; He will do the rest. Even if He willed to make you like Himself, and to let you die amidst what seemed the ruins of the work of your life, after your Good Friday would come its Pentecost."

The Streatham Convent, with its wide apostolate and this great cross to overshadow and bless it, developed rapidly until 1923, when the work was transferred to a large property in the neighbourhood purchased from Sir Henry Tate and known as "Park Hill." Russell House was suitably remodelled and changed into a home for aged ladies, named "St. Mary's." Here they are happy and free, and nursed lovingly whenever there is need. The old and ever-new apostolate is carried on as fervently as ever in both houses. "Park Hill" was re-named "St. Michael's Convent" at its take-over, and in recent years, in a negotiated "give-over", part of its land was chosen as the site for the Bishop Grant Secondary School, while at St. Michael's itself, a beautifully-equipped and spacious day-room and other apartments have been built for the resident girls.

From its first group of parishioners in the tiny chapel of the old Russell House in 1888, the congregation has grown to vast proportions. It is a glorious sight to view at the Parish Corpus Christi Procession, when the Clergy, the men, women and children, with the Sisters and their protégés assemble to escort their Eucharistic Lord around the lovely lawn at St. Michael's, to return to the Sisters' magnificent Chapel for the final Benediction. In these latter years in Streatham itself a beautiful and spacious Lady Chapel has been erected, thanks to the efforts of the Very Reverend Canon Crowley and his generous benefactors. Certain it is that the English Martyrs have reason to rejoice in Heaven over the restoration of the Streatham portion of Our Lady's Dowry since the happy dawn of its "Second Spring," and for which they laid down their lives.

It will be remembered that Mother Magdalen, after her 1886-1887 visitations in England, returned to Rome, and while there in the February of 1888 had a visit from the Archbishop of Dublin, His Grace the Most Reverend Dr. Walsh, who asked if she were willing to take over the management of a charitable institution, one of Dublin's greatest charities, which already existed. His Grace's parents had been among its best benefactors since he was a small boy. Mother Magdalen accepted in the same spirit of zeal for the welfare of the poor as His Grace had offered it, and by August 1888 she and her nuns were at St. Joseph's, Portland Row, Dublin. They were received at the Church door by the Very Rev. Canons Fricker and O'Donnell, and a Mr. James Murphy, who, with Dr. Blake, before the latter became Bishop of Dromore, had long pondered over the sad condition of aged single women in the city. It is on record that His Lordship came from Dromore no less than seven times to preach on behalf of his beloved St. Joseph's. Father Tom Burke, O.P., also is named, and the famous Oxford convert, Reverend Frederick Oakley, afterwards Canon of Westminster, preached in Dublin on behalf of St. Joseph's almost immediately after his ordination to the Catholic priesthood, while the great "Liberator", Daniel O'Connell himself, took up the collection. These sermons were generally preached in Gardiner Street Church, where, through the goodness of the Jesuit Fathers, the pulpit was lent once a year for the benefit of St. Joseph's.

When the Sisters came to the Institution, Mother Magdalen saw at once that the initial difficulties were great. Three old dilapidated houses formed the "Home", and some ladies had even to be lodged in adjoining houses, thus involving further expense. The place was heavily in debt. There was plenty of discomfort of every kind, but the nuns were cheered at hearing that plans were under way for a new wing, the foundation stone of which was laid by His Grace the Archbishop on May 19th, 1889, and he also gave a cheque for £1,000 towards the cost of the projected work. Canons Fricker and O'Donnell were present, while the zealous and untiring Mr. Murphy headed a party of the "Friends of St. Joseph's." One great friend of St. Joseph's was missing from the scene in the person of Miss Ellen Kerr, the former Matron, who had died the year before, and who had been for years devoted to this charitable work. Until the Sisters took over, the work was entrusted to her Asssistant Matron, a Miss Catherine Kiely, who in a most loyal and generous spirit assisted the nuns until her extreme old age, when she too had to retire and was nursed and cared for till her death at St. Joseph's in 1916.

The Reverend Father Henry Young was another "friend" missing on that memorable day. Appointed Chaplain to St. Joseph's at the age of 70, and noted for his great holiness, crowds flocked to his confessional and to his sermons, as they did in France to his saintly contemporary, the Curé of Ars. Father Young lived under the same roof as his Eucharistic Lord, and was known to have spent nights alone with Him in prayer for the world and for St. Joseph's. Mr. Murphy also, even to the last, was prayerfully interested in his beloved St. Joseph's and took up each Sunday's collection with happy gratitude to the last weeks of his life. Whenever a special pressing need for money arose, Mr. Murphy's quaint advice to the Sisters was: "Make a novena, pet!"

In 1909 there was no way to make room for the ever-increasing number of applications but to demolish the old tottering houses, one of which had served as the convent, and a fine new building soon filled the space. A further addition was made in the 1940's by way of single rooms and other renovations, and now in the 1960's, the fine old building has been completely re-modelled and modernized from roof and ceiling to its foundation. Oil has replaced coal for its adapted furnaces, its electric system has been completely checked and re-wired, while a splendidly constructed elevator has been built in, for the comfort of the dear residents.

What has been neither changed nor re-modelled is the spirit of St. Joseph's — that holy atmosphere of continual prayer that goes on from day to day, year in and year out, since its first institution in two rooms in Clarendon Street, whence it was transferred to Portland Row on the Feast of St. Teresa, 15th October, 1830. "How long ago it seems!" wrote someone in the Centenary Year of the Institution. "Leo XIII was a student preparing for the priesthood. Queen Victoria was a girl under her mother's eye in Kensington Palace. Louis Phillippe reigned in France. Daniel O'Connell had successfully achieved his 'bloodless victory' in the cause of Catholic Emancipation. Mother Magdalen Taylor, Foundress of the Institute of religious who were later to take charge of St. Joseph's, was but four years old!" This quotation has been taken from a brochure entitled: "A Shrine and a Story," prefaced by the late Father Stanislaus, O.D.C., and dated 15th October, 1935. Much of the matter of the brochure had been hitherto written by Mother Magdalen herself in a former history of St. Joseph's. In the Foundress' first visit to Portland Row as Fanny Taylor, she had wished for a fairy wand that she might put the Institution under the care of Sisters. This was as far back as 1867, when she wrote of it in her book "Irish Homes and Irish Hearts." Little did she dream at that stage that she herself was to be the fairy god-mother whose children were one day to make St. Joseph's what it is. That "Shrine", as it is fitly called, has been ever supported by the Christ-like charity of the people of Dublin. Since the days of Dr. Blake and Mr. Murphy, of Helen Kerr and her Assistant Matron, of the saintly chaplains, Father Henry Young, Fathers Curtis and Kavanagh, S.J., and the saintly Brother Doyle of the same Society, generous and faithful friends and co-operative and self-sacrificing benefactors had given of their best, and have continued to do so to the present day. Canon Fricker (who afterwards became Archdeacon) with Canon O'Donnell were not only Trustees of St. Joseph's but friends in every sense, and sent many zealous aspirants to the Congregation in their time. There were also its loyal medical doctors, from Drs. McSweeney

145

and O'Connell of the first years down to the present time. And what is to be said of Dublin's dear Archbishops? From the days of Dr. Walsh, all succeeding Archbishops deserve the Sisters' heartfelt gratitude for their co-operation and encouragement. Our present Archbishop, despite the great responsibility and pressure which the phenomenal growth of the Archdiocese has had, and is still having during His Grace's period of government, has not forgotten St. Joseph's, as he has not forgotten the poor and the lonely everywhere. Helped by his loyal Vicar-General, Monsignor Fitzpatrick, who was its one-time chaplain, Dr. McQuaid has truly deserved the Sisters' deepest and most prayerful gratitude for his paternal kindness and his always sincere and trustful co-operation for the good estate of St. Joseph's.

The names of other benefactors are too numerous to mention here, but let it be their consolation that the names of these are written down, never to be forgotten by the Sisters or their protégés. The old ladies (as they are affectionately called) pray daily with the Community, and, after Our Lady's time-honoured Rosary, prayers "For the Church and the Holy Father," "for our Archbishop," "for priests," "for our benefactors, living and dead," "for those who have asked our prayers," "for the peace of the world," "for the souls in Purgatory," etc., are said. Adoration of the Blessed Sacrament is kept up daily, as one white-veiled lady relieves another each half-hour. Passers-by drop in for a moment, say a short prayer, light a candle to Our Lady or St. Joseph, and hurry off to work. It is said that Matt Talbot often did so on his way to and from work. Only God knows the number who give Him a call at St. Joseph's daily, and who receive grace in return. First Friday devotions, always preceded by Thursday's Holy Hour, have gone on from Father Young's time, as have also the May and October devotions, at which times the Church is crowded. The Feast of St. Teresa — birthday in 1836 of the Institution — is observed annually with great solemnity, as is also the anniversary of the opening of, and first Mass at the Church, 20 years later on the same date, when Dr. Blake came from Drogheda and preached at St. Joseph's for the last time.

Many, indeed most of the old ladies are Tertiaries of one or other of the Old Religious Orders of Dublin, or are affiliated in some way with others, and one of their joys after their own Mass and breakfast is to make for their favourite Church and assist at as many Masses as they can. One such lady, now dead, was overheard by the Brother Sacristan, who was arranging flowers in the sacristy of a certain church one day, to say aloud: "My loving Lord, I thank God that no man ever asked me, that all my life is yours, all my Masses, all my Rosaries, all my pains. Take them all to console your Heart, and tell Your Holy Mother I'll expect Her at my death in St. Joseph's." The dear old lady's spoken joyful outburst was a consolation to the Brother, and as both are long dead, one feels free to relate the episode.

The Annual Sale of Work is a great event at St. Joseph's, and is opened with due ceremony by a great friend or notable benefactor. The workroom is a busy spot in preparation. The ladies, except the bedridden or rheumatic, are much interested, and create lovely and useful specimens in embroidery, children's dresses, knitted work, etc. One old lady told the visiting Health Authorities that her target was 20 pairs of knitted socks! There is usually a raffle of expensive articles. The Sisters give of their best, and so do the communities of other houses. Friends of the Sisters and of the ladies come to help at the sale and to entertain the crowd, and altogether it is a joyful occasion, when young and old are all as happy children in one mingling mass. The pages of St. Joseph's, Dublin, justly close with the very prayerful and lasting gratitude of the present Mother-General of the Poor Servants of the Mother of God to all and everyone, even to the little child of six who gave her ice-cream to St. Joseph "for his Baby Jesus" on a very hot July day in 1964! Dr. Blake, Mr. Murphy, Archbishop Walsh, and all who were responsible for the birth and early growth of this great Dublin charity in the nineteenth century, must have rejoiced in Heaven at its progress down the years, and that the Bank of Divine Providence, as Mother Magdalen used to call it, still opens to the Sisters' knocks, by virtue of the unfailing Christian charity of the "Friends of St. Joseph's."

From the meeting of Mother Magdalen and Dr. Walsh in the parlour of the Roman house in the February of 1887, the development of both Streatham and Dublin to the present day has been described. Mother Taylor loved to consider St. Joseph's

147

as being "an Irish cousin" of the Roman house. The negotiations for its take-over began in the Roman parlour. Its Golden Jubilee was blessed by Pope Leo XIII, and its drawing of prizes and bazaar for the occasion were enriched by His Holiness with the beautiful gesture of a valuable painting of St. Joseph and the Holy Child on porcelain, encased in crimson velvet. A further link in the relationship was the celebration of St. Joseph's centenary in the same year as that of the Golden Jubilee of the Roman house.

Back in Rome in 1890, Mother Magdalen saw the Divine Will for yet another Tabernacle, and this in the heart of Paris, where numbers of young English and Irish governesses and students were in need of a protecting hand. She herself had often visited Paris as a young girl, and was very conscious of this need. A rich but eccentric French lady whom she had met in Rome promised financial aid, and Cardinal Richard of Paris was very enthusiastic. House-hunting began in the great city, and after many weeks of useless search, the Sisters set out for what they thought was to be the last useless day. It was September 23rd, Lady Georgiana's birthday, and as they were about to abandon their task, a lady in black suddenly accosted them in the street, and said hurriedly: "If you want a house, you will find one at No. 15 in the next street," and disappeared into the "nowhere" as the Sisters put it. They went to No. 15. There was no "To let" sign. They found the owner, who asked: "How could you possibly have known? We have told no one. We have lost money and wish to break up our household." The house was just the type they needed, and the bargain was concluded that day. The grateful Foundress wrote the news in a circular letter to her Institute, and attributed the miracle not only to Lady Georgiana's prayers, but also to her dear old ladies at Portland Row, to Father Young, and especially to Mr. Murphy, whose advice in every crisis was: "Make a novena, pet." At the last moment the rich eccentric lady withdrew her promise, but the courageous Foundress again entrusted her cause to the Bank of Divine Providence, and God provided.

These hostels in Paris have been really Godsends from the beginning. The first house was evacuated later for a larger one in the Rue Murillo, and again in the Rue Lord Byron, and in these latter years a fine freehold property was purchased at 26 Rue de Lubeck, near the Etoile, in a most convenient place for the students for bus and underground travel to their respective colleges, universities, institutes or other destinations.

The Passionist Fathers have been kindness itself to the Poor Servants of the Mother of God in Paris. They are our chaplains, confessors, conference-givers etc., and live within a short distance from the Convent. The Holy Ghost Fathers and the O.M.I.'s are also great friends. Naturally there is much talent among our boarders, and each one's birthday is a joyful event for all. Sincere and lasting friendships are formed among the girls, and one of their greatest joys is to subscribe to the needs of the poor and the lonely, among whom the Sisters have a busy apostolate. Quite an old custom too, since the Foundress' day, was and is to invite any Irish or English Sisters from French Communities to spend St. Patrick's or St. George's Day with the S.M.G.'s. Such Sisters would be surprisingly few, but it made, as it does still, for happiness and charity, as does also a splendid and well-attended Catholic Club at the local Passionist Church.

In 1891, Mother Taylor, still in Rome, received a sad letter from that great lover of the poor, the outcast and the distressed — Monsignor Nugent of Liverpool. During a visit in London, he had heard from Cardinal Manning of her great work at Russell House, Streatham, and the Cardinal convinced him that "she was the lady to save the situation." The "situation" was critical in the extreme, as the letter disclosed. No less than 300 "bad houses" had been ordered "immediate closing" by the Liverpool magistrates. Numbers of unfortunate women would be committed to the streets. Would she open in Liverpool a Home and Refuge such as she had done in Streatham? Would she telegraph the reply. Mother Magdalen telegraphed an immediate "Yes", and followed the telegram to England, and within a couple of weeks a temporary refuge was opened in Limekiln Lane, which was later changed for a larger building in Bevington Bush, while that in Limekiln Lane became a night-shelter for homeless women. Many a poor soul has been saved by Mother Magdalen's and Monsignor Nugent's timely work, while the difficulties they had to face therein brought down God's blessing on the dangerous handling of such work by the Sisters concerned. Many branch houses in Liverpool opened as a result. These foundations and their various apostolic works owe their existence, under God, to the fatherly kindness and watchful care of Archbishop Whiteside of blessed memory, whose name is forever enshrined in the Sisters' grateful hearts. His care and concern for the orphan, the homeless, the unwanted, the outcast and the sinner, shared as it was by that other Father of the Poor, Monsignor Nugent, was truly according to the example set by his Divine Master.

In the summer of 1892 the Congregation had the grand news from its Mother that the Brief of Approbation of the Rules and Constitutions had arrived from Rome; it had been delayed some months, owing to the death of Father Cardella, S.J., the promotor of the cause, whose place was taken by Father de Augustinis, S.J., Rector of the Gregorian University. Cardinal Manning was beside himself with joy at the news, and Archbishop Vaughan attended the Thanksgiving Day at Brentford on the Feast of Our Lady of Miracles — July 9th — and gave Benediction. A special reason for joy was that in the approved Rules, to the Foundress' immense gratification, the Sisters are not only *permitted,* but *desired* to regard St. Ignatius of Loyola "as if he were their father."

With all her recent graces, which, after God, she attributed to Pope Leo's whole-hearted blessings, and were therefore, as she loved to think, of Roman origin, Mother Magdalen, having prayed and made her decision about all while in Rome, received the Brief of Approbation naturally as an assurance of God's special approval of the Sisters' work. There was the miracle of the Roman apostolate, commanded by the Pope himself. There in the Roman house in 1886 she decided to open the Streatham house with all its charitable works. It was also in the Roman parlour that she gave her happy and comforting "Yes" to Archbishop Walsh of Dublin for the take-over of St. Joseph's, Portland Row, Dublin. Finally, it was while in the Holy City that the Paris and Liverpool foundations were decided upon, and now from the Holy See came the crowning grace— the Brief of Approbation.

The Foundress thought surely that day of Lady Georgiana's smiling words to her, whenever great ventures in her life were blessed by God: "Prepare now for some balancing cross," was the usual "obiter dictum" of her great friend, who knew and had proved in her life, as Mother Magdalen had, that "all things work together for good for those who love God." The years 1892 onwards were to bring many sorrows and crosses to this brave woman who never refused her Lord anything.

"More things are wrought by prayer than this world dreams of," wrote Tennyson. What a change in England since Dr. Wiseman's Pastoral "From out the Flaminian Gate" and its frightening reception by the English people at the Restoration of the Hierarchy in 1850! Even from Dr. Whiteside's time and his "Epidemic of thunderbolts from Whitehall," whose threatening rumble he so bravely resisted, and prevented the bolts from falling! What multitudinous graces were poured on England since 1529 and the so-called Reformation! Since 1533 and the Act of Supremacy, since 1829 with its Emancipation Bill, since 1833 and the first faint dawn of the Oxford Movement, when Fanny Taylor was one year old! Since 1845 when the movement had gained full and courageous impetus and opened out in its full sunburst with Dr. Wiseman's Red Hat in 1850! What a grand, holy and heroic roll of Churchmen have pledged themselves, especially since Wiseman's and Manning's time: to pray, to work and to win back to Christ His Mother's long-lost Dowry!

Who would ever have foreseen or dreamt in 1529 or 1533, or even amid the uproar of 1850, that a Prime Minister of England would be present at a concelebrated Mass in Liverpool Cathedral at its opening on May 14th, 1967? World War II had delayed its major construction and artistic detail, but big things move slowly and God waits. It would seem as if in this case He waited until His Grace, Archbishop Beck, who edited that unique masterpiece of English Church History, "The English Catholics, 1850-1950," had become Archbishop of Liverpool, and Liverpool's previous Archbishop had become Cardinal Archbishop of Westminster, so that the elder sister Cathedral could, through the Pope's chosen Delegate and her own eminent representative congratulate her sister of the North and its gracious Archbishop in the name of England's ancient and restored Hierarchy. She would congratulate her in the names of the martyrs, the confessors and of all who lived, worked, prayed and died for the conversion of England. St. Augustine, England's chief apostle, would have rejoiced with St. Patrick in Heaven at the Cardinal's sermon. So would St. Paul of the Cross have rejoiced with Blessed Dominic Barberi that their united yearnings, prayers and sacrifices in Italy gave them the conversion of England as their avowed vocation. A further reason for their rejoicing was that a famous scion of England's own aristocracy, Lord George Spencer, became a convert to Catholicism, a priest of the English College in Rome, and finally, by God's grace, a humble Passionist who could deliver God's message to England's people in their own tongue.

Dr. Whiteside's successors, Archbishops Keating, Downey, and Godfrey (before being made Cardinal) followed in his footsteps in their paternal kindness in helping and co-operating with the Poor Servants of the Mother of God in their various apostolates for the Church in Liverpool. His Eminence, Cardinal Heenan, also has left his name engraved forever in the hearts of the Sisters, and especially on those of their children at Knolle Park. He played with them, feasted with them, recommended his intentions to their prayers. They loved His Grace, and even his dog, who was their precious charge and "boarder" during his master's absence. They cried bitterly when they heard of their Archbishop's change to Westminster, and one little lad of five asked Sister: "Will our Grace's dog be going to London with our Grace?"

Chapter 15.

THE MOTHER AND HER CHILDREN

Nothing, naturally, gives a mother's heart so much pain in this life as the loss of a devoted child. Holy Scripture has many instances of a father mourning his child's loss, when perhaps it is also the "only son and heir" (as the saying goes) who dies and leaves his parents disconsolate. Some would have it that a father's grief is deeper and more poignant than is a mother's, because the latter weeps more easily, and tears are often a soothing relief. A father's feelings, instead, are all within, and it could happen that the suffering is greater. Yet, the poet puts the mother first when he says:

"A mother's love, how sweet the name!
What is a mother's love?
A noble, pure and tender flame
Enkindled from above."

When sons or daughters leave the parental home in order to consecrate their lives to God, it is often looked upon as a living death; it was very much so in the early ages, and even in our day, many otherwise devout Catholics look upon a boy or girl who enters Religion as completely lost to the family. They educated their children, perhaps, at great cost and many sacrifices, and then God's call comes. Deep down in his or her soul, the boy or girl hears Christ's "Come, follow Me," or "He that loveth father or mother more than Me is not worthy of Me," and His call is obeyed. God gives His grace. After some years that father and mother kneel for their son's blessing at his ordination, and it is they who call, and who hear their privileged son called "Father". Likewise parents, at their child's Vow ce-

153

K

remony, hear their daughter called "Sister", or later "Mother". For one "father or mother or brother or sister or houses or lands" which they forsake, Priests, Brothers and Sisters have to "father" or "mother" hundreds or perhaps thousands of families in the spiritual world of souls to which they are called, and where God's graces await them in every place, while He Himself replaces them in their human families, and blesses their parents' loss, as they soon realize.

Fanny Taylor was the youngest child of a most loving and happy family. It was she who saw her father and mother leave her and die. She had many sorrows and bitter disappointments before and after her conversion. She had heard the "Follow Me" in the Crimean Hospital at Koulali. She was first introduced to Christ's Mother there by the Reverend Mother from Kinsale. She "mothered" the wounded and dying Irish soldiers, and at a risk where she had to cut through much red tape to do so. She wrote letters of love and pain for them, as they confided to her their last dying messages with love and trust.

Later, when the then twenty-two year old Fanny became a nun, and at the head of a little flock of young postulants, they realized that she had learned the lovely art of "mothering", and was perfecting that art by its daily practice. She would not be called "Reverend Mother", she was "Mother". She had long realized that love for her child is a mother's God-given gift, her heaven-enkindled flame. Mother Taylor knew of the sacrifice that both mother and child are asked to make for Him who calls, and that she herself had the Christ-given responsible office of "mothering" that child and of training her for a holy vocation, while the child's love for her earthly mother is meanwhile increased and spiritualized the more. The Lord, by the words of the prophet, puts a mother's love superior to all loves, and yet qualifies it with an "if" and a "yet": "Can a mother forget her infant so as not to have pity on the son of her womb? And *if* she should forget, *yet* will I not forget thee" (Is. 49, v. 15).

And who does not know Our Lord's own beautiful simile with reference to the destruction of the Holy City? "How often would I have gathered thy children together, as a hen gathers her young under her wings, but thou wouldst not" (St. Luke 13, v. 34). In Our Lord's Boyhood at Nazareth He must have often watched the beautiful scene — the mother-hen senses the hawk hovering overhead, ready to swoop on her innocent fledglings. She gets excited, runs towards them and clucks, and the chicks understand. The same happens when a sudden storm threatens and in a moment one can only see the many little feet of the brood, all safely cuddled beneath the mother's wings.

Fanny Taylor well knew the love of a dear mother, and a widowed mother at that. The wound she had caused that mother by her conversion and its consequent difference in their spiritual world never wholly healed, although Mrs. Taylor was too noble and loving a mother to consider her child the less. She believed that any tendency she had towards the Catholic Church was a subtle temptation, arising from their mutual love. Mother Magdalen's ardent prayers and hopes for her mother's conversion were never realized.

In her first decade as head of the infant Congregation, the Foundress had the grief of seeing some of the most promising of her spiritual daughters taken from her by death. Sister M. Antonia died in 1873, Sister M. Gertrude, who had been appointed Novice-Mistress at Roehampton, died in 1876, Sister M. Clare followed in 1880, and Sister M. Winifred died at St. Helens in 1883. From 1891 onwards, one by one of her first companions who had remained loyal and steadfast through the very difficult years of hard living and generously-continued sacrifice for God were now to be called home, before their grateful Mother could share with them the joys of the Silver Jubilee. Of these latter, dear old Sister M. Elizabeth (known by the poor of London as "herself") was the first to go. All her last years were spent in training the young members in the various forms of social work which she herself had been taught by Mother Magdalen. In this work, which as the Rule reminds the Sisters, requires such patience, abnegation and wisdom, Sister M. Elizabeth was an adept. Love and respect for each individual with whom she had to deal were Sister M. Elizabeth's traits all her life. At the sad news of Sister's death, Mother wrote from Rome:

"In came the post with the news of poor dear Sister M. Elizabeth's death. I can only rejoice that she is set free from the burden of this life. She worked hard for God, and did so

155

much good amongst the poor. Only on Wednesday Mother Aloysius Austin and I were talking of her, and saying how much real humility she had. Well, one of *us three* who first had the black veil is gone. Sister M. Evangelist is printing some mortuary cards. I should like them given to the Sisters. I will have enough done for all. She died while the Sisters here were starting for the Vatican, as it was the Pope's Coronation Day, and he is carried in state to the Sistine Chapel. Things are so sad nowadays, and we have seen such sad things among ourselves even, that to die *safe* in Holy Church and in religion seems only peace and joy..."

In the "Catholic Times" for March 1891, Monsignor Talbot wrote:

"My good old friend and fellow-worker for many years, Sister M. Elizabeth, fairly wore herself out by her zealous labours in our parish, walking long distances when she was scarcely able. I am happy to think that all her steps were counted for her on the road to heaven."

Sister M. Colette lived a few years longer. "A perfect Community Sister," the obituary notes reveal. She was a great prop in the early years. "The life and soul of the Community recreation," wrote another Sister, and a shining example to younger Sisters while training them in the art of book-keeping, as well as superintending their studies, their cookery lessons etc. As long as she could hold a pen, much of the business of the Institute was entrusted to Sister M. Colette. Little could be written of her interior life; it was a life "hidden with Christ in God," but example revealed the secret within, where the power-house of the Sacred Heart lay.

Sister M. Rose was another of the grand group, and when she died in 1893, Mother Magdalen's letter from Rome speaks spiritual volumes:

"Rome, June 8, 1893.

"My dear Children,

Though I wrote to you so recently, I feel I must send a few lines to you all on the occasion of the death of our very dear Sister M. Rose. She is gone from us, leaving behind her a fragrant memory. She has been twenty years in the Community, and as I look back on those twenty years, I cannot recall one painful thought about her. I think we may, without presumption, say she was our 'Saint' on earth, now our saint in heaven. She came to us with an upright will, a total disregard of self, and a heart given to Jesus Christ. She was a true lover, a faithful spouse of His, and a true Servant of Mary. How was her life spent? In most lowly offices. The world knew nothing of her. She did not shine as 'Good Sister Rose,' 'Useful Sister Rose,' among priests and ladies. No conversions were attributed to her. She was never chosen as Superior, or to rule over others. Her life was spent in the laundry — there she became a saint. Two means she had for this. First, untiring industry; she laboured, as the Rule enjoins, 'with industry, eagerness, intelligence and interest.' She never rested until she learned how to manage the steam boiler, and then for years she rendered the most valuable service to the Community. The second means was prayer. She was not seen at any extra prayers, she did not spend long hours in the chapel, but she prayed always. If things went wrong she prayed — if they went right she gave thanks. There are two more virtues I wish to remark in her — first, her zeal for the Community — her perfect loyalty to Superiors, so that they could lean upon her as on a strong pillar, sure of her perfect truth and fidelity, her constant charity towards her Sisters — each and all she loved — and, secondly, her spirit of gratitude. This last was, I think, her chief, her distinguishing virtue. She was a living fountain of gratitude — in health and also in sickness — sickness, which often tries the virtue of so many, did not overcome her. She was not only patient, but joyful, grateful; grateful to the end. 'Are you happy?' she was asked. 'Happy, indeed,' she answered, 'What else could I be? How could God have done more for me than call me to religion!'

People often say, when a nun dies it is like breaking a pane of glass. You put in another. But it won't be easy to put in another Mary Rose. If I could I would put up a painted pane to her memory. It should shine with bright rose colour, and in the midst would be the word 'Magnificat'. That was her motto. She lived and died saying 'My soul doth magnify the Lord.' It was strange that she should have received the religious name of 'Rose,' for truly like a rose she bloomed amongst us, casting a fragrance around her — truly she has left a sweet and fragrant

157

odour behind her now that she is gone to bloom for ever in the garden of God's Paradise.

Your affectionate Mother in Christ,
Mother Magdalen of the Sacred Heart, S.M.G."

Cardinal Vaughan visited Sister M. Rose on her death-bed, and expressed his admiration afterwards of her joyous spirit of content and her overflowing gratitude to God and her Superiors.

The Silver Jubilee of the Congregation was due for celebration in 1894, and if Mother Magdalen's affectionate heart could regret anything on that blessed day, it was the absence of those devoted daughters who had lived, loved, laboured and prayed with her, their Reverend Mother, from the birthday of the Congregation, September 24th, 1869. Many others who were missing on that occasion had made an honest "try" of their vocation, and, after prayer and spiritual advice, had taken their leave. Others were judged as unsuitable for one reason or another, and were escorted home according to their parents' wishes, or helped towards some suitable post in England or Ireland, while others still, like dear Sister M. Antonia, made their holy Vows on their death-beds.

On the whole, the Congregation had very much increased by 1894. Mother Magdalen's circular letter to the Communities for the occasion of the Silver Jubilee is here given 'in extenso', and explains itself:

"Rome, March 25th, 1894.
"My very dear Children,

With a full heart I write you these lines which are to reach you on the day we have chosen to keep our Silver Jubilee, and the day chosen by the Church this year to celebrate the feast of the Incarnation of Our Lord within His Holy Mother, our dear Lady, and when the Sacred Hearts of Jesus and Mary beat in unison.

A quarter of a century has passed away since a very small and lowly band began in a very humble way to serve Our Lady and the poor.

They did not foresee the future, they hardly thought about it. They were content to do what God wanted at the moment, and left all in His hands. How can we thank that good Providence of God, through the hands of Mary, for all that He has done for us?

A spirit of deep gratitude ought to animate us all the days of our lives, for I want you to consider that while God blesses all religious Orders, yet when He has vouchsafed to give to any one Order very special marks of His power and His love, so that people wonder and are struck — the members ought to have very special gratitude that they have been called to that Order, because they know their call must have been a very special and marked one.

As I let my memory travel over those first years, I see a little set of hired rooms in the midst of vast London. What a contrast between the turmoil of this great city, full of business and strife and sin, and our simple ceremony when the first little statue of Our Lady was put in its place as Lady, Mistress, Queen and Mother of the Institute, and our first Litany rose up to her in Heaven.

I see our first little house — our hard work, our hard days, when we had little to eat and much to suffer. I see our first little chapel, where we received the holy habit and made our Vows. And now I see our great house in Rome — our large school, and our numerous other houses, with our orphans, sick, penitents, old women and others — and I am wonder-struck, and I feel no one can help saying: 'Lo! the Finger of God is here!'

How many souls has it been given to the Institute to save! First, how many giving themselves to God, and persevering to the end, have become the Spouses of Christ, the Servants of Our Lady, and are now, we humbly trust, among the elect in Heaven! Then our orphans, how many saved from danger, rejoice the Heart of Jesus! Our old people made happy — our penitents brought back to their Shepherd and Redeemer! Let us rejoice and give thanks!

In all our houses let there be a Magnificat sung, or where this cannot be, let it be said three times, and let us all resolve that after this Silver Jubilee, we will work more earnestly for God, be more closely united to the Hearts of Jesus and Mary, and so strive to please Our Lady as faithful Spouses of Her Son,

159

that one day we may shine like stars around her throne for ever! Pray for me, dear children,

Your loving Mother in Christ,
Mother Magdalen of the Sacred Heart, S.M.G."

The Cardinal Vicar came across to the Roman Convent to greet her and the whole Congregation, in the name of the Holy Father, and on a beautiful little "ricordo" from himself was written: "Each day I pray for your happiness," and on the reverse side: "How canst thou be Mine and I thine, unless thou be both within and without freed from all self-will?" (Imitation of Christ, Book III, ch. 37).

Another joy on that day in Rome was the receiving of a few pencilled lines from Father Dignam. After a printed prayer of supplication to God and His dearest Mother, for their tenderest blessings on her and her children, he wrote on the back of a picture of St. Mary Magdalen: "God bless you, you are a comfort, my child." Father Clare, now ageing at St. Beuno's in Wales, wrote to her in April 1894 a letter which, for its wisdom, is given 'in extenso' here:

"April 1, 1894.

"My dear Sister in Christ, P.C.

...I was delighted to hear from you, and to get such good news about your holy Institute, and to find you are celebrating the Silver Jubilee of its existence. You need not recall the early days; for, though on most things my memory plays me false, on this my recollections are vivid enough. First, you yourself were quite tried enough in the fierce furnace of tribulation, and it was only by the special grace of our good God that you did not break under the heavy trials you had. And what a blessing it has been for those who have been under you, as by it you learned to 'have patience and compassion for those who are in ignorance and error, because you yourself were surrounded with infirmity' (Heb. V. 2). Again you must remember how it was reported that I was establishing a new Order of Poor Clares, and that without authority! Which at first the General believed, until he was better informed. That too gave me confidence that you would succeed, for trials coming from such sources were a sure sign that the Finger of God was in your work...

160

You have enough to do, it is true. At the same time, I cannot but think that it is suited to your disposition, and as long as you make no compromise about your spiritual duties, and insist upon them in all your subjects, I have no fear; as long as everything is made to yield to them, all is sure to go right...

There are two things that cause me some anxiety... first, the absence of a supply of well-trained local Superiors. Oh, how rare it is to find, even in long established Orders, persons really fitted for the work of guiding others, and of keeping alive the religious spirit in their subjects, and that in great love and tenderness, combined with firmness. The second point is the great danger arising from the great variety of duties... It certainly is a very large undertaking, and to be well done requires persons most thoroughly devoted and impregnated with the spirit of self-sacrifice; persons formed on the two contemplations which comprise the whole essence of our Society, I mean the 'Contemplation of the Kingdom of Christ,' and 'Two Standards' and on 'Three Classes of Men.' I do not write this, my dear Sister, to depress you, but to show you how necessary it is that you should have your subjects thoroughly well grounded in the principles of religious life, more especially in the spirit of prayer and union with our dear Lord, and in the spirit of detachment.

I am glad that you are in better health, and I pray that our dear Lord will long preserve you to preside over and train your subjects to carry out the work which for His sake you have undertaken.

Believe me, Yours sincerely in Christ,
James Clare, S.J."

This shows clearly the spirit in which, under God, he and Father Dignam trained the Foundress and her first Sisters in the early decades of the life of their Congregation. It was, and truly is, the "spirit of the Foundress," for which the Sisters ever thank God, as they ask themselves to-day, and within sight of the Centenary, "What would our Mother Foundress do now, were she living in our period of Renewal?" And our Head Superiors of to-day, acting in her name, have already answered: "Our Mother would certainly have conformed her whole will and all her spiritual energy to obey the requirements of the Holy

See for Renewal, as set forth in the Council documents and decrees," and this, please God, the Congregation, in perfect loyalty, is all out to do, trusting in the Holy Spirit's Divine Light and in Our Lady's protecting aid.

Their Rule demands that they ever remind themselves that the true spirit of their Congregation is: "Life for Jesus Christ, labour for Jesus Christ, zeal for Jesus Christ, and all things through Mary, His most sweet Mother and our Mistress." Three times daily the Angelus reminds the Sisters "that at the first sound of the bell and in the most profound silence and with great and loving devotion, the Sisters will devoutly recite the Angelus, remembering that 'the Word was made Flesh and dwelt amongst us.'" Père Olier's beautiful prayer was another loving one adopted by the Foundress as expressing the spirit of the Congregation from its beginning. Each day it is recited as: "O Jesus, living in Mary, come and live in Thy servants, in the spirit of Thy holiness, in the fulness of Thy might, in the truth of Thy virtues, in the perfection of Thy ways, in the communion of Thy mysteries. Subdue every hostile power to Thy Spirit for the glory of the Father. Amen."

The Apostleship of Prayer and its diffusion throughout the world (thanks to the zeal of the Society of Jesus) was another fervent aim of the sighing soul of Mother Magdalen. She was Father Dignam's zealous ally in promoting the Apostleship in England. The Sisters to-day, wherever they are to be found, have their promoters, their Register of Enrolment, the monthly leaflets, and, of course, the well-known "Messenger". The Morning Offering, giving the Holy Father's special intention for each month, begins the day in their every Convent chapel, school, hospital, or wherever their lot is cast among souls, and so each act of every day is sanctified for hundreds, while it pleads to the Sacred Heart for all Its intentions in the Holy Mass throughout the world. Well might dear Mother Magdalen's last words on her death-bed be: "Invoke the Sacred Heart!" She knew she could trust that Divine, merciful Heart, for whose consolation she had worked so hard all her religious life.

In the September of the Silver Jubilee year, Father Dignam died. "I have lost one of my best helps on earth," wrote the Foundress to a friend, and after the funeral, she sent the following circular letter to the Communities, most of whom had known and been helped by their venerated Father:

"I must write to you about our dear and venerated Father Dignam, whom God has pleased to take from us. Many of you never saw him, or at least never knew him. Perhaps you do not even know what great services he rendered us; but in every house there are some who knew what he was, and they can tell the others.

He was a true Father to us. He spent himself for us, forming us to be true Religious, after the spirit of St. Ignatius. Only God knows fully what we owe him — and, after God, only myself and a few of the older Sisters.

He was the greatest gift God has ever given us, sent to us in our early days, and not taken away till we were solidly planted and confirmed in the Church. He compiled and wrote our Constitutions, which were so highly thought of in Rome. And to him we owe that spirit of sincere humility, which I can say to my immense consolation, is, I believe, thoroughly grounded in the Institute. We have many faults, but I think all are ready to own them and to be sorry. That was his one great teaching — humility, contrition, confidence in the love of the Sacred Heart.

Dear children, I know you will pray for him as he would have wished. Later on I shall tell you more about him.

We were allowed to see him in his coffin, and so beautiful! All traces of his illness gone, except that he was thin and worn, but such a smile on his face! It reminded me of the lines in the Messenger:

'I smile,' said he,

'Because no one can take my God from me.'

He was in his vestments; his crucifix and his rosary in his hands. A large cross of white flowers was made and sent by us. We could not go to the Mass as it was in the private chapel, but we were allowed to go to see him buried at 9.0 a.m. No others were there save his whole community, and 21 of us. The sun was shining. We threw white flowers for those who loved him, but could not be present.

The Brother Infirmarian came to see me. He said he had never nursed so patient an invalid. He had been in the Infirmary over six months, and never once an impatient word, never a complaint. The Brother went to the Rector and said: 'Surely he must have something to complain of!' But no, never a word, perfect submission to God's Will, perfect patience with others. His last food on earth was Holy Viaticum — he could swallow that, but nothing else.

Your affectionate Mother in Christ,
M.M. of the Sacred Heart, S.M.G."

She lost another of her "best helps on earth" in a little more than three months after, in the person of Mother M. Philomena, who had been appointed Novice-Mistress at Roehampton in 1888, a post which she fulfilled until her last illness in 1894. A letter from Mother Magdalen to her sick daughter, written in January 1895, reads:

"My very dear Child,

I have not written to you for you are so weak, but sent you messages, and you know how much I am with you in spirit. My first thought daily almost is for you, and I watch for the post, and felt it hard during the snow, for we had no post for nearly two days.

Well, dear Philomena, are you really going to see our dear Lord, and His sweet Mother, and all His saints, about whom we have so often talked, and for whom you have laboured in your own poor little way to the last, and you will meet our dearest Father. Ask him to come and see me if God will permit — tell him we will all try to be worthy of his teaching — and tell all of *ours* whom you meet, how we care and think of them.

You say 'Forgive me.' My child, you know I never had a thought of you except love, aye, and gratitude for all you have done, for you have lifted a heavy burden off my shoulders for many years. God and Our Lady be with you.

I found in our Father's letters to me beautiful words about death, how we can make it a grand act of faith — going to God with perfect trust. You'll do this, I know, and pray for me. I shall feel your loss deeply. Fiat voluntas Tua."

And when Mother M. Philomena died, the following circular was sent to the Communities from what, one can conclude, was a bruised, but fully resigned heart, which had beaten ever in full accord with the Sacred Heart of her crucified Lord:

My dear children,

I feel I must write you a few words about our beloved
Mother M. Philomena of the Sacred Heart. God has been
pleased to take her from us, Blessed be His Holy Name! It is
a terrible loss, but Our Lord knows best; He wanted her to
come to Himself, and we must not grudge her her rest and her
reward. I think Our Lord said to her: 'Arise, make haste, My
love and come, the winter is now past, the rain is over and gone.'
Yes, for her the cold winter of life is past, and she has gone
where there is eternal Spring. But now, my dear children, consider why we have these happy thoughts about her — why can
we apply to her these blessed words? Because there are other
words in the same sacred Book that also apply to her closing
religious life: 'A bundle of myrrh is my Beloved to me, He shall
abide between my breasts.' Myrrh means bitterness, and Mother
M. Philomena bravely took up the cross and bore every sort of
trial that could make her more like her Beloved.

From the very first she strove to form herself, and be formed
to religious virtues. How perfect was her obedience! She was
literally like the old man's staff that St. Ignatius says we ought
to imitate. She was naturally very timid, and shrank from responsibility, but when she saw that, by coming forward, she
would lessen my burden, she threw aside all thought of self, and
took up her cross in this respect.

At one time she was Superior of our house at St. Helens,
and on one occasion she said she would give her life to save
me pain. I thought this was rather too strong an expression,
because her life belonged to Our Lord, and said so to Father
Dignam. He replied, 'I see nothing in such a desire contrary to
her fidelity to Our Lord, for, in God's dear Name, what could
be more true fulfilment of her vows to Our Lord than to give
her life for her Superior.' And then he went on to say, 'She is
as true as steel, and you could not wish to have a community
of your Institute serving God with greater reverence and edification than hers.'

Now there is another text in the Sacred Book which applies
to her: 'Catch us the little foxes that destroy the vines, for our
vineyard hath flourished.' For many years she was Novice-

Mistress, and how hard she laboured to catch the little foxes that destroy the vines of religion. So calm — not minding the great big things that could excite or interest, but the *little* things, over and over again, the same teaching, the same training, the same moulding. Such weary work of nature — but she never wearied, early and late, day by day. Her strength was worn out in her long faithful task — and what was the result? 'Our vineyard hath flourished.' The Novitiate has been little or no anxiety to me because of her fidelity, her self-sacrifice. Now and again I said to her, 'Child, you must have rest. Where will you go?' And she always said: 'To St Helens, please Mother, that I may see the Father, for then I shall gain fresh strength and courage.' And this she desired, not for her own soul, but for her charges. Now I want to appeal to all of you:

1. The Sisters who were her novices, remember her teaching and act upon it.
2. The novices who have been led by her up to this. Be as she wished. Let us always know those who were her best novices, and do all you can.
3. Teach her spirit to those who will come after you.
4. Those Sisters who were not her novices try to imitate her virtues, and be, like her, *faithful unto death.*

So now I may safely say, may I not, her crown is great, and Our Lord has said: 'Arise, My beloved, and come.'

Your very affectionate Mother in J.C.,

M. Magdalen of the Sacred Heart, S.M.G."

While two great sorrows, then, followed upon the joys of the Silver Jubilee, a great joy was soon in store for the big-hearted Mother whose continual soul-thirst, like that of the Founder of the Passionists, St. Paul of the Cross, and of the Saint's spiritual sons, Father Ignatius Spencer and Blessed Dominic Barberi, was the restoration to Our Lady of her long-lost ancient Dowry of Catholic England. This "great joy" for Mother Magdalen was the proposed erection, in the Roman Church of St. George and the English Saints, of a shrine of Our Lady, Queen of Prophets, a precious copy of a fresco in the Catacomb of St. Priscilla, set on a marble altar slab supported on four pillars of roughened stone, after the pattern of ancient altars hewn out of stone by the early Christians in the Catacombs. The famous de Rossi had written in 1863 that Roman painters and archaeologists of note had considered the original fresco as one of the earliest specimens of Christian Art, perhaps even earlier than the days of the Antonines.

The work represents Our Blessed Lady seated with the Divine Child in her lap. In front of her is the figure of a man, holding a scroll in his left hand and pointing towards a star with his right. It is understood at once that the painting represents Isaias himself, or the long line of prophets who foretold the rising of the star "out of Jacob" and prophesied the Incarnation, Life, Passion and Death of Christ.

In 1895 came Pope Leo's famous Apostolic Letter, "Ad Anglos Regnum Christi in fidei unitate quaerentes" into which the great English Churchman and future Cardinal, Monsignor Merry de Val, Privy Chamberlain to the Pope, poured his best efforts in translation, and in fact, as was little known at the time, composed the beautiful "Prayer for England" which it contained, and which was and is recited still after Benediction throughout the land. Father Bonavenia, S.J., Professor of Archaeology at the Gregorian University, had longed to see the aforesaid fresco of the Catacombs venerated overground, and, thought he in 1896, "Where could it find a more fitting place than in the Church of St. George and the English Saints?" It would, he thought, in this year of special intercession for England, appeal to English Protestants, as it linked up devotion to Our Lady in the first centuries with the well-known devotion of the English people to the Old Testament.

Leo XIII gave his hearty approval to the idea, and when the copy was painted, His Holiness himself blessed the picture and sanctioned fully its veneration under the title "Regina Prophetarum", suggested by Mother Magdalen's friend, Cardinal Parocchi, His Holiness' Vicar. The Guild of Ransom for the conversion of England, founded in England in 1887 by the Rev. Philip Fletcher and Mr. Lister Drummond, had already been canonically erected in the Roman Church, which was considered the natural centre for prayer for England's conversion.

The erection of the new shrine was the occasion for a Papal Indult for a Proper Mass, to be celebrated annually on January

27th, the newly appointed Feast of Our Lady, Queen of Prophets. For many years following upon the erection, and more particularly since World War I, the Rector of the Beda, the Right Reverend Monsignor Duchemin, and his students took over the morning celebrations at the shrine, and the Rector and students of the Venerable English College performed the evening ceremonies, and the beautiful custom is happily continued by their successors.

A handbook containing the story of the shrine was compiled by Sister M. Campion of the Community in 1906, six years after the death of the Foundress. It gave the complete history, details of the opening ceremony, the sermons preached on the occasion by the learned Cardinal Parocchi, the Reverend Father Porter, S.J., and the Reverend Philip Fletcher. Many other well-known English Churchmen loved, when in Rome, to say Mass at the shrine. Monsignor Merry del Val, Abbot Gasquet and Monsignor Hinsley — three future Cardinals — were frequent celebrants. Priests from the Irish, English, Beda and Scottish Colleges, after their ordination, loved to celebrate their first Mass there, to the great joy of their relatives who had come to Rome for this unique and blessed occasion.

The Sister M. Campion mentioned above in relation to the shrine was herself a convert from Protestantism, and was an Anglican nun for a number of years. When she got the grace of conversion, she was recommended to the Foundress by Rev. Father Gallwey, S.J., who declared her to have received great graces and to have a true call, although well on in years. He knew his postulant had great talents, especially for music and literature, but he said he had forewarned her that such talents did not argue a vocation to the Poor Servants of the Mother of God, except she trade with them for God's glory. Father Gallwey advised her that what she had to work at in the beginning was the attainment of humility, obedience, charity, self-effacement, and that self-abandonment to God's Will which Père Caussade called "the Sacrament of the Present Moment." Dear Sister M. Campion did not forget! A few of Mother Magdalen's letters are quoted here to show how much the Mother did to train the already formed character and way of her old child. She was sent to Rome when she made her first Vows.

Hers was evidently a very sincere and noble character. She was very open with her Superiors from the beginning, and especially with Mother Magdalen, whose policy was ever to "train her subjects as Our Lord trained His Apostles." Such was always her admonition to local Superiors, and over and over again she would counsel: "Never drive — lead." She would quote Our Lord's words: "Let us go…" "Children, have you any meat?" or "Bring hither the fishes which you have caught." Our Lord ever showed His Apostles how much He, their Master, was one with them and interested in all their efforts and in their simple joys, while continually supplying their needs.

In his "Life of Mother Magdalen Taylor" published in 1927, Father Devas, S.J., says: "Sister M. Campion had prepared a considerable amount for a biography of her beloved Mother, much of which is incorporated in these pages." She used her musical and literary talents solely for the Glory of God, and gave lessons in both to her Sisters in religion for many years. She is described by contemporary Sisters as "keeping fresh to the very end her spirit of fun and keen relish for the humour, even, of Religious Life."

When Sister M. Campion was a postulant in 1886, Mother Magdalen wrote to her brave convert:

"I was very glad to get your note. I think it will be good for you to write to me from time to time. I shall thus get to know you better, and then also that want of sympathy, which it is most natural you should feel, may be in a small measure satisfied. As to this, I should be glad if it were, but as to anything more — you cannot find it, it is part of the sacrifice we almost always find in religious life, and to minds like yours the want of solitude, and 'praying by rule,' are also part of it. But I know, dear, you will be glad to have a sacrifice to make. I hope God will grant you sufficient health and strength for your duties. As you go on, you will learn to understand religious life, how it means doing God's Will and not our own. We don't become nuns because we like it — because the life attracts us — but solely because 'The Master has come and called us,' and you will see that the true joy of religious life is exactly in proportion to your self-conquest."

L

And again in 1888:

"Try and fill your soul with thoughts of Jesus and Mary and the Saints — as facts, hard facts. A holy priest once said to me that real spiritual life consisted in saying vocal prayers well — meaning them — and it struck me so much, because we have to say vocal prayers. See how the Church binds priests to the Office — that shows her mind. See what stress the Pope lays on the Rosary — and therefore every community is sure to have vocal prayer of obligation and devotion. We have to say them, and if said badly they will hinder, not help us in our path, and if said well we are making mental prayer also. If, however, you find vocal prayer difficult, I would not add on more on my account."

To the same when in Rome in 1898:

"... The principle with you should be interior self-conquest. Great distrust of self, and to see things with the eye of faith. You know many things which a Sister by your side does not. I had to explain to a Sister the other day what a crocodile was, and I laughed at her, and then came the thought, 'In Heaven where will be my place compared with hers? And even on earth may not Our Lord caress her and not me?' I had been praying long for a favour, and did not get it, she wrote a letter to Our Lady, and it was granted in an hour! Oh, sweet humility! Oh, sweet self-distrust! Let us try for these, and then, if our poor bodies are weak and want a bit of coddling up, Our Lord will not grudge that to us — nor will our Sisters either.

If you were a living fount of sweetness and consolation to all around — never a harsh word, nor cross look, always showing much interest in other people's work and troubles — you would become a treasure in the community. That is the mission of old nuns. So you see I don't want you to bother about external things as to forget or weaken your battle inside. That is a common trick of the devil, to throw dust into our eyes. Addio! Now I am really better, though the heat did pull me down. St. Austin brought the rain and cool."

The final note before Mother Magdalen's death in 1900 runs:

"Dear Child,

Blessed Edmund Campion's day is not far off, and I think

170

it is the first of your feasts that I have not been in Rome. Changes and chances will come to young and old, except that God never changes, with Him is 'no shadow of turning.' So I wish you more and more of the charity and generosity which makes us like to God, because our fellows can say of us: 'She is always the same — you can depend on her,' and I wish you many other gifts besides..."

Dear Sister M. Campion outlived the Foundress by eight years, dying in August 1908 at La Quercia, whither the Sisters had gone for a few weeks from the great heat of Rome. She was buried at Viterbo on August 31st, after a Requiem Mass. Annually on her anniversary, the Roman Community visits her grave.

Sister M. Campion saw fulfilled before her death a heartfelt wish of her great Mother, viz. to have a second convent in Italy, where the Sisters could go for a change of scene, and have a good rest in holiday time. In 1907, a convent and school were opened in Florence, the beautiful city of the Renaissance. The Foundress and Sister M. Clare, it will be remembered, spent one night there on their visit to the Eternal City. The Florence foundation will be dealt with later on.

It may be of interest to relate here that among the Sisters who were "polished off," as they expressed the process, at the organ and piano by Sister M. Campion in Rome was a certain Sister M. Rose of Lucan in Co. Dublin (who got the name of the saintly Sister M. Rose who died in 1893 and who was also a great lover of music and possessed a rich voice). One free Wednesday afternoon she sat at the piano and played the tune to "Father O'Flynn". Sister M. Campion heard the air and came curiously to see who the very rhythmical musician was! There and then she had to be promised that Sister M. Rose would make her a copy of the song, which the latter was only too happy to do. When ready, Sister M. Campion asked Sister M. Rose to stand by while she rehearsed song and music. The Sister critic could not get her pupil to pronounce certain words as they were spelt, and especially the Irish words in the chorus. After "Here's a health to you, Father O'Flynn," Sister M. Campion, composing her own lines, to the amusement of all, sang:

"Sings an old English Sister again and again,
Powerfullest preacher and tenderest teacher
And kindliest creature of old Donegal!"

After dear Sister's death in 1908, her "special song" ceased to feature in Community concerts, but the memory of the dear old "English Sister" will ever be associated with the Roman convent and its historic shrine of Regina Prophetarum.

C h a p t e r   16.

PRAYER, PEN AND PAIN-LIFE

The years 1894 to 1896, as has been seen, had their special joys and special sorrows for Mother Magdalen and her Sisters in their further development of the Congregation — the Silver Jubilee, the erection of the Roman Shrine with its own Feast of Our Lady Queen of Prophets, granted *in perpetua* by His Holiness Leo XIII were joys indeed. But, as she was often heard say in her spiritual talks to her Sisters: "There must ever be a healthy intermingling of crosses in our joys, if they be of God," and now in the few years of life still left to the brave Mother, an illustration of the truth of her saying is certainly evident in her own case.

In the May of 1894, Mother Magdalen had to mourn the death of her maiden sister, Lucy Taylor, who had remained a staunch Anglican all her life. Her death was followed within a few months by that of their bachelor brother, Mortimer. Unlike his sister Lucy, Mortimer had been staunch to nothing in life. He played at many religions and scoffed at them all. Mother Magdalen, however, had the great consolation of seeing her brother being received into the Catholic Church on his death-bed, and make full peace with his God; he himself having asked for a Catholic priest.

Alluding to this unexpected conversion as a miracle of prayer, Sister M. Thomas, a most saintly Sister who outlived the Foundress, related in after years that one night, as she was about to retire, she found that her little holy water font was empty, and she tiptoed downstairs to get a refill from the common stoup. As she approached the chapel door from the old St. Paul's dormitory, she heard a deep sigh, followed by a pleading prayer

173

from someone inside the old chapel, which now is the large front parlour, opening on to the lawn. As she came to the yet closed door and courageously opened it quietly, she recognized Mother Foundress kneeling before the tabernacle, in the glow of the sanctuary lamp, and heard her say pleadingly: "Oh my God, *do, do* give me the soul of my brother!" Sister M. Thomas felt so moved, and had such pity for Mother Magdalen, that she slipped out quietly, closed the door gently, and knelt outside to say a Rosary for the same intention. When she had finished the five Sorrowful Mysteries, Mother Magdalen was still in her place, praying. Sister M. Thomas felt free to relate the story to Mother Aloysius Austin after the Foundress' death. To her surprise, she had told nothing that was a revelation. Mother Aloysius Austin's reply was: "Child, is that all you know? Our Mother spent countless hours at night before the Lord in the tabernacle, and He alone knows what went on." Here one remembers Cardinal Manning's advice in the first difficult years of Mother Magdalen's "seeking". "Knock at the tabernacle for bread," was his counsel, and we know how well the Lord answered her every knock. Bread, as such, had never failed the trustful, matter-of-fact Foundress, who, like St. Paul, while work could be had, would gladly undertake it, lest she and her children "should be chargeable" to anyone.

She knew well from long experience that "man liveth not by bread alone." Her "bread" was ever to do the Will of God. She had knocked and prayed, and sought and found. Also her Holy Hours before the tabernacle must have often recalled her father's explanation of the word "Seek" in his sermon on that far-off Thanksgiving Sunday in Stoke Rochford Church. Fanny Taylor's whole life was one long search for souls whose love and generosity for Christ, their Divine Hunter, would soothe His Calvary's "Sitio".

Naturally Mother Magdalen's love for, and interest in her near relatives would have been deepened and spiritualized by her having become a Catholic and a Religious. Except for her sister Charlotte and her brother Mortimer, she had not the great joy on earth of knowing that the first half of the 20th century was to see the majority of the third and fourth generation of Taylors all fervent Catholics, with one grand-nephew — the Rev.

174

Charles Taylor — a Redemptorist, his sister a Sister of Mercy — having chosen the name of "Magdalen" in veneration of her great-aunt — while a niece of hers again is a Presentation nun. A blessed co-incidence has to be related here. During the special General Chapter at Roehampton in September 1969 this Presentation nun, Sister Beatrice Taylor, paid a visit to the Community of the S.M.G.'s. It was as if Mother Foundress herself wanted to assure them of her interest. One feels certain that Mother Magdalen's relatives always benefitted by her special prayers. She was interested, naturally, in all that concerned their religious lives, while being very humanly interested in, and affectionately united to each. Typical of this interest, both spiritual and natural, is a letter she wrote in 1882 to a Catholic girl who married her yet Protestant nephew, Alfred Taylor, in Australia.

"My dear Mary,

I must write you a few lines of welcome as my niece, though so far away and — though we may never meet — we are now joined in a bond of relationship which must make us take an interest in each other.

I daresay you will have heard from Alfred that you have Catholic relations in his family, two aunts and four cousins, thank God! I can't go further without sending my best love to Alfred, and all sorts of good wishes on his marriage. I am sure he is a very lucky young man, and you are going to make him a splendid wife.

I hope you will write to me, dear Mary, and tell me about yourself. I don't even know your maiden name. How many brothers and sisters have you, and are your dear parents alive? I suppose your people didn't much care for your marrying a Protestant. When Alfred reads this, how angry he will be because I call him this. Alas, 'tis true — he *is* a Protestant, no matter what amount of Catholic doctrine he holds, for there is but one Church, there are not two — one Church always the same and never erring. I have been a Catholic 27 years, and day by day I bless the more the goodness of God Who gave to me the precious gift of faith. Perhaps you born Catholics hardly know the joy of the convert, finding year by year new beauties in Holy Church."

Mother Magdalen tells her niece-in-law about the relatives

at home — her cousin-in-law, Charlotte's family. How Cyril Dean, Charlotte's son, attended Cardinal Newman's School and carried away lots of prizes, that he was a fine type of the Catholic layman, that Lily, Dora and Amy were "tall, pretty and sweet." The letter closes with a promise to pray for a "mutual special intention" which can be easily guessed at to be Alfred's conversion.

In the November of 1894, a month after Father Dignam's death, Mother Magdalen returned home, and although suffering much, began, after what one would call "an enforced rest" her famous "Memoir of Father Dignam." She surely owed this labour of love and gratitude to the holy priest who, with the encouraging permission of his Superiors, had helped her to form her Congregation and give it its true spirit. Father Dignam gave the Sisters as many as fourteen Annual Retreats, not to count the many triduums, conferences and other intermediate helps and counsels which aided many an individual Sister to bridge a dangerous ditch in her spiritual path.

When Mother Magdalen (as yet Fanny Taylor) returned to England after the Crimean campaign in 1855, she was determined, and was advised by Miss Stanley, to take up her pen and lay bare the sad condition of the Eastern hospitals and what the soldiers condemned to them had to endure, prior to, and even after the coming of Florence Nightingale and the Catholic Sisters, and what the latter did to embetter and humanize the whole atmosphere for the dear wounded men. For this very important work, Fanny took the responsibility, and "Eastern Hospitals and English Nurses" was the outcome. The book was widely read and ran into three editions. She exposed without personal reference what the Catholic Sisters had to endure, the cold, often cruel, biassed and unnatural opposition which they had to encounter, as well as the bigotry which met them at every turn. On Mother Frances Bridgeman's noble and sweet, undaunted spirit through it all, Fanny commented highly, and thanked God for all the inspiration the humble nun gave her.

Later, in the same tone and in the desire for reform, she exposed in pitiful and painful phrasing the sad state of poor orphanages, work-houses, prisons and lunatic asylums, the woeful condition of neglected street urchins, of so-called homes for destitute and abandoned women, etc. It is comforting to know that almost for a century now, the Congregation which Mother Magdalen founded has had, and still has, repetitions of all types under their protective care. Superiors see to it that the Sisters themselves are trained in the various sciences and techniques that are helpful and necessary for the training of their protégés, in order to make them happy and useful by the feeling, nay, the conviction, that they are part of the life around them. It is usual to find some who could never concentrate, for example, on the "three R's" as children, learn by heart and by ear a most difficult passage of prose, especially if it be drama to be acted. Others play a most fulfilling part in Church or chapel functions, and quickly pick up the words and airs of the most beautiful hymns, psalms, etc.

Mother Magdalen's second book, "Tyburn", was published in 1857. It was judged as a fine standard Catholic novel, not unworthy to rank with Cardinal Wiseman's "Fabiola". "Tyburn" was, one remembers, the original means of introduction that bound its author to her lifelong friend and benefactress, Lady Georgiana Fullerton, who, on its perusal, urged Fanny Taylor to "write more and more." "Tyburn" has been a pioneer in promoting devotion to the English, and especially the Tyburn Martyrs. The book ran into several editions, and even in the 1950's a further edition was asked for, and welcomed and honoured in its Preface being written by the Right Reverend Monsignor Duchemin, the then Rector of the Pontifical Beda College, Rome.

"A Pearl in Dark Waters" by "The Author of Tyburn" was written to honour Blessed Claude de la Columbière, who was the first to preach in England the devotion to the Sacred Heart.

In 1861, Mother Magdalen became responsible for the production of a series of original essays entitled: "Offerings for Orphans," brought out in aid of a "Fund for Orphan and Destitute Children." The author was, at the outset, happy to enrol names of generous working-people of a few parishes who volunteered to help her, and who put her in touch with others who would also help in this worthy cause. God blessed the venture, and soon persons of station, wealth and influence added their names to the author's list of contributors. London opened its amazed eyes to see such names as: Newman, Faber, Bowles, Fullerton, de Vere, Proctor, D. F. McCarthy, H. R. S. Dalton, the Honourable Susan Pitt, the Earl of Carlisle, the Honourable Mrs. Norton, Barry Cornwall, Mrs. Greville, and, as the author of two poems, "Stonyhurst".

In 1862 "Religious Orders" appeared, giving short sketches of most of the religious orders and congregations then existing. In 1862 also, Fanny became proprietor and editor of "The Lamp", which was highly valued as an admirable Catholic magazine. Many of her friends wrote for it also, but she had reluctantly to abandon it in 1871. Financially it had proved a failure.

Meanwhile, on the advice of the Fathers of Farm Street, in 1864 Fanny Taylor took on the surprising responsibility of the editorship of a new periodical, "The Month". The difficulties of this undertaking, of course, were great, but the young editor, we are told, held it on for a year, at the end of which she handed over editorship and proprietorship to the Fathers, who, she is careful to say, paid all expenses of paper, printing, etc., though most of the contributions were given gratis. Of her own contributions, Fanny says nothing, but "Hope for the Prisoner", "Lunatic Asylums", and "Half out of the World" were supposed to be hers, as her sympathies with the afflicted were very great. The first Sisters, who knew their Mother so well, have often been quoted as saying that she had hated the designations "Lunatic Asylum", "Lock-up", etc., as applied to the insane, where no good resulted from this cruel confinement. How she would have welcomed the more kindly name "Mental Home", in which, in our more humane century, every effort is made through psychiatric and other treatment to restore the poor patient to health and comparative happiness again.

The story of "The Dream of Gerontius" and of the "waste-paper basket as being considered a myth" is well known. Mother Magdalen Aimée, who was the Foundress' niece and a nun of her Congregation for 70 years, negated the assertion every time, saying, "Aunt Fanny could not have sold the 'Dream', had he not given her leave, and when she told Dr. Newman of the price, he was overjoyed, saying 'I thought it was worth nothing.'" In fact, in the Archives of the Poor Servants of the

Mother of God is the copy of the receipt sent to the "Trustees of the British Museum" for the cheque of £30 paid for the original MS. of Cardinal Newman's "Dream of Gerontius." It bears the penny postage stamp of Queen Victoria's reign, and across the stamp is written in her own characteristic hand the name "Fanny Margaret Taylor." That Dr. Newman himself thought this great work inferior and flung it into the wastepaper basket is easily understood. His great soul's ideal in many of his aims was, like Fra Angelico's in his particular world of art, beyond his reach. It is said of the latter that he suffered agony until his soul's conception, the image in his master-mind, became living on the walls of San Marco in Florence, and yet he suffered more from his inability to reproduce the perfect image. That Sir Edward Elgar's music has enhanced the literary beauty and soul-stirring message of "The Dream of Gerontius" is beyond contradiction.

Mother Magdalen (or rather, Fanny Taylor as yet) relieved of the editorship of "The Month", brought out in 1869 "Irish Homes and Irish Hearts" published by Longmans, Green & Co., a book that was warmly welcomed at the time. Many of its chapters were written in Ireland itself, while other parts had already appeared in "The Lamp". In 1869 she translated from the French "Practical Meditations for Every Day in the Year, revised by a Jesuit Father" (Father Clare). Two smaller books of Meditations from the Italian of Father Rogacci, S.J., followed, and she was also largely responsible for "Heart to Heart with Jesus" from the Italian of Padre Maresca, a saintly Barnabite and an apostle of the Sacred Heart in Rome.

In 1889, after the S.M.G. Sisters took on the work at St. Joseph's, Portland Row, Dublin, Mother Magdalen wrote the "Life of Father Curtis, S.J.," a holy priest to whom the Community owed much. Her pen was also responsible for "A Marvellous History", the life-story of Jeanne de la Noue, Foundress of the Sisters of St. Anne of Providence; "Forgotten Heroines", life sketches of nuns in Germany and France who suffered for the Faith, including those martyred at Orange and beatified by Pope Pius XI.

After Mother Magdalen's visit to the Shrine of St. Winifred, already alluded to in a previous chapter, she wrote a "Life of

179

St. Winifred", to whom she promised that there should always be a Sister bearing the saint's name in the Congregation, which promise has been faithfully fulfilled.

Other books or booklets from the ever busy pen of the Foundress were: "The Catholic Pilgrim's Guide to Rome" (3 editions); "Dame Dolores", "Lost, and other Tales". Added to all this unceasing work, Mother Magdalen's contributions to magazines, especially to the American "Ave Maria", were legion. She has left on record that one day in 1896 the Community funds had greatly diminished, and she went across to the Sacred Heart Chapel in Farm Street, to "ask", to "seek" and to "knock", and poured out her anxieties into that Heart that had never failed her. Full of faith in Our Lord's promises, she returned home, to find that Father Hudson had written to ask her to become a regular contributor to the "Ave Maria". Payments for her articles were immediate and generous, and the Community difficulties on that occasion were solved "soon and sudden."

Mother Magdalen was a gifted story-teller all her life. Some time in the 1880's, two London Sisters entered the Congregation. One, who, at her religious reception received the name "Sister Paul Magdalen" had been trained in art needlework as well as in painting. She had been Directress of the girl staff at Peter Robinson's, and boasted innocently all her life of having designed and then supervised the making of three dresses for Queen Victoria. Even as a nun, she had a great "say" in things at Peter Robinson's, and during sales collected much for the poor by way of clothing, etc. Mother Magdalen, taking advantage of Sister Paul Magdalen's influence with the firm, bade her at her next visit solicit some carpet cuttings or upholstery material that could be made into hassocks on which the postulants could happily sit around her during their recreations, while she, their Mother, told them stories. Sister Paul Magdalen's prompt obedience had her next day with her sister, Sister Anne Ignatius, sitting, spectacled, at a counter at Peter Robinson's sketching out on paper the pattern of her hassocks. Not only did the firm supply the cuttings, but fourteen hassocks were made to her requirements and delivered gratis within a week. Many a jaunt did those hassocks enjoy! For picnics at Kew Gardens, Hampton

Court, Old Windsor, etc., they were an essential part of the postulants' luggage.

Mother Magdalen loved to encourage new ventures by way of contributory stories to Catholic magazines, and whenever she discovered such talent, she was the first to bring it into the field and help to find an editor.

And now in Rome, with her rich and ripe experience of a long, holy and well-spent life for God and souls, she must not yet lay down her pen. She owed it to the two great allies and special, saintly friends of her life and of her Congregation, that she leave a spiritual legacy that would enrich, for all time, those whom God would yet call to the Congregation to work for souls. This, her "last will and testament" was to consist of no less than four precious books, each one of which still reflects, as in a mirror, her own interior life, as well as the sources from which it drew light and strength for the fray. These were: "The Memoir of Father Dignam", "Retreats by Father Dignam", "Conferences by Father Dignam", and the "Inner Life of Lady Georgiana Fullerton". These came out in rapid succession from 1895 to 1899. All were appreciated immensely, and even a new edition of "Retreats" and "Conferences" was demanded as late as 1962. All four books were written and printed in Rome. In the Preface to the fifth edition of "Retreats" the late Very Rev. Father Janssens, S.J., General of the Society of Jesus, wrote:

"I am pleased to have this opportunity of welcoming the fifth edition of Father Augustus Dignam's 'Retreats'. That another edition should be needed is an indication of the lasting worth of the book and of the help and encouragement which the words of Father Dignam continue to bring to souls to-day as in the past. The decision to keep those words unchanged, just as they appeared in the first edition, was a happy one; to have attempted to modernize them would have been to spoil the warm, homely style which speaks straight to the heart.*

Anyone who wishes to make a private retreat or who is unable to find a Retreat Master to direct him according to the plan of Saint Ignatius' Spiritual Exercises will find in the

* The decision not to change or modernize any part of Father Dignam's "Retreats" or "Conferences" in the 1962 Edition was that of His Holiness Pope Pius XII.

'Retreats' a sure and helpful guide; but for your own Congregation of the Poor Servants of the Mother of God they have an altogether special efficacy and importance. They owe their existence in their present form to the loving care of your valiant Mother Foundress, Mother Mary Magdalen Taylor, who saw to it that each sentence and each word was preserved as it was uttered in the course of the fourteen annual retreats which Father Dignam gave to your first Sisters. They are, in large part, the record of the guidance by which, under God, the spirit of your infant Congregation was formed. In them is expressed the spirit of your Mother Foundress and of Father Dignam, her Spiritual Director.

It is my prayer that all who use this book may discover that spirit beneath the simple words and learn to make it their own, for it is the spirit of total selfless dedication to the service of others for the love of God, which is no other than the spirit of Our Lord's own Sacred Heart."

During the time of writing, correcting and re-writing her MSS, the Foundress occupied a small room on the first floor of the Roman house. (To this day it is set aside as "Mother's Room" by her loving Community.) Here in this sanctum overlooking a large courtyard that served, and still serves, as the school-children's playground, she worked away in loving, peaceful patience, undisturbed by the noisy laughter underneath. She loved to see the gay Italian children enjoying themselves, and the Sister who supervised enjoying herself with them.

Mother Magdalen's mental energy was miraculous; she worked far into the night at times. Our Lord in His Sacrament was near, in the tiny tribune near by which looked on to the sanctuary, and which she could enter at will whenever she wished. So time passed all too quickly and happily, every moment given to God in loving service.

In the spring of 1899, when her last book was published, and she was for returning to England, her Roman doctor forbade the journey for health reasons, unless she promised to break it and take in Vichy on the way. Mother Magdalen submitted as ever, and felt the better for the visit, as the waters helped much to restore her now failing energy. Before leaving Rome, she paid what was destined to be her last visit to St. Peter's, although she did not know it, and did not ask for an audience with the Holy Father, saying: "I'll be back in August."

While in England, she became interested in two new foundations — one in Selkirkshire, Scotland, the other in Wales. Neither of these succeeded, and the great woman of prayer and determination abandoned the project, yet, strange as it may seem, after her death, in the years that followed, her Sisters went to both Scotland and Wales, and settled permanently in both places, doing very fruitful work for souls and attracting many to God.

While in England, also, Mother Magdalen assembled what was to be her last General Chapter, at which, in spite of all her loving protests, she was re-elected. His Eminence Cardinal Bourne presided. After this meeting the delegates dispersed happily to their convents, while their Mother made North for St. Helens, where important work in her dear Providence Hospital awaited her. She next went back to Liverpool, to examine matters there. The work in this city was very dear to Mother Magdalen's great heart. There was the Home for wayward and homeless poor women, there was the Night Shelter and the Orphanage, which works she took on with all her heart in response to dear Monsignor Nugent's crying wish in 1891.

From Liverpool, Mother Magdalen had intended to cross to her beloved Ireland, and was on the eve of so doing when she had to abandon the journey for unforeseen reasons. She much regretted this turn in events, as it involved the question of taking over, or not taking over Rathdown Union Workhouse in Co. Dublin. So determined were the authorities on getting the Poor Servants of the Mother of God to staff the Institution that one of their number came all the way to Brentford to negotiate the business with the Foundress, before her intended departure for Rome in October. He returned with a happy answer and was able to tell his fellow Guardians that all was well, and that the Sisters would be in Rathdown before Christmas.

Mother Magdalen liked to connect all her important decisions with the feasts of Holy Church, and in the case of Rathdown it was decided that the Sisters should take up work there on December 8th, 1899. On the previous day, accompanied by a Mother Assistant from St. Joseph's, Portland Row, they were

183

received by His Grace, Most Reverend Dr. Walsh, Archbishop of Dublin, who greeted them most kindly and expressed his delight that the poor of Rathdown should henceforth have the loving care of the Sisters, and cited their work at St. Joseph's as an example. On arriving at Rathdown, the nuns were met by the Board of Guardians in a body. Canon Quin and Lady Gilbert led the procession to the altar-rails, where the Canon spoke for about five minutes. He explained to the people that he thought it best to take the Sisters first to the Chapel. After the "Veni Creator" had been sung, he prayed the way to the Convent parlour, where he said: "Now you are duly installed, and may God bless you." He said quietly afterwards to the Sisters that they did not seem a bit frightened, and bidding them good-bye for the present, he left them. No wonder the Canon used the word "frightened"! Workhouses in those days were blots on the landscape in England and in Ireland, and few knew their internal condition as did Mather Magdalen, who wrote from Paris to the new Community on their opening day:

"My dear Children,

This is to welcome you into your new house. May our dear Lady bless you a thousandfold in your new and blessed work! I was thinking the other day that we never had a work which is more completely suited to the Servants of the Poor — for those you are to look after are the poorest of the poor. You know perhaps that in France the workhouse is called the "Hotel Dieu" — God's House, or God's Inn. You will need this thought often in your mind to sustain you in what will certainly be very hard work.

Now, what I want you to bear in mind is this; be very obedient and united, and obey in faith — if you do, God will take care of you. Always and to all, a bright, cheerful, courteous manner. Sometimes you must be brave and firm, of course, but never look weary or cast down. When you have to give up Mass, or any spiritual duty, remember, charity is before all. When you feed these people think of these lines:

'Hungry, by Whom saints are fed
With the Eternal Living Bread:
Thirsty, from Whose pierced Side
Living waters spring and glide.

184

Mother M. Lucy
Mother General from 1900 to 1915
(See Chapter XIX)

Mother M. Stanislaus
Mother General 1915-1922

Mother Rose Joseph
Mother General 1922-1936
(re-elected 1929)

Mother M. Angelis
Mother General 1936-1945

Mother Anne Xavier
Mother General 1945-1952

Mother M. Geraldine
Mother General 1952-1966
(re-elected 1959)

Mother M. Azevedo
present Mother General
elected 1966

Poor and bare He comes, Who never
May put off His robe of light;
Homeless, Who must dwell for ever
In the Father's Bosom bright.'

There — you'll never have time to read all this — my heart and soul will be with you on Friday. How we shall talk about you, especially from five to six, that is our 'talkee' time.

May the Sacred Heart bless you all.

Your loving Mother,
M. Magdalen of the Sacred Heart, S.M.G."

Mother M. Dismas was the first local Superior at Rathdown, having had to her advantage ten years' experience of the Providence Hospital and its Community.

For many years now Rathdown Workhouse has gone "off the map" as such. It has been replaced by the fine General District Hospital, Loughlinstown, with its beautiful Church open to the public and served by the parish clergy. A neat corridor connects the Sisters' Convent with their Oratory, which in its turn looks on to the Sanctuary. The Hospital, being at a distance from the City of Dublin and its hospitals, caters for emergency cases, road accidents, etc., as well as for its district patients. Very often itinerant families who roam the countryside have their patients at the hospitals. These families are well known to the medical and nursing staff, and Mother Magdalen Taylor surely rejoices in Heaven as she sees her Sisters to-day helping, in one way or another, these romantic wanderers of the wild, who somehow have a charm all their own. A Sister who had prepared a small group of itinerant children for First Communion — materially as well as spiritually, having provided frocks, veils etc. for the beautiful occasion, was being thanked by the Itinerant-in-chief at the parlour breakfast table on that special morning in these words:

"Now, friends, we all thank the priest and the nuns for all they done for us, and we promise them we'll go to Mass on Sunday everywhere we settle, and if we can't, we'll never curse or swear again anyhow."

This father, stalwart and strong and weather-beaten, spoke from his heart as his eyes moistened and he must have rejoiced the Sacred Heart at that moment.

185

M

December 8th, 1899, as has been said, saw Mother Magdalen at the Paris Convent on her way to Rome, as she had anticipated, but God meant otherwise. Christmas was passed at the Convent, where the valiant woman, already far from being well, busied herself making the season happy for the poor, the lonely and for those who were away from their English, Irish or American families for Christmas. It will be remembered that the Paris foundation, like that of St. Joseph's, Dublin, was inspired by an institution which already existed, with the difference that the Paris house was for English or Irish governesses, many of whom were very young, and also for business girls, students etc., for all of whom lodgings in the great city were provokingly dangerous. A Miss Murray, well known to Mother Magdalen, ran a rather good boarding-house for some time in Paris, but by the end of 1890, the lease was up and Miss Murray acquainted Mother Magdalen of the great charity it would be if she saw her way to come to the relief of so many Catholics in those very anti-clerical times. Mother Magdalen was overjoyed, and began house-hunting, asking Heaven to help her. Cardinal Richard was enthusiastic. When in Rome, a rich French lady to whom the Foundress was introduced, offered to help her financially, but afterwards when she returned to Paris, withdrew her promise, because of some personal difference with the Cardinal. The Foundress, however, had gone too far to turn back, and the "Bank of God" did not fail her once again.

The New Year, the first of the 1900's and the Jubilee Year, was about to dawn, and at the desire of the Holy Father it was to be celebrated throughout the Catholic world with Exposition of the Blessed Sacrament and Midnight Mass. On the night of December 31st, in Paris, Mother Magdalen wrote in her diary: "Adoration begun. So ends this year, which I cast into Thy Mercy. Great is Thy goodness, Oh, Heart of Jesus, and sweetest Heart of Mary." She dedicates the New Year to God the Holy Spirit, to the Sacred Heart of Jesus and to the Immaculate Heart of Mary, to St. Joseph, to her beloved St. Francis Xavier, promising that if a "certain favour" be granted, she will do something very special in honour of the Holy Spirit and Our Lady of Sorrows.

In the height of her suffering, she consoles herself by sending a special message to the Providence Hospital Committee at St. Helens, voicing her great anxiety that some beds be speedily set aside for the returning Lancashire wounded of the Boer War, for which the Secretary of War sent her his warm gratitude for what he styled "her public-spirited offer." Father Miller, O.M.I., who was confessor for the Paris Community, had been to South Africa and was able to give the already experienced war-nurse a full account of the campaign. Father Miller was afterwards appointed by the Holy See the first Vicar-Apostolic of the Transvaal. He was a great father to the Paris Community and an untold comfort to their failing Mother at this period. The O.M.I. Fathers, ever since the days at Tower Hill, have been great friends of the Congregation in Dublin, Paris and Rome, and their O.M.I. Sisters have been equally friendly and gracious.

Mother Magdalen's medical advisers made her intention of travelling from Paris to Rome dependent on a little longer rest and a visit to Vichy also, in the hope that it would again help her and restore her lost energy as on a former occasion. As ever, her obedience was prompt in executing their orders, and she determined to visit her beloved Paray-le-Monial en route as before. Her ever-burning love for the Sacred Heart of her Lord gave her fresh courage while there, but her stay at Vichy had an opposite effect this time on her fast-failing health. The doctors, seeing this, ordered a return to Paris at once. Poor Rome and her children there! How was she to break the news? Much business too was awaiting her there, the chief being to be present and give replies to questions on and reasons for certain amendments and adjustments made in the Rules and Constitutions, preparatory to their final approval by the Holy See.

For the Feast of the Annunciation, Mother Magdalen wrote the usual circular letter from Paris to her beloved and absent children everywhere. Neither she nor they ever dreamt that this was to be her dying message — her "last will and testament" from her Mother's overflowing heart:

"Paris, March 21st, 1900.

My dearest Children,

I am writing you a letter to reach you on our dear and holy

187

feast. I think that our dear and venerated Father Dignam has taught us to understand the beauty of our feast more than many do. He loved to call it the feast of the Incarnation, when the Sacred Heart began to beat, and so we feel it is the Feast of Jesus and Mary in one, and such is the model of our lives — to serve Mary and Jesus — to imitate her life of prayer. Imagine how she must have prayed when our Lord was hidden within her — and also her life of labour, for she went about her duties, comforting others, helping St. Elizabeth, going in haste, preparing for her journey to Bethlehem, and then travelling. How often we have to go in haste to travel — to pack up — to be off somewhere — how we have to live for others.

Oh blessed life! To tread in our Lady's footsteps, and to meet her in Heaven. What will our habit be like in Heaven? I often think about it in my sleepless nights. All is white, of course, no black there, for penance will be over — but I think each Order will have its mark, and ours will be blue. The Italian sky is not only of a deeper blue than ours, but sometimes it seems dissolved into a sort of blue light, all shining, and as girded gold, with seven jewels. Oh, let us love our habit, let us kiss it on the 25th, and ask God to die rather than lose it.

I remember one sermon at a Clothing, and the preacher said, 'Bring forth the best robe and put it on her.' Those words so often ring in my ears. The best robe — the *best*. Oh, can we ever cast aside the best robe that our Lady gave us with her own hands? Surely never. But it is not a robe of ease — it is for those who are content to suffer, to find things hard, to overcome, to bear, as our soldiers teach us; never to give up, to storm the hills of our passions, our pride, our self-will, our love of our own opinion, and take them. To bear weariness and depression, to fight temptations and so be conquerors, and not conquered by our enemy, whose favourite pastime is to rob us of vocation by any pretext.

One word more. Many of you have written to me during your Triduum. I know you don't expect answers, but I want to tell you all how pleased I am with those letters, what a good spirit they display. How I thanked God as each one passed through my hands, and I *know* you know I answer you each in my heart, and say with Father Faber, 'Time and obedience are enough, and thou a saint shalt be.'

Pray for your loving Mother,

M. Magdalen of the Sacred Heart, S.M.G."

On the Feast itself came the news of the death of Cardinal Mazella, S.J., the Protector of the Congregation and its very devoted friend, who was responsible for the passage of the Brief of the Final Approbation through the offices of Propaganda — the then responsible body to the Holy See for what the Sacred Congregation for Religious does now. This death was a new disappointment for Mother Magdalen, and her message to the Roman house was her usual "Fiat", and "May God reward him for all the good he has done us. It does seem such a cross but Our Lord knows best."

The Final Brief of Approbation of the Rules and Constitutions of the Congregation of the Poor Servants of the Mother of God was granted by the Holy See on 19th July, 1900, a little over a month after the Foundress' death, exactly 21 years after the Lauda in 1879 and a little over eight years since the first Decree in 1892.

Another letter, written evidently to one of her nieces, undated, is given here to show that she had still high hopes for her journey, and was not unduly preoccupied about her condition. From its content one can judge it was written early in the New Year. It speaks for itself, and its length shows her mind to be clear and interested.

"Paris.

Dearest,

You will be glad to hear I am getting on well. The weather is intensely cold — they say colder than known for years — and yet I am standing it well, and in fact quite enjoying the bracing air. I did suffer much from sleepless nights, but thank God these have improved, and perhaps will get better still as time goes on.

I hope you like your new house, and are comfortably settled in, and feeling fairly well, and I hope Willie and family are well, and the Lloyds...

This is a terrible winter with which to close the century.

189

I can hardly bear to hear the war news. Our confessor here has lately come back from Africa. He says it is a most difficult country to know and to deal with — our people really seem to have far under-estimated the difficulties. I expect it will be a very long and terrible war.

The Pope expressed his wish for many prayers to be made on the last night of the year and the morning of the first day of 1900... If I had seen you again before I left, I meant to have told you that I did twice, *as I believe,* have a glimpse into the other world — of course this is *entirely for yourself,* dear.*

Once was after my dearest mother's death. I saw her in heavenly rapture, but the singular part was that she was beautiful and young, and yet exactly like herself; I can't explain how, but I seemed to understand how we shall recognize our own in eternity.

The second time was eleven years later. I had lost a Sister who was very dear to me, and I was kneeling in a church before a big crucifix in a dark corner, and I saw this Sister with our Lord. He was like a picture of the Sacred Heart, only unutterably more beautiful, and she was pointing to Him and also to me, as if to say: 'Look at Him — I have found perfect joy.' Here again was the same thing — this Sister M. Clare was very plain — a homely face — now she was beautiful and yet herself. I shall never forget the consolation of those few minutes.

Now, have I not written you a long history! This letter is to bear you my loving wishes for the New Year. May you, dear, see many years in this new century, and spend them all glorifying God, Who has done so much for you and for me and for all. How grateful we ought to be, and how we ought to trust Him — He seems so to long for trust. 'Blessed are those who have not seen, and yet have believed.'

Amy sends you a lot of love. Kind wishes from her and myself for Maud.

Your loving old Aunt Fanny,
M.M., S.M.G."

---

* As Mother Magdalen herself referred to the second of these experiences in her Memoir of Sister M. Clare, we feel at liberty now to quote this letter.

Chapter 17.

OBEDIENT UNTO DEATH

Mother Magdalen had her heart set on having the coming First Friday at Paray-le-Monial, but the Lord intended otherwise, and instead of her visit to the Shrine on that beautiful April morning of 1900, her loving acts of reparation and thanksgiving were made on her sick-bed; later she was taken across in a wheel-chair, and one can imagine how she poured out her heart's love in agonizing prayer to Him Who saw that her desires were all for His glory and to win Him souls at any cost to herself. After her visit, she and her companion set out for Vichy. Here she grew from bad to worse, and for the really first time her hope lessened, and she realized that her illness was not temporary. Anxious that the Congregation should not be the sufferer, she stipulated that her accompanying Mother Assistant should go to England. The Sisters with her, however, objected, and telegraphed for another of the Mothers to come. When this latter Mother arrived at Paris Station, she met the faithful Father Miller, O.M.I., to learn that he also had been wired for, and was on his way to Vichy. When both arrived, they found Mother very much changed for the worse, and with the sudden, complete failure of her bodily powers, she, the strong woman, always so serenely calm and self-possessed, had now become so dependent, so clinging, so fearful. But the agony was short-lived. The fear, spiritual and physical, was doubtless the Evil One's diabolical action on her great soul, and completely disappeared in the presence of God's priest. She was too well trained not to obey and respond quickly. The Father brought her Holy Communion next morning, to her great consolation. After all this spiritual refreshment, faith and courage returned to her weary soul. She, whose loving words to encourage others in their trials and sorrows were usually: "Be still and see that I am God," or those others of the Psalmist: "Though I walk through the valley of the shadow of death, I will fear no evil, for Thou art with me," was soon able to recover her usual serenity. When her mysterious soul-battle was over, and having been refreshed and invigorated by Holy Communion, she showed a happy and childlike abandonment to the will of others. To everybody's surprise, she asked the Mother by her bedside to get pen and paper, as she was about to dictate a letter to England. This she did, and when she began to dictate, she seemed to get new life and energy. The letter was for the Council Mothers, resigning her office into their hands, and asking forgiveness for many things "about which I cannot write," she said, "I hope after this you may have a better Mother."

Everything that could be done was done, and her doctors urged wisely that the patient be removed to her home immediately. Being thoroughly conversant herself with the French language, she saw that they were absolutely sincere and personally interested, and their allusion to the word "home" was not anybody's suggestion. The travellers therefore left Vichy as soon as possible, and reached Paris on May 25th, where Father Miller brought her Holy Communion immediately. Neither he nor the brave patient knew that this was to be her Viaticum — "the pledge of future glory" — to accompany her on the remaining stage of her soul's perilous journey, when the enemy of souls might again try his last card, and take advantage of the body's weakness for the final combat.

On May 26th, at the insistence of the Paris doctor, and with the prudent advice of Father Miller, the dear patient left Paris for Soho Square Convent. As usual her thoughts, even at this stage of her dying life, were for others. This time it was a young Sister, a trained nurse and a convert, who was sent from England when the bad change came over her Mother at Vichy. In Paris, on the homeward journey, the patient suggested that her nurse remain behind to visit and see some of the glories of the Catholic Church, especially Notre Dame, the Madeleine, and above all Notre Dame des Victoires. The nurse would not dream of the suggestion, but was deeply grateful and edified at the Mother's unselfish childlike obedience, and added: "She whom hundreds obeyed so lovingly and exactly obeyed me like a little child."

When the travellers arrived safely at the Soho Square Convent, the Mothers were again called upon to come to a painful decision. The medical consultants thought that the patient might yet obtain a cure if she were removed to a private nursing home in the City, where nothing, not even the presence of a Sister, could distract her, or even the beloved habit remind her of all her past work and worry. At first she dreaded the separation, and her Sisters, who knew the wealth of love for them in that great heart, understood. But when Father Scoles, S.J., her trusted friend, and her barrister nephew, Cyril Dean, said it was a duty to make the sacrifice, the Mothers and Sisters felt that they would never forgive themselves if they did not follow St. Ignatius' maxim and pray as if all depended on God, but also use all natural means as if all depended on themselves.

Mother Magdalen begged the doctors with pitiful and touching pathos to allow one Sister to remain with her. The only concession granted was that a Sister should accompany her to the Nursing Home, but not stay with her. This decision she accepted also, whispering to a Mother beside her: "He was obedient even unto death." The next day the doctors saw the patient and realized that they had put a great strain on her by depriving her of the companionship of one of her own, and said that one Sister could sit with her. To see again one of her Sisters in the dear familiar habit was her dearest wish, and was also a consolation to her London Sisters. Nevertheless, things worsened, ånd Father Scoles, S.J., who had already seen her, was sent for and heard her confession. Although death did not seem imminent, she begged to be anointed. It was Sunday; on Monday she received the last rites of the Church, and passed into a heavy, unconscious state. The next step for the Sisters was to get the dear patient home to the nearest convent, which was her beloved Soho Square. The doctors no longer opposed this decision, and, strange as it may seem, as she was being carried into the hall, and thought by all to be in a deep coma, she uttered one smiling word — the sweet word "Home!"

A crusade of Masses and prayers began in the various com-

193

munities. Only a miracle could save Mother Magdalen now, and even that was hoped for. The dying Mother seemed already wrapped in the calm of another world, unconscious to all around her. The chaplain of the convent was passing to another room to take Holy Communion to a sick Sister, and gave a last blessing to the dying nun, to the joy of the kneeling Sisters.

Another surprise was in store after this blessing. Sister M. Ignatius, her devoted nurse and her "messenger" for many years, broke down completely and the prayers ceased for the moment. Mother Magdalen opened wide her large blue eyes and looked around at each of her beloved children in turn, with a seeming look of reproach for their want of faith and trust, and in a low, pleading voice said: "Invoke the Sacred Heart." These were her last words. She lay unconscious all that day, and at midnight, surrounded by her loving, praying children, and with the copy of the Vows, her Rule and her crucifix beside her, she peacefully passed away to her Spouse and her Judge, for Whom she had lived, loved, laboured and suffered until her last breath. It was June 9th, 1900.

His Eminence Cardinal Vaughan was one of the first to come in person to console the Sisters in their grief, and although suffering from the mortal disease that had so cruelly attacked his tall, vigorous and very dignified frame, he made a brave effort to go upstairs to where the dead Mother lay. The visit was described by a Sister who was present:

"The scene was a contrast to the whirl of life in the streets outside. Great, too, was the contrast within. He, one of the Cardinal Princes of Holy Church, bent, not so much by years as by labour and pain, yet bravely fighting on to the 'last gasp' for God. She, the simple nun, Poor Servant of the Mother of God, her course run, her battle over, with that calm, restful look which seemed to bespeak to all Father Scole's advice to herself in some difficult hour, and which she loved to quote: 'Plod on, you don't see beyond'." The Cardinal prayed for her children and left them comforted in their loneliness.

The ties of sisterly affection were wonderfully strengthened in the entire Congregation by this great cross of their Mother's death, as in each house the Sisters tried to be brave and support one another. Telegrams and express letters were dispatched immediately to all the houses, and from all came messages of sympathy.

If the void in the Sisters' hearts caused by their Mother's loss was great in England and Ireland and Paris, what it was in Rome, the following letter to the next Mother Assistant will give a hint. The Roman Community, who expected their Mother surely that spring, had hoped against hope for her coming. They had awaited, as usual, the final news of the arrival, stating the day and the hour that she was to be at Rome Station. Of her repeated set-backs in Paris and Vichy they were not wholly informed.

"Rome, June 11, 1900.

My dear Mother M. de Sales,

Just a line to convey to you my deepest sympathy in the great sorrow and grief that has come upon us all in the loss of our first and dear Mother. I know you will feel it very much, as we all do, no matter what our spirit of conformity to God's Will may be, and we especially here, who have had our dear Mother so much in our midst. I do not know how we feel, and I am sure you will pray for us, as we will all pray for one another.

Friends have been exceedingly kind in offering their sympathy. We had a visit of condolence from dear Cardinal Parocchi, who had been Cardinal Vicar when our dear Mother first came to Rome and for many years afterwards, and helped in all things in which she had recourse to him. He has always been so full of real esteem for our good Mother. He spoke some nice, consoling words to us, and made us sit around him like so many children.

My poor, dear little Mother de Sales, what shall we do now but continue trying, as we always have done, to do what would please our dear Mother best? And one thing would be that we maintain that true spirit of the Institute which she taught us.

Believe me,

Always your affectionate Sister in Xt.,

Sister M. Thecla, S.M.G."

The following poem was evidently composed before Mother Magdalen set out for Paris, to be sung that year 1899 on her

195

arrival. She never saw the MS. nor heard the poem. It was
found in the Roman house among old worn-out sheets of music
as late as 1955. It is inserted here, not for its literary value
nor for the aptness of its metaphor, but as a proof of the lovely
family spirit of simplicity and unity that existed among the
Sisters, in their appreciation of their Mother and her work for
the Congregation. It will be quite new to many of the Congregation now living, and, it is hoped, an inspiration to those yet
to come to the service of Our Lord and His Mother Mary.

"Where the Anio runs down to the Tiber,
    And old Tiber rolls on to the sea;
Where the fireflies hold revel till moonlight
    And dance 'neath the shade of each tree; —

Where the olive boughs glint in the sun rays
    Silver leaves 'gainst the sapphire blue sky,
And the night wind aye moans through the branches
    And the heart answers back with a sigh;

For the olive is laden with memories,
    And we think of the night long ago
When they sheltered the God-Man's long struggle
    And kept His Heart's secret of woe; —

Where the sun ever rises in gladness,
    Heaven's Manna descending as dew,
And each bird, flower and insect rejoices,
    There, Mother, we're praying for you.

We think of you far in old England,
    And we picture the lilies around,
White-veiled, holding rich golden treasure
    In their hearts as a chalice profound.

There too are the sombre clad olives,
    Black veiled, but still glistening with joy,
And laden with oil for the altar,
    Pure oil, well refined from alloy.

Lily novices offer gold heart's love,
    Prayer's incense perfuming the air,

And the myrrh of life's small mortifications
   (Crushed petals yield balsam most rare).

First Vows, like the olives, shine brightly
   'Neath sunbeams and Heaven's azure dome
But Professed bear the chill of the night wind,
   Their heart is the Sacred Heart's home.

When crushed in the press of affliction,
   The Sacred Heart's secret they know;
Their work feeds the lamp on the Altar,
   Their unction is balm in life's woe.

So, Mother, we bless you who train us
   And lead us a step at a time,
And we pray a light zephyr to waft you
   Our love from Italia's fair clime.

May each Feast Day see masses of lilies
   Perfuming the grass at your feet,
And rich olive branches to cheer you
   With silver-leaved promises sweet;

While closely surrounding your table
   May the fruit to maturity grow,*
Their Mother's heart strengthening and shielding
   From every keen blast that may blow.

Flow on, gentle Anio, flow quickly
   From Tivoli down to the sea
And bear from the far distant branches
   This song of the old olive tree!

On Tuesday, June 12th, the coffin was taken from the
Convent, Soho Square, to the Novitiate House at Roehampton,
Surrey. There, their Mother's dear "white veils", the novices,
and her "black lambkins", as she liked to call the postulants,
kept watch in turn beside the open coffin. Sisters came non-stop
from the local convents. A group of boarders from the Apostolic
School of Brentford which she had founded, came in white

* Psalm 127.

dresses which Mother Foundress got specially made for them
the year before for the Corpus Christi procession. Over these
dresses they wore black shoulder bands, and the Chapel itself
was draped in black and silver.

The Solemn Requiem was celebrated on June 13th by the
Jesuit Fathers from Manresa House, Father Lumozzi, assisted
by Fathers Goldie and Corrigan, in the presence of Dr. Bourne,
then Bishop of Southwark, who gave the Absolution. Cardinal
Vaughan, being too ill to participate, was represented by his
brother, the Right Reverend Monsignor John S. Vaughan.
Reverend Father Scoles, S.J., preached the funeral oration, and
the Manresa novices did the singing effectively in beautiful
subdued Gregorian chant, as they did also at the graveside in
Mortlake. Many of the clergy from the Westminster and Southwark dioceses were present also, to pay a last tribute to her
whom they styled their "inspiratrix".

The chief family mourners were Mr. Cyril Dean and Mrs.
Frank Mason, nephew and niece of the deceased) but the real
"chief mourners" on that day and for months afterwards were
the Foundress' dear Communities, who had a lonely turning
away from her grave after the interment. One consolation was
that some Sisters and novices went every Sunday afternoon to
teach catechism in St. Mary Magdalen's Church, which ad-
joined the cemetery, and so could visit and pray at the grave.

In the mourning congregation also at that Requiem Mass
were numbers whom Mother Magdalen had loved and helped
and served in her life, as well as some dear London-Irish ve-
terans whom she had nursed in the Crimea 46 years before.
There were the women of the Mothers' Guild which she and
Lady Georgiana Fullerton had founded. There were many girls
whom she had saved from disaster in earlier days and set on the
right path, and she had had the happiness of seeing them become good responsible Catholic mothers. And lastly, there were
the many women and young girls from Roehampton, Putney,
Mortlake and Wimbledon who had steady employment in the
public laundries she had set up, and in spite of much criticism
had sent her Sisters as far as Antwerp to be trained and fully
initiated into all the secrets of the laundress' art. Electric power
had not as yet established its supremacy over coal gas in the

working of machinery, nor had machinery itself reached the perfection it boasts of to-day. A most pleasurable interest came into the lives of many women from the growing knowledge of "best ways" of doing things, and also when they began to improve their standards of living in their own homes.

It was consoling to hear in after years the Jesuit Fathers, in the course of annual retreats, referring to their having been novices on that eventful day of Mother Magdalen's funeral, and having sung the Requiem and at Mortlake. Archbishop Goodier of happy memory was one who knew her, and Father Peers Smith, who was a War Chaplain in World War I, and was happy to say that on his way home from France he celebrated Holy Mass at Ars in the vestments which belonged to St. John Vianney. He gave conferences to the S.M.G. novices while he was novice-master at Manresa for a "Rosary of Years," as they loved to call the period of fifteen years. Always on Clothing Day he would refer to having been at Mother Foundress' grave and to the large congregation at the Mass, giving proof of her Christlike love for, and wholehearted interest in souls. Then there was Father Gretton, S.J., who took over the editorship of the "Messenger" for Father Dignam, Father Wilson, S.J., and other already professed Fathers who had known and revered the deceased Mother. Lastly one must mention her dear co-worker, Canon Murnane, called the "saviour of the slums," who used to relate that from the gains from her vast contributions to Catholic literature, she often helped him financially to provide a poor bride's trousseau, etc., and she had only to send Sister Paul Magdalen to Peter Robinson's for other necessities.

Father Peter Paul Mackey, O.P., writing from Rome after news of Mother Foundress' death, said:

" . . . It has never been found that the death of one who has established an Order has brought anything but blessing to the children left behind. Certainly it would have been a great happiness to the Mother if she had seen her Congregation receive the last word of approbation; still she had completed all that lay in her, and best thanks are due to God that during her lifetime your Society received its complete formation... I offered my Mass this morning for the soul of the Mother, and I will always remember her in my prayers, while I shall always cherish the memory of a most estimable and esteemed friend."

From Father W. Ronan, S.J., from whom she received her First Communion at the Crimea:

" . . . She was a noble character, and a splendid religious. I will always remember her as one of my oldest and best friends... Your good Mother had at times great spiritual trials, but she was always brave under them, and never deterred on account of them, from doing what came clearly before her as the will of God. She was a great worker, and had the singular power, on account of her special gifts, of doing much work in a short time. Nobody could understand how she was able to keep the "Month" floating before she gave it to our Fathers. During all that time she was editor, and indeed everything connected with it. On one occasion and when she was about to give it to us, she came over to Ireland wearied and worn out by her super-human exertions. I did all I could to persuade her to have the transfer effected at once, as an act of self-preservation from disease and death. I always found her most unselfish — a great soul in every sense."

From Father Clare, S.J., who with Dr. Manning had decided her vocation and directed all her early steps:

"I sincerely condole with you and all the Sisters in your great sorrow. Your Congregation has incurred a very great loss, and one which it will be hard to repair. However, our dear Lord, than Whom none is stronger nor wiser, none more loyal and faithful, will not abandon you, but will bring you safely through your great trial, if only you combine in prayer to Him, and throw yourselves in loving confidence under His protection. I said Mass for the repose of your Rev. Mother's soul this morning, and I pray our dear Lord to watch over, to protect and bless you all, and to preserve you in holy union and charity."

From Father Gretton, S.J., Father Dignam's successor as Director of the Apostleship of Prayer in England:

"I beg you to convey to all the Sisters of your Congregation who know me, and who know what kindly relations existed between the late Rev. Mother General and myself, my deepest

The Sacred Heart pleading for the world. Painted in Rome on Mother Magdalen's idea.
— (See details in book).

The moment of the Incarnation.

"And the Angel departed from her" (Lk. 1 : 38)

Church of St. George and the English Saints — built by Mr. Fullerton in memory of his wife, Lady Georgiana Fullerton.

Shrine of Regina Prophetarum
in the Roman Church of the S.M.G.'s.

sympathy with them and with the whole Congregation in this great and irreparable loss.

It is too well known how much the Apostleship of Prayer owes to her and to you all, for me to have to assure you of my prayers for her soul and for your welfare. God has taken away a soul which was the soul of all of you, and it seems to you as if you had all lost part of yourselves. But have confidence in Him, Who gave her to you, and through her brought you to Himself. He will in His own way strengthen you all, and console you, and the great work and its increase will continue as heretofore.

The scene in Mortlake cemetery was a grace to us all, the beginning of many graces to come, which will now be given to you for the sake of one who has finished her work and won her crown. May she speedily come to the Beatific Vision, where she will see you all, individually, in God."

From Father Bernard Vaughan, S.J.:

"Do all you can to speed her, like a bird flying to its nest, on her way to the Heart of Jesus. Her place will be high up..."

From the Cistercian, Father Henry Collins:

"How grieved I am for the loss you have sustained, and the whole Church in England. A valiant woman, one with true sterling piety — one with common sense. She always considered her new Institute as an enlargement of the Cistercian life for those who could not fast — labour and prayer."

From Father W. Miller, O.M.I.:

"My knowledge of Rev. Mother M. Magdalen dates only during the last months of her life. When I met her, she was suffering from the illness which proved fatal. What impressed me most with her was her great faith and her great humility. Her trust in God was boundless. To Him she committed the entire care of the religious community which it pleased God to entrust to her care and which she founded.

Early in her illness, or rather early in our acquaintance, she mentioned to me her conviction that her illness was incurable, and when I ventured to encourage her by saying that our Divine Lord would spare her to continue and consolidate the work He had given her to do, she said, 'Father, it was Our Lord

N

Himself Who has enabled the work to subsist, and I have never been necessary — I can leave it entirely to Him. My whole concern now is about my own soul.' Her great concern during the time I knew her was to be ready for death. She feared a sudden call or rather she feared to pass away while asleep. Her desire was to retain her consciousness to the end so that she might merit more, and also so that she might have an opportunity of repairing any acts of impatience which suffering might occasion. Her sufferings were great indeed, and she bore them with much patience.

Many little incidents showed me her spirit of charity and kindness for others. Obliged to ask the aid and assistance of others in her illness — aid and help so willingly and devotedly given — she sometimes expressed to me her sorrow at what she considered her want of consideration. But she always had a thought for each one who was near her, and her words of gratitude were heartfelt indeed. Her zeal for souls too struck me. She seemed to me to be one who would fear no risk and shirk no danger to aid and help souls in any danger.

She was very pleased at some words of appreciation uttered by me concerning the work of her children in Paris. She desired them to work humbly and without any advertisement. I considered it a favour to have known one who has done so much for God and for souls, and who has left to the Church a religious family who labour so devotedly for those who are most in need."

From Sir J. B. Leach, Chairman of the Committee of the Providence Hospital, a non-Catholic:

"I learned to-day of the death of our dear deeply lamented and much loved Mother General. She has finished the good work God gave her to do here on earth, and has now gone to the reward of the faithful... She lived a good, noble and unselfish life, and we are all the better for having had the great honour and privilege of assisting, under her able direction, the operation of her large-hearted charity and love for her helpless poor and afflicted fellow-creatures, for of all good works this is the greatest, to follow in the steps of the good Lord.

On behalf of myself and the Committee of the Providence Free Hospital, St. Helens, permit me to tender to yourself and the

Sisters our deepest sympathy and sorrow at the unspeakable loss
you have been called upon to suffer, and to say that our prayer
is that the Good Master will help you to suffer, and sustain
you in continuing the institutions which are so successfully
doing her work. I beg of you to rest assured that anything I
can do to help shall be done with the greatest joy and pleasure,
and I may say this on behalf of the many friends of the Hospital
here. I count it no small honour to be engaged in any way
with you in the good work you have in hand."

From Aubrey de Vere:

"My prayers will not fail to rise for her. But it is to *her*
prayers for others that we must now look for the aid they will
draw down upon them."

From Mr. A. J. Blount, of Messrs. Blount, Lynch and
Peters:

"Fitzalan House,
Arundel Street, Strand,
London, June 12, 1900.

I am greatly grieved to hear of the death of your most Reverend
Mother General. She was a very old client and friend for whom
I always entertained the greatest veneration and affection. I had
not seen her for many years, but her image and her wonderful
personality were indelibly impressed upon my memory, so that
if I were to live to a hundred, I should always see her before
me. May she rest in peace, and may God comfort and watch
over her spiritual children."

From a Religious of the Sacred Heart in Roehampton:

"I must tell you how, many years ago, I knew your holy
Foundress. I was a novice at our Convent at Roehampton when
she spent a month there while undertaking the building of your
Convent at Roehampton. I remember several times going to
the Chapel to tell her her meals were served, and finding her
so absorbed in prayer that it was difficult to make her understand
what I wanted. Then she would smile and say, 'Oh, thank you,
Sister.' I had a great veneration for her, and a few days ago
when there seemed some difficulty about getting Berthe to
Brentford, I prayed to your holy Foundress, and begged her to
arrange it all, and D.G. how well she has done it!"

From her beloved Kinsale, where she often stayed since Crimean days:

"We had general Communion for her on the 9th (the day of her death) and will have another for her dear soul. We all here very sincerely sympathize with you and your Community in your sorrow, and are grieved at the death of your dear Mother General whom we loved and revered as a sincere and kind friend — a very much valued special friend and fellow-labourer of our beloved Mother M. Frances Bridgeman."

Finally there are three letters from Australia. From Mother M. Stanislaus, Convent of Perpetual Adoration, Brisbane:

" . . . Dear Mother, how generous she was, and how anxious to help everyone and every good work. She did all she could for us when we were in Rome, and then in letters after our return she would enquire about all our little affairs, as though she had not the responsibility of all her own children and their good works. She loved the Nocturnal Adoration and asked that she might have a share in it... How her dear eyes glistened whenever she spoke of our Holy Father (Leo XIII). In one of her letters she relates how, when one of her Sisters wished a a patient in the hospital at St. Helens 'A happy Christmas' she exclaimed, 'We are always happy with you!' That little word seemed to give her much consolation, as her soul longed to comfort others, especially those in sorrow."

From Sister M. Gertrude, an Irish Sister of Charity and novice-mistress in Australia:

"I have dear Mother-General's postcard in her own writing, which reached me after we left Rome. It is put away in a little box with relics of the saints and other treasures. Perhaps you have a photo or some little pictures that she used during life? Would you think of poor little me out in Australia, though I have so little claim. But I know and feel that she will help me and pray for me. She read my heart so clearly at the first interview. Surely she will know it better now, and will help me to become a holy religious, and to lead others closer to God... I cannot keep back the tears all day. How good God was to let me meet her and know her ever so slightly! It was a privilege indeed. May it be my happy privilege to meet her in eternity."

From the author of "A Modern Pilgrim's Progress" — Miss Anstice Baker:

"When first I knew your dear Mother Foundress I was a Protestant. Your convent was near, in the district of Seven Dials, at that time one of the poorest and worst in London. It consisted of a few rooms in a little street, the name of which, I think, was Green Court. Not far off was a Providence Night Refuge, kept by 'Sister Zillah', an Anglican Sister with whom your Mother was on very friendly terms. Soho Square was not very far off, and even in those days dear 'Mother Taylor', as we used to call her, hoped to have a convent there some day. I think it must have been through Father Christie that I first made her acquaintance. I was an Anglican by birth and education, but had become an agnostic, and yet yearned for something more satisfying, and knew that nowhere except in Catholicism should I find what I needed.

'Slumming' was the rule just then, and I was sick of the usual round of social amusements, and wanted to work among the poor. Father Christie introduced me to your dear Mother, and she let me work with her and with her Sisters. I lived in Dover Street, and used to go up to the convent in the morning and stay a great part of the day. After a time I went to Paris, and when I next saw Mother Taylor I was a Catholic, and she was at Mount Street. To me she was ever the kindest of friends, and I feel I owe much to her... I always think 'Tyburn' the most beautiful Catholic story that has ever been written — here at the other end of the world it is influencing thousands, and your Mother is working for God after her death by means of her books, as truly as she did when alive. May He reward her for all she has done for souls! One of those to whom she was good will never forget her, and will always feel a deep interest in all her convents."

The following is an extract from the sermon preached by Father Scoles, S.J., at Mother Magdalen's funeral: (taken from the "Tablet" of June 30, 1900)

"Things which God intends to bless are not done in a hurry, and some years passed before her scheme took definite shape. At last Father Dignam, S.J., appeared, who stood by her till his death. With his guidance and help the Rules were formed,

205

which are drawn chiefly from the Constitutions of the Society of Jesus. In the year 1879 the Brief of Praise (or Lauda) was obtained from Rome. In 1885 she went to Rome to obtain the formal approbation, and at this time a suggestion was made by the Cardinal Vicar of Rome to found a house there. This was not her suggestion, but the Pope's own special desire that they should have a house and school in that city. This desire was complied with, and both the house and school are now in a flourishing condition. The formal approbation of the Rules and Constitutions of the Order was obtained in 1892 from the Holy Father, Cardinal Mazella, S.J., being appointed Cardinal Protector of the Institute. In 1892 she felt that she had finished the work which God had given her to do, "consummatum est opus meum." From then until her death her life was mainly one of pain and suffering. Dear Brethren, does it not seem strange that Almighty God sends trials and sufferings to the great souls He loves most, so that He appears almost needlessly to try them. It has been so with founders of Religious Orders; the gold is tried in the furnace — the price must be paid for the work to last. Apparently in all work done for His sake, it seems at times to be recompensed only with great trials. 'My God, my God! Why hast Thou forsaken me?' I say 'it seems' only, for we know it, of reality, to be far otherwise.

Such was the work of the life of the great soul that has passed away. What was, and what is, the spirit of her Order? It is truly a religious spirit, intense hatred of worldliness, great esteem of poverty, and deep confidence in God; no external show, but true internal spirit; for God alone — quite at variance with the spirit of the 19th century, which looks alone to things that are showy and grand, and does not appreciate the unseen work of the Sacraments. Works external may strike the eye, but they may not be "full" works. It is the Spirit who gives life — the flesh avails nothing. We know the works of God, and in His dealings with us He looks not upon externals, but upon the desire of the heart — His love of poverty, humility, and the work done amongst those whom the world shuns. See the thousands of poor and orphans gathered and sought out of the by-ways, and brought in touch with religion — the schools founded, hospitals erected — these she has left in the care of her children, who have been well tried in virtue and suffering before they undertake the external works of the Order. Her powers of guidance and imparting the religious spirit were exceptionally great, and she satisfied herself that each individual soul was able to undertake the works and understand the spirit of the Institute. 'Let her works praise her in the gates,' for they were full works. This is the history she has taken with her to account for at the Throne of God.

As with her model, the Son of God, she was brought to the depths of physical pain and mental suffering, so that she could, in a sense, say as He — 'My God! My God! Why hast Thou forsaken me?' Let us lift up the curtain. Of late her life has been one of unutterable pain, but all through her long sufferings she has been buoyed up with the spirit of thankfulness at being allowed to be an instrument in God's hands. She was ever humble in asking guidance. Her conformity to the will of God was most striking. She found great consolation in the words 'Thy will be done', and this was not said for the occasion. She knew her God, and knew His hand was upon her. The clouds were lifted up at last, and she realized at length the peace of soul those enjoy who cling to God in suffering. She waited, and waited in patience. I was called to her bedside shortly before her death. Her last words to me were: 'The will of God be done. The will of God be done.'

We too are called to do great works; we are called to live in her spirit. Let us seek to imitate her in her true spirit of humility, and like her, strive to obtain the true internal spirit, dreading any show that may strike the eye or the senses. 'He hath regarded the humility of His handmaid.' We must wait and hope and trust, and we shall find we have not trusted in vain. Let us seek that deep faith that teaches us that behind the cloud God does really love us; that our God is very near us. Let us not look back. Let us place all confidence in Him and never admit of any distrust in Him. 'Her works follow her.' Her works *will* follow her, and all the good she has done, every act of conformity, every suffering borne, will follow her to the Throne of God, and put a further meaning to the text, 'Her works follow her.' With pain and prayer she has left a perfect work. We may thus hope confidently it will last to be a help to the needy, the helpless and the suffering. May her spirit of poverty and humility and confidence in God be instilled into the hearts of her companions. She has finished the work God gave her to do. May her soul, then, rest in peace. 'In Thee, O Lord, have I hoped. Let me not be confounded for ever'."

Fifty-nine long years, with their major events, were to make history in Church and State, and Mortlake Cemetery was destined to see another sight. On September 24th, 1959, the anniversary of the very day, ninety years before, that Archbishop Manning had authorized Father Clare, S.J., to receive as postulants Fanny Taylor and her first companions, and therefore the birthday of her Congregation, her precious remains were removed from Mortlake Cemetery to Maryfield Novitiate Chapel, Roehampton. In the spring of 1959, when the then Mother-General was having a private audience with the saintly Pontiff, Pius XII, and the question of the exhumation was discussed, His Holiness graciously said: "Tell your Bishop of the diocese where your Mother is buried that he may give you every permission you ask." This message was for dear Dr. Cowderoy, Archbishop of Southwark, who immediately put the matter into the hands of his Vicar-General, the Right Reverend Monsignor Provost Hubert Gibney, parish priest of St. Mary Magdalen's, Mortlake.

The Secretary of the Home Office, Mr. Butler, had next to be interviewed, and he in turn passed the business on to Mr. Head, Secretary of Housing and Local Government, who gave an unconditional "yes", asking that the costs involved would be given as a donation to the "Life-Boat Association", and the following reply letter dated 25th June, 1959, speaks for itself:

"Dear Mr. Head,

Thank you so much for having brought our business to a successful finish. We are most grateful, and will never forget your noble gesture and the helpful spirit you have shown.

I will happily do as you say with regard to the Lifeboat Association, and will pray for you and your dear ones while I live.

This business may have had to have been very official and

bureaucratic, but for us it is all love and reverence, hence our gratitude.

I am, dear Mr. Head,
Your very sincerely,
Mother M. Geraldine, S.M.G."

R. E. Head Esq.,
Minister of Housing & Local Government,
Whitehall, London, S.W.1.

When on July 22nd, Mother Magdalen's grave was unearthed, and all ecclesiastical and civil requirements had been complied with, naturally, as was foreseen, the elm coffin which had enclosed the leaden one, had much deteriorated except for its identity plate, which was not even rusty. The leaden coffin was intact, showing neither the slightest dirt nor rust stain. If it had been found faulty in the least degree (as we had hoped it might be), we had Pope Pius XII's order to remove the remains, get the bones reverently cleaned, bound in silk and placed, with all the dust found, into a new leaden case and then into a new oak coffin for re-interment. If the original leaden coffin, however, were found still wholly intact, the process of viewing the remains was strictly forbidden for the time.

On the eve of the 24th September, all was checked and prepared in the crypt at Mortlake, and very early next morning, "while it was yet dark," the Mothers set out to meet the motor hearse that bore their coffined treasure and accompanied it to Maryfield, where all was ready for the re-interment.

The following exact account of the further proceedings in the event is copied from the circular sent from Maryfield, Roehampton, to all the convents of the Congregation after the re-interment, and dated 24th September, 1959:

"The great day has come at last, and our beloved and venerated Mother and Foundress is at home with us, and while her precious remains rest in the Sacred Heart Chapel, the influence of her spiritual presence is everywhere felt. In fact, once the final permission was given and the men began the preparation of the vault, even the youngest postulant wanted to be "up and doing" to prepare for Mother's home-coming.

Since July 22nd, when the remains were exhumed and the

209

intact leaden coffin enclosed in the new oak one, the crypt at Mortlake saw many Sisters kneeling beside Mother, and as the big Retreats came and went, some hundreds of Sisters in all had this privilege.

Monsignor Gibney, Vicar-General of the Diocese, was "in the scene" all the time, and rejoiced at seeing the Sisters come daily; we owe a great debt of gratitude to Monsignor for all the help he gave in Mortlake itself and for his kind interest in Mother, to the point even of asking that he himself be the celebrant of the High Mass on the 24th, and so he was, with Canon Monk for deacon and Father Rector of Manresa sub-deacon.

Wonderful, too, was the enthusiasm with which all concerned prepared the little vault in the Sacred Heart chapel. The marble slab, having the same inscription as that on the plate of the original elm coffin, is imbedded in the parquet flooring and done so neatly that one would wonder how it all could happen. Mother faces the Sacred Heart altar — the Sacred Heart of her Lord, for whom she had done so much! St. Joseph's statue is also in the chapel, so the position illustrates exactly her favourite ejaculation: 'St. Joseph, friend of the Sacred Heart, pray for us.'

On September 24th, the great feast then of the 90th anniversary of the birth of our beloved Congregation, we had the Community Mass at 6.30, and in due time afterwards, Mother and Mother M. Lewis went to Mortlake to accompany to Maryfield our dear Mother's coffin in its quiet hearse, as all had to be done very privately until we came inside our Convent gate. Here the hearse was met by a Guard of Honour of Sisters, Novices and Postulants with Monsignor Gibney, Canon Monk and seven acolyte novices from Manresa, with Dick Dean and three others of the Foundress' family, also Father Simon Hayes in his beautiful Carmelite habit. All carried lighted candles, held in pale blue Lourdes protectors. It was a beautiful sight, flooded in bright sunshine.

As the heavy coffin was shouldered from the hearse to the chapel door by eight men, including Dick Dean (the Foundress' grand-nephew), the choir sang 'In Paradisum'. The procession moved slowly up the chapel, and when the vault was blessed

210

the coffin was lowered on to planks above the vault, and then very gently and slowly fixed in position inside. Tears were shed by many of the old Sisters who remembered that other day fifty-nine years ago, when Mother was laid in Mortlake cemetery. Father Peers Smith, S.J., wrote a beautiful letter for this occasion; he was one of the Manresa novice-choir at Mortlake on that other day in 1900.

The clergy now, having sprinkled the coffin, retired to the sacristy to vest for Pontifical High Mass, and gave a quarter of an hour for the large gathering of Sisters, Novices and Postulants to sprinkle also.

High Mass began at about 9.45. The choir burst out joyfully as the clergy entered the sanctuary. It was all joy and jubilation, and once again in Heaven one could imagine Mother uttering the sweet word 'Home', as she had uttered it on arriving at Soho from Paris to die. It was a coincidence that an old Soho child — Mary O'Connor, who knew Mother and who helped to prepare for that sad home-coming, was here with us. She came from Clapham for the occasion and remained till evening. One felt that she knelt there as a symbol of our great Mother's love and redeeming work for the outcast and the poor — and Mary's personality and refinement were proof of their success.

All the forthcoming Chapter Sisters without exception were present, and it was grand to have dear Mother M. Germanus with us and to see her look so well. Her heart must have been full of joy at seeing Mother come home to that Maryfield where she and the Mothers of the terrible World War II period had their full share of the Cross.

After Mass, at which Monsignor Gibney preached the appended little eulogy, we had the full choir Magnificat and then the Blessed Sacrament was exposed till 4.30 p.m., when Benediction was given by Monsignor, assisted by Father Rector.

A lunch worthy of the great occasion was prepared for the clergy, who invited Dick Dean, as Mother Foundress' grandnephew, to their table. They saw in him the fine gentlemanly figure of a great Catholic who could confer with them on any topic. Dick's sisters dined in another room, and were entertained by some of our senior Sisters who had known them from childhood. Meanwhile the Community, of well over 100, were faring well in our refectory when a telegram bringing congratulations from our Sisters in America was handed in. We were very much in spirit with them all, and with all our other absent Sisters who were not forgotten in our prayers. Certainly our spirits had no limitations on the 24th.

Relays of Sisters from the local houses to the number of 94 came and went all the afternoon to visit and welcome our Mother home at last. At 5.45 our Catholic builder, Mr. Hussey, came with his artist brother (who wanted to share in the ceremony) and just as the Angelus rang, the slab was being placed perfectly and neatly over the finished vault.

As the sprinkling of the holy water had ended in the morning, and just before High Mass had begun, Mother and Mother M. Lewis placed two beautiful sheaves of white gladioli and asters on Mother's coffin. One had come from her own dear Brentford and was first laid on the prie-dieu in Mother's room there. The second was from St. Philomena's, Euston Square. We now offer our grateful thanks for these and also for all the other generous and rich gifts sent by Superiors of the other houses and which helped to make the day most happy and festive for all.

We owe great gratitude and prayers to His Holiness Pope Pius XII, and to our dear Bishop of Southwark for having given their sanction and blessing to our proposal from the beginning. The Home Office Authorities and the Ministry of Housing were also most kind and sympathetic and helped us in every way. But certainly it was dear Mother Foundress herself who finished the affair so satisfactorily. It was most remarkable that, as our dear Mother in life loved to fix dates to her graces, the month of June brought the final document, the 22nd July the exhumation, and lastly, September 24th brought dear Mother Foundress herself home to her children."

*   *   *

Eulogy given by the Right Reverend Monsignor Provost Hubert Gibney, V.G., Parish Priest of St. Mary Magdalen's, Mortlake, and as the Bishop's representative, celebrant of the Pontifical High Mass on September 24th, 1959.

"My dear Sisters in Jesus Christ, I am not going to speak to you this morning about the life and work of your Foundress — Mother Mary Magdalen Taylor. After all, it is all known to you much better than it is known to me. You have been brought up with her and all of you are being trained in her spirit. The sacrifice you are making is because of her example and your aim is to be like her as far as you can be, according to your ability and according to the grace of God which He is giving you.

This morning I will speak to you about one aspect of Mother Magdalen. You know the saints have many qualities, they differ in so many ways, but there are certain fundamental virtues that they all possess. Speaking of Mother Foundress, we try to find in her the qualities of the saints — the qualities of those who gave their lives to the service of God and to their fellow creatures. Our Lord said 'Learn of Me, because I am meek and humble of Heart,' 'Blessed are the meek for they shall possess the land.' Some look on meekness as a poor kind of thing — a weak person — one who has not much spirit — one who allows herself to be led by others — one with no thoughts of her own, but this is not correct. Meekness is strength. It comes from the fact that you are single-minded. It means self-sacrifice. 'Learn of Me, for I am meek and humble of Heart.' Surely Our Lord was not weak — He was strong. He had one purpose — to save mankind — even to the Cross, nothing would deter Him. So it is with the Servants of God. Their one purpose in life is to serve God and His creatures and nothing will stop them.

Mother Magdalen — you realise how much she gave up and yet how much she got back. In her whole life she never hurt a soul — never said anything to hurt a sensitive nature. She gathered round her friends who were to be loyal supporters

213

— she saw to the wants of others. Mother Magdalen, who began with nothing, ended with all that could be given her. When you stand at the graveside of the great, of those who have made history, shaped the destinies of nations, perhaps, the thought might enter your minds: 'What is left now but a little dust in the earth?' Here lies one who was unknown, one who has never impressed others, yet one who has left so much after her. She who began with so little has left behind her a monument that shall never be forgotten. When you think that she began from nothing, she had even to search for the true Faith — she was not a Catholic, and then she had this call to serve God! She tried so hard to find elsewhere what she wanted but in the end she had to found her own Congregation, as she knew it to be God's Will.

Then came the years of growth. Some of you may not know what responsibility is, and what it is to make a serious decision. Real responsibility means to take full charge of things. As you read the life of Mother Taylor, you realise how often she took a step in the dark. Each new convent was an act of virtue, of hope, of charity. She founded her Congregation and God called her to Himself and she could go happily to her reward.

This is a happy day for you and for your dear Mother Foundress in Heaven. After being in the grave at Mortlake for over fifty years, she has come back to-day to be among her own Sisters, to be in her own convent, to be in her own chapel, to be at the Feet of the Master Whom she loves so well — a great happiness to you, and I am sure to her. To-day, I feel that from her place in Heaven she is looking down on us, happy and smiling. She is not counting the cost of the sacrifices she made nor the sufferings she endured, nor the pain. These things matter no longer. She has left behind her a memory and a monument which we hope will never be forgotten, and which we hope will flourish as long as the Church exists. She realises the sacrifices we have made in order that we may carry on her work. She is looking down on her Sisters and on the work they are doing. She is happy because *her* work is done. In the Name of the Father and of the Son and of the Holy Ghost. Amen."

Chapter 18.

"BY THEIR FRUITS YOU SHALL KNOW THEM"

Who has not experienced, at one time or another in life, the feeling of loneliness and frustration that invades one's whole being when a beloved one, on whom so much depended, is called from this world? Such loneliness and frustration are not proofs of weakness nor of lack of resignation to the Divine Will, rather are they born of that love which later on energises one's depression and spurs one on to begin life, as it were, all over again.

When Mother Magdalen died in June, 1900, doubtless many Sisters asked themselves Sister M. Thecla's question to Mother de Sales: "What shall we do now?" to which she herself gave the one entirely correct answer: "What shall we do now, but continue trying, as we have always done, to do what would please our dear Mother best. And one thing would be that we may ever maintain that true spirit of the Institute which she taught us." It has to be acknowledged that the Foundress had marked a straight path for her children to follow. Some six weeks after her death, the Final Decree of Approbation had been given to the Congregation which she had nurtured. She had left behind her a group of spiritual, well-trained women whose united aim was her own, and who loyally loved and lived and laboured as she had done for the glory of God and the good of souls. And now, the "Kindly Light" of the Holy Spirit was to lead them on in their work for God.

While the whole Congregation was still lamenting the loss of its first dear Mother, it knew well she would not have the Sisters "looking up to Heaven." Only "Up and doing!" she would counsel. When the July Retreats were all at a happy ending, and the Sisters had been spiritually refreshed for the combat, the second General Chapter of the Congregation assembled at Brentford, and at the end of the deliberations and special Retreat, the delegates came to Roehampton for the election. It was presided over by Bishop Bourne, then of Southwark, and Canon Murnane, an old and valued friend of the late Foundress. The results were: —

Mother M. Lucy	Mother General
Mother Magdalen Aimée	Mother Assistant
Mother M. de Sales	Mother Assistant
Mother Aloysius Austin	Mother Assistant
Mother M. Imelda	Mother Assistant

The Chapter certainly had the guidance of the Holy Spirit in its choice, and the wise direction of the Manresa Fathers to help the delegates in their work.

The new Mother General and her experienced Council knew that their late Mother's wish was to build a special Novitiate at St. Mary's Roehampton, and this was the first work of the early 1900's. It will be remembered that on the Feast of the Annunciation, 1876, Mother Magdalen secured three small houses, and got them thrown into one, until a proper convent could be built by the Congregation. The allotted space for the new site was rather small, but the competent architect "aimed high" and built a magnificent four-story convent, with room and to spare for the many applicants to the Congregation in those first years of the 20th century. Here also came the Sisters of the third year's probation or Tertianship, preparatory to the making of Final Vows. The former noviceship quarters were fitted out with dormitories, refectory, class-rooms, etc., and "St. Mary's Orphanage" came into being. Their young years were made happy and their religion safeguarded for many otherwise destitute and neglected children, and especially was this the case during and after World War I.

It will be remembered that the League of the Apostleship of Prayer, or of the Sacred Heart, was introduced from Le Puy in France into England and Ireland by Father William Maher, S.J., in 1865. After his death, the devotion had declined somewhat, to be renewed by his successor, Father Dignam, S.J., in

1884. Mother Magdalen Taylor became one of Father Dignam's most zealous allies in spreading the devotion, and the little "Penny Messenger" brought the message of the Sacred Heart monthly and regularly to the doors of rich and poor. It was printed by Brother James Stanley at Manresa Press, Roehampton, and in his day, and in those of his successor, Brother John Griffin, the printed sheets came in bulk with the pink covers, to be folded, stitched and cut in the "Messenger room" by the senior girls of St. Mary's Orphanage. This "holy work", as the children liked to call it, helped considerably in the financial upkeep of the Orphanage, and in the part it played in the work of the Crusade of Rescue. One very intelligent and bright child, who is known to many S.M.G.'s as "Madge", came to St. Mary's in 1912, and remained until 1926, when she entered with the Benedictines at Bergholt, on December 6th of that year. Madge took the name "Sister Magdalen", having had great reverence for Mother Magdalen Taylor and the Sisters. For many years Madge was mistress of the "Messenger room" at St. Mary's, and was much loved by the junior children, as well as by her own age group. She is now at St. Mary's Benedictine Abbey at Hazlemere, and a very useful member. The Benedictines there love to think that their one-time renowned Lady Abbess was Lady Woollett, whose brother, Father Woollett, S.J., had received Fanny Taylor into the Church at the Crimea.

In 1903, the Sisters were asked to take charge of the Mental Hospital, Youghal, Co. Cork, an institution for over 400 patients, male and female. They accepted this, and served successfully and happily for over 60 years. In the spring of 1963, the Superior General was reluctantly compelled to withdraw the Sisters, owing to shortage of staff. His Lordship, Dr. Aherne, Bishop of the Diocese, regretted their leaving the Hospital, as did the devoted clergy and people of Youghal, whose kindness over the years the Congregation will ever remember.

In 1904 the taking over of a fine feudal property at Portslade, Sussex, and all the business involved, began to be negotiated with the Congregation. The ruins of the ancient pre-Reformation manor are within some yards of the present Manor House, which evidently was built about 1807, and where the last Lord of the Manor died in 1879, while his wife lived on there till her death

217

o

in 1899. The house was occupied again until 1904. The fine old pre-Reformation Church of St. Nicholas, a few yards off from the ruins, is still in excellent condition. It dates back to the 12th century. The present chancel is of the 13th century, and one of the original consecration crosses can still be seen on the south doorway.

When the Sisters took over the property, naturally there was much to be done by way of adaptation. The existing "Portslade Manor" became the convent. A large room was fitted out for a chapel. The destined work was to be for mentally handicapped girls and those needing care and protection. As time passed, a new home was built for these girls, and a fine modern laundry gave them their means of support, while later still, a spacious chapel and sacristy were built on to the convent, where the parish overflow at the Manor end of the town and from the direction of Mile Oak could find ample room until such time as a further church could be built there, as had already been planned and happily accomplished for Southwick at the other side of Portslade. Now the sanctuary of this spacious convent chapel has again been adapted to the Liturgical requirements of Vatican II. The neat little Catholic Church of Our Lady, Star of the Sea, at Portslade itself, the first since the Reformation, was greatly aided by a Mr. and Mrs. Broderick, who were considered to be "two wandering Irish saints" in their day. They often accepted charity from the people by way of food and other necessities, but only a special few knew that they were intent on helping to give Portslade its first church. A Catholic school soon followed in its wake. As attempts to get this recognised by the Education Authorities failed at the time, the Sisters, in co-operation with His Lordship Dr. Amigo, Bishop of Southwark, and Reverend Father Kirwan, who was chaplain, saved the situation by working it as a cheap private paying school for many years. So much was this appreciated that many non-Catholics also begged that their children too might be admitted. As the Catholic population grew, not only in Portslade, but in the outlying districts, and as the school was already too small for even the number of Catholic children attending, another petition and a public enquiry, as well as a prolonged period of free teaching on the Sisters' part, led to its being recognised as a public Catholic Elementary School under the Sussex County Council Education Authority, whose members and their successors, independent of creed or class, have ever been kindly interested in, and co-operative with the clergy and the Sisters. In late years another extension has been added, and since the system of education calls for a still more comprehensive scheme, Portslade envisages further necessary work to meet the future developments.

The grounds of Portslade Manor offer every convenience for the Parish Corpus Christi procession, which has taken place annually there from the beginning. The people of the parish and from far outside it, the Sisters and children from St. Anne's, Brighton, and the Manor Community with its women and girls of the Home, the Sisters who teach in the school, with their boys and girls, all assemble to form a vast procession on the winding lawn. On one such occasion, a dear retarded girl of the Home said to a Sister: "Sister, the birds stopped singing to listen to us as we were taking Our Lord for a walk!" One thanks God for the growth of the Catholic population of Portslade from the twenty or so of 1907 to its present proportion. The Golden Jubilee of the Parish and Convent was celebrated in 1954, when His Grace, Archbishop Cowderoy, celebrated High Mass. Many of the Sussex and Surrey clergy attended, and the parishioners were there in numbers. Mother Magdalen Taylor and the Sisters of the Heavenly Community must have rejoiced in the celebration of the fifty years' triumph. Her Sisters in Portslade had lived in the fulness of her spirit all those years. That spirit, as expressed in their Holy Rule: "Life for Jesus Christ, labour for Jesus Christ, zeal for Jesus Christ, and all things through Mary, His most sweet Mother and our Mistress" has faithfully and loyally inspired all their life-work in their busy apostolate. Carrying on the Foundress' apostolate in the schools, in the visitation of the poor and lonely, in their instruction of converts, in their charitable training of their poor handicapped girls, in their catechetical classes elsewhere and in their endeavours to help their devoted Bishop and clergy in every possible way, they strive with God's never-failing grace and Our Lady's help to renew in themselves that interior spirit of holiness and union with God from which alone comes true strength for their lives in community and for their work among the many souls they contact.

In 1905, the Sisters took over the workhouse and district hospital in Youghal from their beloved Sisters of Mercy of Kinsale, with whom they had close ties of friendship through their Foundress since Crimean days. The present writer visited Kinsale with another Sister in 1927. We were not expected, but as the purpose of the visit was to deliver some messages from our Mother General, and a book, "The Life of Mother Magdalen Taylor", by Father Devas, S.J., just published, the call was to be brief, as we thought. What was our surprise when we heard that our taxi driver had been paid and sent off, and that we could not go home until morning! The Reverend Mother, who recalled many memories of Mother Magdalen's visits to Kinsale, told us at supper that night the story of one special evening. Mother Bridgeman and she were seated on a window-sill in conversation. Mother Magdalen moved her hand and, not seeing a crack in the window-pane, accidentally smashed it outright. "Ah," exclaimed Mother Bridgeman, smiling, "that's an English fist!" Her friend returned, holding up a bleeding finger: "And that's Irish glass, see, it has paid me off!" The older nuns remembered our Mother well, and the loving intimacy that existed between them until Mother Bridgeman's death. The Poor Servants of the Mother of God will ever remember with gratitude what they owe to the Crimean heroine, Mother Frances Bridgeman of Kinsale, who was the first to teach Mother Magdalen how to meditate on Our Lady's "Magnificat", and that while preparing an Irish soldier for burial at Koulali Hospital in the Christmas octave of 1854.

The year 1907 saw a much-needed Girl's Home opened at Edge Lane, Liverpool, and a Home for Crippled and Invalid Children at Brighton, Sussex. Wherever the Sisters went to work among their dear poor, they became busy with their parish apostolate, and won the sympathy of the people. The work in these two 1907 foundations was of its nature an intensely charitable undertaking. One remembers Monsignor Nugent's first pleading letter to Mother Magdalen to come to his aid, and her prompt "Yes" telegraphed from Rome in 1891. Mother M. Lucy, her successor, was re-elected in 1907. Her previous record as a nun, as well as her first term as Mother General, proved how well she had imbibed the spirit of the Foundress, especially in her practical love for the poor, as in her Christ-like compassion for the abandoned, the irresponsible, the orphan and the homeless of that desperate age.

The Home at Edge Lane relieved the work of Paul Street, Bevington Bush and of the Nugent House Night Shelter for Women. The purchase of the very suitable property at Mossley Hill at a later date, and the foundation of a Home there, gave security to the continuance of Monsignor Nugent's and Mother Magdalen's work of rescue. The Paul Street premises began now to be remodelled, extended and fully equipped as a hospital for the poor, while a number of single and double rooms were set aside for the rich, according to a certain phrase of the Rule, which reads: "The Sisters are permitted to receive such persons (the rich) into their hospitals or other houses, as a means of gaining aid for the poor."

The Paul Street Home became a real "home" with the new name "Lourdes Hospital" in 1929. The Welfare State, with its Councils, its Regional Boards and its other varied forms of National Assistance was still in the offing, but the kind Liverpool people with their Penny Fund, the 8th Royal Irish Regiment with its generous subscriptions, the interest alone on which gave a further £50 annually, all of this, with the addition of the endowment of two beds by benefactors, a Linen Guild and repeated "Bring-and-Buy" and Jumble Sales, Flag Day, etc., kept Lourdes Hospital well on its feet until enemy action during World War II rendered it partly useless as a hospital and extremely dangerous for further habitation. Nothing daunted, however, the brave Sisters set themselves to other work in Liverpool and outside of it, until the war was well over, at which time their house-hunting had succeeded in the purchase of a building in the environment of Sefton Park, which, though not very suitable, was speedily adapted, and "Lourdes Hospital" began its temporary career once more: "temporary" because plans were already being drafted and the site secured along the Greenbank Road for the new hospital, which was completed in 1955, and to which its temporary forerunner had the well-deserved honour of being united and re-adapted and equipped as a very modern Maternity Block, to the immense satisfaction of Dr. Godfrey, the then Archbishop of Liverpool, who, after His Grace had delivered a fitting eulogy to the assembled crowd at the solemn opening, cut the white ribbon to declare the Maternity Block open in June 1956, and, in the presence of all, handed the Reverend Mother a cheque for £700 from an anonymous donor, "to help the good work." Now, in the current year, 1969, a further extension to the main Hospital is under way, and the Convent Chapel is being brought up to date to meet the Liturgical requirements of Vatican II.

Mother Magdalen Taylor, after having received so many blessings in Rome in the late 1880s, was encouraged to pray and long for a second house in Italy, where the Sisters could have a change and some relaxation during the months of July and August, when the great heat of Rome is intensely weakening. Not until seven years after her death was her wish realised. The Reverend Father Strickland, S.J., knowing from experience the danger to which children and others were exposed in the days of anti-clericalism in Italy, and knowing that religious instruction did not figure on the curricula of the State schools, made up his mind to do something to solve the problem. There were numbers of English and American Catholic families whose children usually went to non-Catholic private schools, of which there were many, and Italian children frequented them also for lessons in English.

Father Strickland, knowing of the work begun in Rome some years back, and knowing the results for rich and poor alike, implored Cardinal Mistrangelo of Florence to beg the then Mother General of the Congregation for even a few Sisters to take on this most necessary apostolate in the city. The Cardinal, himself a religious of the Order of St. Joseph Calasanctius, was overjoyed. The Superiors, knowing their Foundress' wish and so receiving the message as the will of God, purchased an already existing school building, with a gymnasium attached, drafted some Sisters of the Roman house to Florence to begin the work, because of their knowledge of the language, and began, as Pope Leo had advised for Rome, "on a small scale." The work grew phenomenally, and the Italian children themselves were soon in the majority. The Florence school followed the plan of the Roman one, as advised by the Education Authorities in Mother Magdalen's day. When Mussolini came into power, the old system of education was completely re-modelled. Not only was religious instruction restored to the schools, but the very text books used in the teaching of the Humanities gave much Catholic knowledge, and of course Dante's and Manzoni's priceless works lived on. The grades or classes were re-organized to consist of the kindergarten (or "Giardino dell'Infanzia") followed by the five elementary classes, with an internal examination in the 3rd and 5th, success in the latter giving admission to the "Scuola Media" (middle school). This is followed by three years in the "Ginnasio" classes. The third year's successful examination here means entrance to the Lyceum (or "Liceo") which in turn, if successful, means the University. After the Lateran Treaty, all was well for Sisters' and Brothers' schools, and after test examinations for both teachers and classes, the same legal rights were afforded as to status with internal examinations etc., but of course with no cost to the State, they became "Parificato" as private secondary schools.

At this point one may well ask oneself: "Did Mother Magdalen then found her Congregation for the well-to-do as well as for the poor?" The Rule of the Congregation says that the Sisters may receive the rich into their hospitals or other houses as a means of gaining aid for the poor. Pope Leo in her own day commanded her to open the Roman school, impressing on her through his Vicar-General that no poverty was so sad as the spiritual poverty of the rich. The Rule also says that "Every talent which may be discovered in the Sisters, whether for government or labour or works of zeal, must be carefully trained to perfection." Why? That their Superiors may not merit the Gospel reproach of not having traded with those talents. How fine was Mother Magdalen's philosophy! While to help the poor of every type was her cherished aim, the rich were her means to its achievement, therefore the contacts with the latter, while being materially important for the poor, were and are, exceedingly so, spiritually, for themselves, while the Sisters and their talents, by God's grace, are His privileged go-betweens in humbly serving both.

The children's First Communion Day, usually on a Sunday,

is naturally the happiest in their lives, and their parents participate fully in their joy by being recipients also on that day. The First Fridays and all devotions concerning the League of the Sacred Heart are scrupulously observed, as are also the annual Lenten Retreats for all classes, according to their ages and needs, from the First Communion class on. The season ends with the Women's Retreat, when the numbers are generally increased by mothers or spouses-to-be.

The visitation of the poor and the lonely in the City itself, the catechetical instruction of the young, and all the helps that can possibly be given to the Missions, for the hungry and for the heart-rending appeals sponsored by charitable associations, are all financed, as far as possible, by the proceeds of school concerts, bazaars, garden parties, raffles, etc., to which the pupils love to contribute. The dear Italian children are excitable and joyous and generous by nature. A little one of five or six may be seen putting his or her lire into the slot outside the assembly hall, where he or she will soon giggle and jump for joy at seeing Pinocchio or Micky Mouse or such, projected on the screen, but the child is more delighted still that the money in the slot is going to "i bambini poveri." In these latter years a new gymnasium with all the necessary equipment has been built, and extra class-rooms added, according to the Ministry's recommendations and for health reasons.

There may be much greater and more universal need to-day than in Mother Taylor's time for all this charity, but there are also greater means, perhaps, at people's disposal than in her time. One thing is certain — her great heart would take advantage of them all, and so, in this as in everything, her Sisters strive to do as she would do were she among them now.

On 28th August, 1907, the third General Chapter of the Congregation was held at the Convent, Brentford. His Grace Archbishop Bourne of Westminster presided. The Mother-General (Mother M. Lucy) was re-elected, as were three of her former Council. Mother Aloysius Austin, who had died on August 18th, was replaced by Mother M. Dismas.

In this year a Home for crippled and invalid children at Buckingham Place, Brighton, was taken over by the Sisters at the invitation of the then Most Reverend Dr. Amigo, Bishop of Southwark. It had been run for many years by a kindly Catholic Matron, who by 1907 felt that the management, with all its responsibility, was getting beyond her now declining health, and so she retired happily from her very charitable work at St. Anne's Home (such was its name) when she realised it was being placed under the care of nuns. The situation of the Home was ideal for its purpose. The sea air had proved a powerful tonic for the very poor children drafted from the London slums by the Southwark Rescue Society and for other holiday children needing change during the summer. The dear Brighton people were prodigal of their charity in their welcome visits to the Home, in their many and generous donations and other gifts towards its renovation and decoration in these first years. The Community too were cheered at the thought that their Sisters in Portslade, only a mile away, were so near to help in many ways, the two chief ways being that Portslade undertook the whole of St. Anne's laundry weekly, and on its delivery day sent a generous basket of fresh fruit and vegetables from the Manor farm as a welcome gift for the children. Especially was this a blessing during World War I, when the Home opened its doors to a group of refugee Belgian children.

First Communion preparation and choir practices, lessons in the classroom, visits to the beach, outings and picnics on the Downs, children's plays in the Home, and visits to pantomines, especially at Christmas, were the happy variety for St. Anne's children down the years, until World War II changed the scene. One eventful day in 1940, a bomb hit the beautiful glass dome of St. Anne's, falling into the spacious day-room and carpeting its floor with the splintered glass. Fortunately all the children but one were away that day, and this poor child became the victim of the raid. The building was badly damaged, and considered unsafe for further habitation, so the Sisters and children were evacuated to Lourdes Hospital, Greenbank Road, Liverpool. Immediately an intense search began for a suitable house away from the danger zone, but not until the War was ended did the effort succeed, when a friend of the Congregation helped the Sisters to find the present property, known as "Claremont", in Lansdowne Road, Hove. The building had formerly been a boys' school, and had been occupied by the military during the

War, hence it may be concluded that the premises needed much renovation, but the faithful architect and his competent builder, notwithstanding the slow business of getting license from the Ministry, had the work completed in a few months, and St. Anne's Community and their children took happy possession again in 1948.

The altar in the new Chapel, the gift from our Roman House, has for its frontal a beautiful and valuable carving of the Last Supper — which fact caused difficulty and delay in procuring its release from the British Customs until it was explained that it was an unsolicited gift from a great friend to our Roman Sisters some years before.

In 1949, "Woodside", which adjoins Claremont property and grounds, was purchased and converted into a beautiful nursery and kindergarten unit for the "under-fives", at the request of the Home Office, whose authorities have lately sanctioned further alterations and helped with the costs.

In 1914 an already existing Home at Knolle Park, Woolton, Liverpool, was taken over by the Sisters. German nuns had managed this foundation magnificently for years, but owing to the War, were obliged to withdraw for political reasons. God has very visibly blessed the great work at Knolle Park down the years. The paternal interest of Liverpool's Archbishop and local clergy, from the days of Archbishop Whiteside, has been an inspiration and a grace both for the Sisters and their charges. Not a few of the Knolle Park girls have become zealous nuns in various Orders, and one of its chief joys is to welcome back its "old children", as holiday Sisters. Having had the advantages of a good primary and secondary education in the various Liverpool schools (especially the John Almond Secondary School, where our Sisters teach and where Sister M. St. Gertrude is the deputy Head), and having grown up in the kindly atmosphere of the Home itself, these dear children have every opportunity of being good, fervent Catholics and responsible citizens. The kindness of the Home Office and of the officers of the Liverpool Regional Hospital Board has been outstanding, and the beautiful new nursery, towards the expenses of which a generous contribution was made, is a monument to the State's appreciation of the dedicated work of Religious Communities all over the country.

In 1915, at the invitation of Archbishop Whiteside, a convalescent home for children was opened at Freshfield, Liverpool, a much-needed haven in the beautiful pineland near Formby, where the rich resin-scented air and daily recreation in the sandhills offered an unfailing panacea for the many ills that impeded a speedy return to health. The unwholesome atmosphere of a large city and the wartime rationing of food had combined to prevent the happy, healthy life of Liverpool's children. However, when World War I was over, the Home was still a convalescent retreat, or a sanatorium for many years, until the wonderfully successful fight against tuberculosis and its after-effects had won the victory in the medical field. Even still there was much for the Home to accomplish even when all fear of infection had disappeared.

At the end of World War II, actually in 1946, our devoted physician, Dr. Garry, invited an American friend of his to see Freshfield. This man was so thrilled at seeing what great work was being accomplished for the children, that through his great generosity the Sisters were enabled to build an entirely new Home, which, by the time it was completed in the late 1950's became known as "St. Joseph's Children's Hospital for Spastics," there being no longer need for its former type of children. Again in these latter years more improvements and adaptations have been accomplished, among them the building of a new convent for the Sisters, and the handing over of their former one to the nurses and staff, while extra annexes have been added to the Hospital itself, thus enabling its personnel to cope more proficiently with one of the most desperate needs of our time.

One cannot thank God sufficiently for all the work accomplished at Freshfield and the other Liverpool Houses since their beginning in Monsignor Nugent's and Archbishop Whiteside's days. We confidently hope that Mother Magdalen Taylor and all the great and devoted Sisters who had so activated the theories and the love of these great men for the poor, in the past, may in the future also be ever an inspiration and a challenge to those S.M.G.'s who continue the work of their venerated Foundress in her unwearying efforts to gain souls for Christ.

In March 1913, the Convent in Soho Square where Mother M. Magdalen had died thirteen years before, had been given up because of the expiry of its lease, and because the locality had become undesirable for its special work, it was considered best not to renew this. The girls were removed to the Home at Russell House, Streatham, as already stated. London's very intensive mission work was continued from the new Convent at Gordon Square, where the Sisters were asked to open a Hostel for Catholic students, business girls and others from many lands.

Some time later a second such hostel was opened at Cambridge Gardens, North Kensington, where a great apostolate among the poor was also carried on. Later on still, after World War II, the work of both hostels was transferred to Euston Square and Pembridge Square respectively, where freehold properties were purchased for this great and most necessary work in London. Cardinal Richard and Mothr Magdalen Taylor had realised years ago the crying need for this work in the great city of Paris, and so her Sisters knew that their Mother would have likewise sanctioned a similar apostolate in London. So taken was His Eminence, Cardinal Godfrey, with the saving work of these two Catholic Hostels in the Archdiocese that he begged for a third, and advised house-hunting in search of a suitable locality, "convenient for travel by bus or underground."

For weeks the "hunt" went on for the house that His Eminence had already named "St. Hilda's". Unbelievable as it may seem, the very week of the Cardinal's lamented death, our agent phoned to say the house adjoining our own Hostel in Pembridge Square was for sale. On examination it was found to be most suitable. When negotiations were completed, the workmen made a few openings in a partition wall, a few new doors, a week's decorative work, and the extension, "St. Hilda's", was a fact.

A united family atmosphere is sensed immediately in the London hostels. Happy and lasting friendships are forged between young people from countries as far apart as India and Ireland, or England, Africa and the United States. The French,

Spanish and Italians, however, are always in the majority. Nuns, missionary and otherwise, are frequent visitors at the Euston Square Hostel, and our Sisters in both houses remember our dear Mother Foundress' exhortation: "We can never be too kind to nuns who are away from their convents" — an experience gained in her own travelling years.

C h a p t e r 19.

WAR, WORK AND WORRY

The Fourth General Chapter of the Congregation, due in October 1914, was by permission from lawful authority postponed for a year because of the War. It was held in Brentford in October 1915, with the Right Reverend Monsignor Butt, Bishop of Cambysopolis, presiding. Although the War was raging, some delegates managed the journey from Rome.

The results of the election were: — Mother General: Mother M. Stanislaus, who, as a novice had been sent to Rome by the Foundress. She had Mother Magdalen as Novice-Mistress for most of her second year, and her First and Final Vows were made in the Roman House. The Assistant Mothers elected were Mother Agnes Raphael, (another Roman), Mother M. Rose Joseph, Mother M. Patricia and Mother M. de Pazzi. These Mothers also had known their Mother Foundress well, both as novices and as First Vow Sisters, and as all lived on to a ripe old age, they imparted to their younger contemporaries her beautiful prayerful spirit of charity, emanating from her union with God, and her utter devotedness to the Congregation He had called her to found.

Mother M. de Sales, who had been a Council Assistant since the Foundress' death in 1900, now became Superior of St. Mary's Convent, Youghal, Co. Cork. This nun was a great religious. To live the "common life" in its every perfect detail was her holy ambition. She was spoken of as a "golden superior", an "inspiring and motherly Novice-Mistress". Mother de Sales was the very soul of Community recreations, and while an Assistant Mother, her visitations of the various S.M.G. convents were looked forward to as refreshing periods for soul and body.

Mother M. de Sales, as well as her zealous, apostolic contemporary, Sister M. Immaculata, were relatives of Cashel's great Archbishop, His Grace the Most Reverend Dr. Croke, between whose sister and Mother M. Magdalen there had existed a sincere and mutually respected friendship. Another contemporary forming the "famous trio" was Sister M. de Britto, who became completely blind in her last years. She had been a local Sister Bursar all her life. When no longer able to follow Community life, she was assigned to live in "Mother Foundress' Room" in Brentford. The present writer remembers Sister M. de Britto telling her that she had "two innocent boasts" — one, that Mother Foundress had slept in her house in Ireland, and the second that she belonged to the O'Connor Don family. On being asked who this *Mr.* O'Connor Don was she replied: "Oh, child, you never call him 'Mr.', you say '*The* O'Connor Don!'" Another little incident, from which much edification resulted, is recalled. I was told by the Sister Infirmarian that Sister Superior said I should have charge of Sister M. de Britto's trays on Sundays (Sister had her meals in her room). "And," said the Infirmarian, "be sure that all is served beautifully and all on the tray spotless, especially the water glass, *because* Sister is blind." "A very reason to be careless," thought I to myself. What exquisite charity!

The year 1918 was fortunate in its flow of promising aspirants to the Congregation. Sister M. Thecla, so often mentioned in connection with the Foundress and the Roman House, had been home from Rome that summer, and during July and August she was in Ireland visiting the Irish Houses. Of course she made for her own dear home in the "Kingdom" of Kerry, where her cousin, the Most Reverend Dr. O'Sullivan, was Bishop. The happy result was the "Freedom of the City" for her apostolate. Sister returned to Roehampton, England, with seventeen aspirants, who naturally received a warm welcome. When they had been given the postulants' "cap and cape", and were admitted into the Community the evening after their arrival, they were soon greeted by a repeated, frightening air-raid signal, for which they were not prepared. As the Superior, with calm composure, came into the room to lead them to the appointed safety quarters downstairs, the senior postulant spoke out: "Look, girls, we'll all go home in the morning, this is no country to come to!" In the morning, however, after a good night's rest and a warm breakfast, the same child cried out to her postulant mistress: "Do you think, Sister, that Reverend Mother will send me home, because of my mood last night?" "Not at all," replied the Sister, "that was only an expression of surprised fear!" "Thank you, Sister," replied the postulant, "if she says 'Go', we'll all say 'No!'" It ended at that. Sister Maria Brendan (the postulant's name afterwards) used to relate this air-raid incident against herself in later years. She was a great nun, of a sweet personality, and beloved by her Community.

The Golden Jubilee of the Congregation was celebrated on the 24th September, 1919, and was an event of great rejoicing in the Houses everywhere.

In the January of 1922, the S.M.G. Sisters took on the management of Rathdrum Workhouse in the Archdiocese of Dublin — a work of great charity which they knew their beloved Foundress would be glad to have accepted. Since the abolition of the work-house system in Ireland, this Institution developed into St. Colman's District Hospital, with sanatorium attached. Later on down the years, the victory in the war against tuber-colosis having been won in Ireland as elsewhere, the new Sanatorium has been fitted out to become a happy home for aged ladies, who live out their last years in this peaceful countryside spot, enriched as it is by the balmy heath and gorse-scented breezes from the Wicklow hills.

In October 1922, the Fifth General Chapter was held, when Mother M. Rose Joseph was unanimously elected Mother-General, with Mother M. Stanislaus, Mother Magdalen Aimée, Mother M. Lucy and Mother M. Prisca as Councillors.

In this year, the Sisters made for the West of England at the invitation of the Most Reverend Dr. Burton, Bishop of Clifton, who authorized the Very Reverend Canon Lee to negotiate. Two foundations were made almost simultaneously. The Sisters took on teaching and parish work at Swindon, Wiltshire. School-work and its attendant apostolic labours for souls were also allotted to the Sisters in Clifton, Bristol, where a wide field was already over-ripe for the harvest, and where the saintly

Mother Margaret Hallahan had sown the seed in her zealous past.

In 1926 a hospital also was opened in Clifton, at Upper Byron Place, to the great delight of Dr. Burton. As well as the Sister-nurses, other Sisters were sent, who visited in the parish, took on the instruction of converts, looked after the poor, the lonely and the lapsed. This Catholic hospital in Clifton, which was named "St. Mary's", was a source of great joy to Canon Lee as well as to the Bishop. As in Mother Foundress' time, no distinction in creed or class was made among the patients, and soon the dear people of Bristol and the surroundings began to understand the vocation of Sisters to be a total dedication of their lives to God and to humanity.

Dr. Burton's decease in 1931 was deeply lamented, not only by his clergy and people, but by all Churchmen in general, for they knew the extent of his Lordship's charity, as well as of his richly-cutivated, yet humble mind and his sturdy North-country outspoken mode of expression, when the need for truth or justice demanded it.

> "A man's reach should exceed his grasp,
> Or what's a Heaven for?"

exclaims the Poet. This was Dr. Burton's axiom all his life, as it was understood by his clergy, his people and by all whom he loved in their united, if uphill ascent to God.

The Sixth General Chapter of the Congregation had been held in Brentford in 1929. The very Reverend Canon Dunford presided for the Archbishop. The Mother-General and two of her former Councillors were re-elected, the other two being re-placed by Mother M. Petrus, the late Novice-Mistress, and Mother Stanislaus Mary, an experienced local Superior.

It was during this régime that a convent was opened at Hayes, Middlesex, when the Sisters took charge of the parish elementary school, and began their usual apostolate in this busy industrial town, which boasts of a great Catholic population. The Claretian Fathers were "fathers" indeed to the new Community, and proved an inspiring example, as they still are, in their zeal for souls and in their showing forth the charity of Christ to their parish flock. As this memoir is being written, it is well to say that further plans are being contemplated for

P

Hayes schools, as for many others, to bring them into line with the ever-changing demands of the Ministry of Education and Science.

The Seventh General Chapter was held at Brentford on October 3rd, 1936, and was presided over by His Grace, Archbishop Hinsley of Westminster, the future simple, outspoken Cardinal of World War II years, and a great friend of the Congregation, especially of the Roman Community. For the first time since the Foundress' death in 1900, all the elected members were new, although long experienced in the religious life and in directing Communities. Mother M. Angelis was elected Mother-General, her four Assistants being Mother M. Germanus, who had been Bursar-General as well as local Superior on and off, Mother M. Thoma, who had been local Superior, as had been Mother M. Martha also, and Mother M. Anastasia, who had been a nursing Sister. These were they destined by God to tide the Congregation through the disastrous, devastating years of World War II. Except for Mother M. Anastasia, all had known the Foundress in their young years, and had imbibed her spirit of lowliness, charity, and utter devotedness to her Tabernacled Lord, Who alone was to support and encourage them in the years ahead.

Bishop Burton of Clifton was succeeded by Bishop Lee, who ruled the Diocese from 1932 to 1948. The new Bishop, who was all out for God and souls, had a thorough knowledge of the work and needs of the Diocese and of the loss it had incurred in the death of its late beloved Bishop and true father; he had resolved, therefore, that Clifton should not take the least step downwards from the high "reach" of its former Bishop.

In 1937, a Home for mentally deficient girls was opened at Weston-super-Mare by the Poor Servants of the Mother of God. The Congregation purchased a most adaptable house named Totterdown Hall, situated in its own spacious grounds. The work, i.e. the training of these mentally deficient and otherwise handicapped or irresponsible girls in need of care and protection — a work most dear to the great heart of their Foundress — brought, and still brings, untold blessings to Totterdown. Being a good distance from the Parish Church, the Chapel was opened to the public almost immmediately. The Sisters took on the visitation of the poor; lapsed Catholics were sought out; catechetical classes were formed at the Convent for the instruction of converts, and altogether a wonderful and ever-increasing apostolate grew, with the kindly co-operation of the clergy and people, with the happy result that at present, after almost 30 years, an extra chapel of ease will soon be necessary. This continual interest and charity of the priests and people of Totterdown and Weston towards the Sisters and their protégés in the parish, and to the Home in particular, has been truly Christian and deserving of God's best blessings for themselves and their families for all time.

Phenomenal it is that from the Foundress' day and her first freehold purchase at Brentford, the very best of the Congregation's houses and adjoining lands have been allotted to these homes for the aged and for the poor, the handicapped and the deprived, and to those who never have known the joys of happy childhood, as little Fanny Taylor knew them in her country village at Stoke Rochford.

Another convent was opened in 1937, in Chippenham, Wiltshire, where the Bishop wished the Sisters to start a school, which had first to be built, and after a certain period of experiment was classed as "Private Efficient". Catholic children were in the majority, but non-Catholic mothers also asked that theirs too might be accepted. After a certain number of years, however, and as the Catholic attendance increased, the decision was made with his Lordship, Dr. Rudderham, the Bishop of Clifton, to make it entirely Catholic, in view of its future recognition as a Catholic state-aided elementary school. Extra class-rooms and other necessary apartments were added to bring the whole into line with the Ministry's requirements. The kindness and generosity of the Parish Priest, Very Reverend Canon Kelleher, during this transition period will never be forgotten. Finally the Chippenham school began as a recognized state-aided elementary school. At the earnest request of many non-Catholic parents, the private school was continued for some years longer in another building, nearer the Convent, until, for lack of the necessary staff, it had to be closed in 1968, to the great sorrow of many fathers, mothers and children. Be it said to the private school's credit that it was instrumental in laying the foundation of solid Catholic training for the children of Chippenham, as well as in creating a healthy and unbigoted atmosphere between the different denominations.

In 1939 a school was opened in Gloucester, also at Dr. Lee's request. Parish visiting and all it involved went hand in hand, and God's very visible blessings attended the wide apostolate undertaken in this city. Very Reverend Canon Roche, the parish priest, with his assistants, proved to be real friends and co-operators. The Sisters teach in the parish schools, to which they set out daily, while the private school has held its own down the years, and the children, both in the catechetical and secular examinations, have done remarkably well. Instruction classes for converts have been regularly held at the Convent, and, if the walls of the Church and of the Convent Chapel could speak, mysteries of grace would be revealed as the results of God's blessings on the work of the clergy and the Sisters.

Gloucester's beautiful pre-Reformation Cathedral attracts many tourists and Churchmen to the city, especially if the latter have the building of a church or a cathedral in mind. Such was the case some years ago, when His Lordship of Galway visited Gloucester. The S.M.G. Sisters of St. Michael's Convent, Gloucester, attributed to St. Michael the joy they experienced when Dr. Michael Brown called on the Community when visiting Gloucester to contemplate various aspects of the Cathedral's architecture, having had at the time his own now beautifully-finished masterpiece in view.

In 1939 also, a house was purchased at Cheltenham, intended for hospital work, but owing to World War II, the necessary alterations and extensions could not be undertaken. Rather than abandon the project, however, it was opened as a home for the aged in 1940, and served a very useful and charitable purpose until 1963, when its residents moved to Corston, near Bath, in Somerset.

The history of Corston has variety in its content. The property was purchased at the outbreak of World War II, when it was decided for safety's sake to remove the Novitiate from the London area. So in the month of October, 1940, the novices, with full authorization from Rome, set out with their Novice-Mistress and other responsible personnel for their temporary

Novitiate. The Reverend Father Collins, S.J., with his Provincial's permission, accompanied the party, to act as their chaplain and spiritual Father. The kindness and concern of the dear aged, but yet very alert Father were an encouragement and a great spiritual support to all concerned.

In 1942, danger seemed less threatening, and the novices, with all in charge, returned to Roehampton. On March 25th of that year the house at Corston was opened as a private hospital. God Himself seemed to be managing the affair, for soon afterwards St. Mary's Hospital, Clifton, was itself severely damaged during an air-raid, exactly as a surgical operation was being performed. As a consequence of this raid, the patients were all removed to Corston until such time as the damages at St. Mary's could be fully repaired. It is an interesting detail at this point to relate that on that very night in far-away Cutigliano, by the Sestione river, Tuscany, Italy, where the Florence S.M.G. Sisters, at the end of the school year, were having a few weeks' change from the heat of the city, they heard of the raid. The B.B.C. "Parla Londra", whose real name of course we did not know, announced the bombing of the Clifton hospital, saying that the surgeon was encouraged by the Matron, "Suor Luigi Gonzaga", to get the unconscious patient, the surgical apparatus and all else necessary downstairs to safer quarters. This was done with the help of another doctor and some Sisters, and the operation was a confirmed success even in candle-light!

On a never-to-be-forgotten night in 1944, the young Community of Maryfield Novitiate itself was awakened by the well-known air-raid siren, and the Convent had its first bomb in a matter of seconds. Luckily it was seen to that all the younger members had "taken cover" in good time, and the more responsible and courageous got active to save all they could from the flames — the incendiary bombs having started a big fire. The Jesuit Fathers and Community from Manresa House across the way came in haste, and using every possible receptacle from a glass to a pail or hose, poured water on the threatening flames from every corner of the house, while others hurriedly pushed or threw furniture and anything that could be saved on to the lawn on one side, or the terrace on the other, so that by dawn the whole place presented a sorry sight, inside and out. The priests and people of Roehampton showed the full extent of their charity and sympathy on that dreadful night. Neighbours came with their cars and taxis to take some of the aged and a few patients to St. Mary's Convent in the village — in fact one patient had to be taken by ambulance. Miraculously, the beautiful Chapel was untouched, and — greatest blessing of all — no lives were lost.

The wise decision of next day was acted upon promptly. The novices, postulants, and all who had to do with them set out as soon as possible to a house in Chew Magna, in the West, and remained there until the end of the War. Chew Magna had been rented "pro tem" for the transfer of Clifton patients after the raid on St. Mary's Hospital, until Corston was ready to receive them. Corston Hospital later on was converted into a beautiful Home for the aged, and at the present time many further facilities are being planned: a new chapel and convent, are being built and the sleeping and recreation quarters for the staff are being renewed. Maryfield, in its safest quarters was occupied by some Sisters whose duties held them there right on to the end of the War. When the Chew Magna party returned, as well as the novices and postulants from Ireland, who had entered there and whose Clothing Ceremony had been authorized to take place at Carrigtwohill during the War, there was a grand and happy re-union when the first Vow Ceremony was celebrated in Maryfield on July 22nd, 1945.

Certainly the Head Superiors of the Seventh General Chapter of 1936 were destined to govern and to administrate during a very trying period of years. Their fortitude, their calm, united charity and their ever-increasing trust in God in the face of calamity were contagious, and could only have resulted from their deep spirit of prayer and union with God, from their devotion to our Eucharistic Lord and to His Virgin Mother, their Mistress and Queen. It was their lot to see bombed out of action the hospitals at Liverpool and Clifton, the Children's Home at Buckingham Place, Brighton, and the General Novitiate at Roehampton. Yet by 1950, all the reconstruction work had been satisfactorily completed, or the houses replaced, as was the case with Paul Street and St. Anne's Home. And while all this work was in progress, their successors did not hesitate when asked in 1948 to operate temporarily a home for poor children at Aberdour in the Archdiocese of Edinburgh. Later on, a temporary Girls' Home was founded in what was Balnakiel House at Galashiels in Selkirkshire. A completely new building for the Home was built later on.

The then Archbishop of Edinburgh showed his paternal interest in this saving work from the beginning, and His Grace's visits to the Home were always much appreciated by the Community and their dear protégés. The girls had taught the budgerigar to chirp "Dr. Gordon Joseph Gray", which it did most clearly. It is to be assumed that after Rome's grand ceremony in the year 1969, the phrase will be: "His Eminence, Gordon Joseph Cardinal Gray."

In 1940 the Sisters were invited by Bishop Parker of the Northampton Diocese to face eastward and open a convent at Chesham in Buckinghamshire, with a view to beginning school work there. This invitation they accepted, and in 1941 was opened a small private school. Since then the number of Catholic children has grown steadily. Recently this private school has been reorganized as "Efficient", and the Schools' Commission expect full recognition as a State-aided Catholic school by 1970 or 1971.

The Brentford school children, with the Sisters in charge, had to evacuate to three places in the Northampton Diocese in September, 1939, when war was imminent. Being a goodly crowd, the children had to be divided between Chalfont St. Giles, Coleshill and Chesham. The S.M.G. Sisters thus got to know the clergy and people, and were no strangers when they settled permanently in the Diocese. Dr. Parker gave another call in 1946, this time to Beccles in Suffolk, where a foundation was taken over from the Servite Sisters, who were leaving. A party of three S.M.G. Sisters took on the parish school of St. Benet's, while others undertook work in the private school. By 1963 the numbers in St. Mary's (the private school) had much diminished, and, with the Bishop's consent, a home for poor children replaced it. These children, except the under-fives, attend the parish school, while their Home is a really happy "home" conducted by other Sisters who have been trained for child care and who are doing a truly great saving work with these dear deprived children.

The people of Beccles have been and are still most generous in their gifts to the Home, and one much valued present was a minibus for the children's use.

The Benedictine Fathers who work the parish have been, from the beginning, kindness itself to the Sisters. Their interest and unfailing co-operation have been an invaluable support to the Community. It is a happy memory for the S.M.G. Sisters that when the English Benedictines were negotiating their Order's business in Rome, and Mother Magdalen Taylor, ful-filling the earnest wish of Leo XIII, had already founded her Convent in Piazza di Spagna, the Fathers lived for a while in what was then the "extern quarters" of the future Convent. Dr. Hedley, Bishop of Newport (the famous Dom Cuthbert of Ampleforth) and his great O.S.B. brother, Dom Aidan of Downside, the future Cardinal, were until their deaths personal friends of the Congregation founded by Mother Taylor. Bishop Hedley, who outlived her by fifteen years, loved, when in Rome on diocesan business, to celebrate Mass at the Shrine of Regina Prophetarum. Abbot Gasquet, called to Rome in 1907 to be President of the Vulgate Commission, was created Cardinal in 1914, and later became Cardinal Protector of the Congregation founded by his former friend. Even after being created a Prince of the Church, His Eminence would announce himself to the Sister at the telephone as "Dom Aidan speaking". His death in 1929 was much and universally lamented, as that of a great Cardinal and a loyal Churchman. This greatness and loyalty were enriched by that spirit of humility, meekness and sincerity which St. Benedict inherited from his Divine Exemplar and bequeathed to his "ever-ancient, ever-new" Monastic Order.

C h a p t e r   20.

S.M.G.'s IN THE NEW WORLD

The Eighth General Chapter of the Poor Servants of the Mother of God, postponed because of World War II, was held at Maryfield, Roehampton, on October 3rd, 1945, and presided over by His Grace, Archbishop Amigo of Southwark. The result was: Mother General: Mother Anne Xavier, (a Roman since Mother Foundress' day), Mother M. Germanus (re-elected), Mother Alcantara, Mother M. Aloysia and Mother M. Xavier as the Mothers Assistant. His Grace of Southwark, on seeing the Maryfield war-damage scene, remarked jokingly: "I came from my ruined Cathedral to see all that Hitler had managed here!"

In 1947 the S.M.G. Congregation heard of its first foundation in the New World. For some time before, evidently, something by way of a small Catholic hospital or nursing home had been a need in North Carolina, but no particular location was named. Mother M. Alcantara, meanwhile, on the other side of the Atlantic, had authority from her Mother General to send occasional gifts in money to a Father Rohrbacher of the Diocese of Raleigh, whose needs were many in his efforts to spread Christ's Kingdom by building a church in some "no-priest-land" in the Diocese. Father, in his letters to his benefactress, expressed his desire for Sisters, and got the authorization and blessing of his Bishop on the project. The nuns, who knew that the great aim of their Foundress was to introduce our Tabernacled Lord into as many places as she could in the England of the Reformation and further afield in time, willingly assented. How gladly, they thought, would Mother Magdalen have come to such a needy place, set up a convent and its tabernacle to in-

241

troduce their Sacramental Lord to a people who had never known Him, or whose emigrant ancestors, having known Him once, lost, in the haze of history, their faith in, and their true vision of, their Eucharistic Lord.

Having thus had the blessing and generous authorization of Bishop Waters, and all else being in order, one of the Mothers Assistant (Mother M. Xavier) was sent with Sister M. Patrice, a local Superior and an experienced S.R.N., to investigate and see what could be done with the help of God's grace in the spiritual uplifting of the people of the South. They met the Bishop on their arrival, and he saw to it that they were conducted all round the Diocese, and they were free to choose the location. The two travellers returned to England and gave their report in favour of the undertaking, and the decision was made for the foundation (High Point) in North Carolina.

Not knowing what was in store, and foreseeing, perhaps, a long term of house-hunting on their arrival in the vast Diocese, what a pleasant surprise and what a pointer to the Will of God, when, on the morning of November 16th, 1947, as four Sisters were about to get into the taxi that waited to take them to Waterloo, en route for Southampton to take ship for New York, and the whole community assembled to bid them "God speed", a cablegram was handed in to Mother General marked "Western Union". It read: "House to rent, are you interested?" The prepaid reply was an immediate: "Yes, negotiate immediately." The four pioneers were overjoyed! They were: Sister M. Patrice, Sister M. Anne Christina, Sister M. Assumption and Sister Maria Benigus, all fully-trained S.R.N.'s. The cablegram was a consolation, and the idea of "vacant possession" and of being handed the keys by the Reverend Father McMillan was also comforting. But on their arrival at "Pennybyrn" in High Point, what was their surprise to find that their future Pastor and many of his kind parishioners, and even his non-Catholic friends had assembled to meet them and to introduce them to their already prepared mission home. It was anything but "vacant possession!" The keys were already in the doors. Father McMillan and his generous friends had cleaned the rooms from attic to basement. Beds were made, kitchen utensils all in place and the first meal almost ready. Within a few days the little

242

Chapel was set up, the whole house blessed, and the Bishop gave leave for the first Mass and the reservation of the Blessed Sacrament. He himself paid a visit to "Pennybyrn" within the week, and also "paid" down a goodly sum of dollars to help towards the equipment of the Nursing Home. Monsignor Sugrue of Chicage, Sister M. Patrice's cousin, furnished the Chapel, even to detail, and sent financial aid as well. The Chicago Mission Club sent donations, Sisters' friends in the U.S.A. were most generous, and our Mothers, in their American travels, sent us all their gifts in dollars. Father Dick Ryan (Sister M. Richard's and Sister M. Catherina's brother) sent many donations from his California Parish. The following is an excerpt from a letter which accompanied a generous donation sent in December 1947: "I can well imagine how lost you are and how strange all seems to you. But the work is wonderful, and nothing breaks down prejudice so powerfully as the presence of Sisters in a community. The first few years will undoubtedly be a struggle, but ten years from now will certainly see a great change. It is a great thrill doing pioneer work." And later — "Doing it for the love of God means so much. It is a great bracer' — to do it for God."

Another letter of Monsignor Sugrue to the Superior and Sisters of the little Community at Maryfield, for their first Christmas in America, was consoling. It read: "I was very happy to know you were having Midnight Mass in your own little Chapel — to have Bethlehem among you on your first Christmas night in a strange land! How blessed we are with the Faith and Holy Mass... At my Midnight Mass I asked Him to keep you all as united in spirit and in love as was the Holy Family at Bethlehem. With faith, love, trust in God's Providence and Our Lady's intercession, fidelity to your Holy Rule and charity, God will bless and prosper your work and sanctify each of you. Pope Pius X once said: 'Show me the Religious who keeps his Rule perfectly and I will canonize him while he is yet alive.' It is your sure way to Heaven if kept in the spirit of charity... I know that each one will do her part to lay the foundation deep and strong and contribute her share to charity."

On re-reading this letter in 1969, one has to say to oneself: "Mother Magdalen Taylor could not have been more emphatic in her prayers and efforts for her dear children, exiled for God's greater glory, to the first American cradle of the Congregation in High Point.

Before accepting patients, it was necessary to have "Maryfield Incorporated" registered in Raleigh in November 1947, and the first patient was admitted on December 12th. The Maryfield Nursing Home with its capacity for 22 patients was licensed by the North Carolina State Board of Health in 1952.

In the meantime, minds were busy. A fine brick-built garage on the grounds was converted into a convent, and the Sisters had but to cross a few yards to the Chapel each morning. As the number of patients increased, and the work became more generally known, the people grew more and more friendly and helpful. They saw a small community of Sisters entirely devoted to Christ in His sick members, there was no attempt at proselytising, as they had first thought there would be, and soon the Sisters were able to employ local help, which was a great asset for truthful propaganda. By hard work and economy, and help from the Bank, the heretofore rented house, "Pennybyrn", and the surrounding grounds were purchased and named "Maryfield Nursing Home." It had now become well known as a place where patients were sure of first-class care and devoted and loving attention.

As time went on, more and yet more applications had to be refused for want of room, and the question of extending the building was raised. This, however, was not considered the best line of action from the point of view of expenses. Finally in 1963 it was decided to form a local Advisory Council to help and advise the Sisters, who on their part had consulted the North Carolina Medical Care Commission as to whether federal funds would be available for the building of a new nursing home. The answer was an encouraging "Yes", if matching funds were possible. So with full permission from Head Superiors and from local and legal authorities, an Advisory Council was formed with Mr. Leo J. Heer as its first Chairman. To his great influence and fine personality the great success of the fund-raising campaign was principally due. What with the results of the Drive, plus an equal amount in federal aid, added to individual and collective donations from personal friends, the new nursing home rose rapidly. The one-storey building contained a beautiful Chapel at the main entrance, sixty beds in private and semi-private rooms; the living-room, laundry, kitchen, heating and air-conditioning were planned on a large scale to facilitate a further extension later and save expense, as prices were rising daily, so another fifty-five bed addition is foreseen in the near future. The new Nursing Home Chapel is a gem, and was furnished by Mrs. M. H. Barthmaier and family, just as Monsignor Sugrue had been the benefactor of the first one in 1947, except that Mr. and Mrs. Settlemyre gave the beautiful Tabernacle.

The new Home was blessed and opened on November 30th, 1965, by Bishop McLaughlin, who also dedicated the new Chapel, in the absence of Bishop Waters. The beautifully-carved Italian wooden Stations of the Cross were erected a few days later by Bishop Waters himself.

The first Nursing Home is now the Sisters' Convent, with its little Chapel fitted out to comply with the requirements of Vatican II. When the Sisters or any of the patients or staff pass from the Home to the Convent, or vice versa, they find the Blessed Sacrament in both places, while it is consoling in the Nursing Home Chapel to see the patients wheeled in to daily Mass and to receive their Sacramental Lord, and to Catholic and non-Catholic alike the readings of the Epistles and Gospels are heard on loud-speakers in every department.

God has certainly blessed the undertaking in the twenty-two years of its existence. Spiritually and materially has He blessed it in the kindly and inspiring, fatherly interest of its Bishop, in the ever-ready help and full co-operation of its pastors, in their devotedness to the spiritual needs of the patients, and in the unity that exists between the Sisters and their nursing and domestic staffs.

What shall we say of the people of High Point? Words would fail to express the Sisters' gratitude to the friends God sent them. Since the arrival of the S.M.G.'s in 1947, the Price and Thomas families have been most generous in their donations and their practical help in many other ways. The Sisters owe them a deep debt of gratitude and they will be always remembered in their prayers. Another great benefactor was Mrs. McKinley Bryan of Greensboro, and Mr. Amos R. Kearns of High Point. There are others too numerous to mention, but all our benefactors and friends are prayed for daily and by obligation when we are assembled in prayer in our every Chapel in every land; and our Extraordinary Benefactors' names are archived, to be read in all the refectories of the Congregation on New Year's Day.

A great service was rendered to the Sisters also by dear Sister Grace Electa, O.P., who for a great many years met the new S.M.G. Sisters when they arrived in New York, gave them hospitality and sent them off safely to the South, where she is often welcomed as a visitor.

The Sisters in High Point, as elsewhere, visit the poor, the lonely and the deprived, feed and clothe the children of the poor, and do all that their Mother Foundress did in her day to alleviate every form of human suffering. "What would that great lover of mankind do to-day, were she living in this sad, war-torn, confused world?" the Sisters ask themselves, and try to do likewise, as they pray for and seek the good of all God's children.

In 1948, when as yet the pioneer Sisters had scarcely found their bearings in High Point, a second foundation was offered in Norton, Virginia. An already existing hospital was for sale, and the Reverend Father Dean, of the Glenmary Missionaries, was hoping and praying that the High Point Sisters might consider its purchase, so he came and made his sad case known to the High Point Superior, who in turn consulted her Head Superiors, who, despite all their post-War anxieties, trusted God and decided to send another group of nursing Sisters to this spiritually impoverished land. The pioneers were Sister M. Colette, Sister Rose Carmel, Sister Anne Christina (transferred from High Point), Sister M. Fintan, Sister M. St. Finian and Sister Agnes Concepta. The Glenmary Fathers from Cincinnati, Ohio, work the parish. The Catholic population was, and still is very small. There is as yet no Catholic school, but there is great hope for the future. Certainly the presence of the Sisters has had an impact on the people. At their first coming, they met with prejudice and much ill-will as "Papists". The neighbouring

State school-children were frightened and ran away at the sight of them, never having seen nuns before. But the Sisters began to pray and to work. In spite of much opposition to the Catholic possession of a Hospital at the beginning, some of its former non-Catholic doctors and nurses were loyal and remained on under the new régime. Soon patients became numerous, and gradually both the white and coloured of Norton realized that they were being humanly treated.

The town of Norton is situated near the great Appalacian chain of mountains, in the heights and on the slopes of which are the numerous coal belts of the region. As a natural consequence, mining has been the principal occupation of the working population for generations. If the wealthy mine-owners live in the great cities, as do the Union Executives, many of both categories are proud to say that their emigrant ancestors were also miners, but by thrift, economy and purposeful, intelligent foresight, they saw to it that their children fared better.

The Baptist church has had a great hold in this part of the U.S.A., and yet Irish and Italian names predominate. The reason given is that when the first Catholic emigrants arrived from Ireland, Italy or Spain in New York or Boston, Catholic priests were already there, but the Irish emigrants in the South, who dreaded the English word "Church" or "Kirk", and had no priests, sought the "Chapel" which was the Baptist place of worship. Likewise the Italian word "Cappella" won the Italians, who also were not at all familiar with the English language. The word "Cappella" means Chapel. However, as time went on, all denominations clung to the Bible, and the Epistles of St. Paul have worked wonders. Priests from Ireland and from the Continent are fairly numerous in this part. Its late Bishop Swint built many new Churches. His Excellency, and his co-adjutor Bishop McDonald were most kind to the Norton Sisters, and much interested in their charitable work. Their present Bishop, Most Reverend Dr. Hodges, is a true father and friend. When His Excellency visited the Roman Convent, unannounced, one Saturday morning during Vatican II, the Sisters were all busy at the various charges (there being no school on Saturday). His Excellency forbade them to remove their blue aprons, and promised them that he would report to the Norton Community how he found them all working. He did not forget to mark his visit by a generous gift.

So the Norton Community has flourished. Its spiritual well-being, with the help of Divine Grace and the light of the Holy Spirit, will grow "from strength to strength" in this precious period of Renewal. With their Eucharistic Lord dwelling with them in the beautiful Chapel, their daily Mass when He comes to be their life-giving Force, and by which He fortifies them with grace for their work among the poor and suffering patients, the Sisters will be His witnesses to all with whom they come in contact. Theirs is a General Hospital with a maternity unit, a children's ward and wards for white and coloured together, without distinction and of all ages.

Their apostolate outside the Hospital goes on apace. The poor, the lonely, those who are ignorant of God and His Holy Mother are their friends, who no longer fear their influence. The Sisters teach the people how to pray, to trust God in their every trial, and many souls have come back to Him whom they call the "God of their fathers." The Sisters also help in the "A.W.A.R.E." Association, which aims at the social, economic and spiritual betterment of Norton and of Wise County. The letters spell: "Appalachian & Wise Association for Rehabilitation and Education" — a completely voluntary and charitable body of workers.

The Glenmary Fathers are ever alert on the trail for souls, and are welcome in every home. Many conversions have been the fruit of their labours, and could the walls of the Hospital relate their story, the chapters would be many. Enough that these are written, nay "engraved" on the Sacred Heart of the Son of God, whose death was the price of the victory over Satan and sin, and whose glorious Resurrection proved the truth and power of the Blessed Trinity for all time.

The Norton Hospital, as well as the nun's Chapel, were extended to great advantage some years ago, and the latter has again been re-modelled to comply with the liturgical requirements of Vatican II. As this story of Norton is being written, however, there is need for more and more space. Head Superiors, like their Mother Foundress before them, are not afraid of risks. Her advice and practice were ever successful: she would "knock at the door of the Bank of God," and the Divine Teller always provided. Cardinal Manning advised Mother Magdalen in the early days of the foundation "to knock at the Tabernacle" in every need. How well she knocked, and how often! Spiritual needs for herself, her Sisters and souls made her knock persistently, and with regard to material needs, we know from a study of her practical life how fully God supplied them and how well and wisely she did her share in the work!

In the March of 1961, a further call came while Superiors from England were on the visitation of High Point and Norton convents. This time it was from Philadelphia, from a certain pastor, Reverend Father Brennan of Holy Spirit Church, who needed Sisters for a new grade school which was in the process of being built. The site for a new convent was conveniently placed, but the school had to be completed first. Father Brennan's pleading words to the visiting Superiors were: "It breaks my heart to see hundreds of our Catholic children being bussed off each morning to the State school." He said that our Sisters were recommended by the Philadelphia Jesuits, who had given the annual Retreats in the Southern houses for the past 18 years. It was seen that the need was great, nevertheless a few more years passed before the final decision was made, in spite of the frequency of Father Brennan's pathetic letters. The haunting thought that hundreds of children of Irish and Italian descent, and therefore Catholic, were faced with the positive danger of losing the Faith defeated every other consideration, however, and soon the pioneer teaching Sisters were en route for Philadelphia. They were Sister M. St. Coleman, of long teaching experience, Sister M. Emmanuel, Sister M. Agnes Paul, and Sister M. Augustine, who was "pro tem." Five other teaching Sisters were sent later. The Sisters of St. Joseph of Chestnut Hill, whose gracious kindness will never be forgotten, gave the S.M.G. Sisters hospitality at their Stella Maris Convent for some weeks, as the foundation stone of their future house had not yet been laid. Soon, however, with the help of their Pastor and dear Sister Grace Electa, they were able to get a vacant house which they fixed up, even to preparing the cellar for a Community feast-day! Leo XIII's advice to Mother Magdalen Taylor in encouraging her to open a house in Piazza di Spagna:

"Begin in a humble way" was certainly the "had-to-be" method in Philadelphia in the beginning. The Sisters' courage could not fail when they experienced the warm and enthusiastic welcome and blessing of His Eminence Cardinal Krol and of Father Brennan and his assistant priest, Father Dominic Chiaravalle. The people of the parish, too, were all out to help them. Mother M. Lalande, of the Sisters Servants of the Immaculate Heart of Mary and the Mother Administrator of their schools, remained many weeks with the Sisters to help them and initiate them into the American system of keeping school registers, records, and the various workings of the school curriculum. The Sisters owe their first year's success with the pupils entirely to Mother M. Lalande's sisterly, correct and unselfish supervision of means and methods.

Among the many other friends too numerous to mention are Mother Sylvester of the Franciscan Missionaries of the Immaculate Conception, Mrs. Tolomeo, President of the Women's Club, and the neighbours of their first house at 17th Street, including Mrs. Golding, who still befriends the Sisters. All our friends and benefactors everywhere, be they living or deceased, have their place in our daily prayers, wherever our Communities are.

The S.M.G.'s were first introduced to American benevolence during World War II, when the Allies entered Rome on the memorable 4th June, 1944, without any of the disastrous fighting attendant on the taking of other European cities, the whole Christian world rejoiced. Winston Churchill called it "a memorable event," and President Roosevelt rejoiced, and referred to Rome as having "the longest history of all cities." What a relieving joy for the Sisters of Piazza di Spagna! Under Vatican protection, owing to the blessing of the Vatican Treaty, and a telegram from Rome that read: "Remain where you are," the Sisters were able to share and help in the sorrows of their dear Italian friends all through the War period, and their school functioned fully all those years. The American and British officers and soldiers were kindness and generosity personified, and are remembered even to this day by correspondence and prayer.

By July the Allies were closing in on Tuscany from every side. The beautiful medieval bridges (with the exception of the

Ponte Vecchio) had been destroyed by the retreating enemy, but Allied engineers with amazing speed spanned the Arno with their iron replacements, and Florence was occupied fully within a few days. The first British press-men were introduced to the Sisters by an Italian doctor friend. They were welcomed as brothers, and through them, our nuns in England got news of our safety, notwithstanding the terrible days of dread before the occupation of the much damaged city. In a few days the Americans came in numbers. They too were introduced to the Sisters, and came to the Convent almost immediately. After the press-men left us, we discovered, two other officers came to fasten to our Convent door a notice signed: "By order of General Mark Clark," which read: "Billeting forbidden in this Institution." The chaplain in chief, Colonel Father Ryan, General Sullivan, the Quarter-Master General, and many, many Americans showed the Sisters extraordinary kindness. A great Christmas feast was given to displaced Polish and other Allied children in the Convent in 1944, even the English and American officers, nurses and others came to wait upon and entertain the children. From October especially until Christmas, great friendships were forged between the Italians and the Allies. Many of the students of the Cambridge Certificate student classes from the Sisters' school were used as interpreters in the various Allied offices, and even many officers' brides were chosen from among them. Mother Magdalen must have rejoiced over it all, and that her great Downside friend, Abbot, and later Cardinal Gasquet, was represented by his spiritual brother from Downside in the person of the Reverend Vincent Cavanagh, O.S.B. As a resident British Army Chaplain in Florence during the long occupation of the city, he gave the Sisters most helpful spiritual conferences in their Chapel, which helped them very much in a time of great strain.

From the above rather lengthy preamble describing the Allied landing in Rome and Florence towards the end of World War II, it will be easily understood how glad the Congregation of the Poor Servants of the Mother of God was to accept the American invitation in 1947, and to extend its apostolate to this kindly land whose people, mindful of their own suffering, exiled or emigrant ancestors, have grown into a nation deserving of

God's blessing in its effort to aid the poor, to smash oppression, and to help every people towards peace and justice. It was not for nothing that George Washington chose "In God we trust" as the U.S.A. motto.

An end-up to our American story, must consist of a tribute of deep gratitude to our present Chairman, Mr. Holt McPherson — Editor of the High Point Enterprise who, in his famous "Good Afternoon" column, has publicised every important event that helps our Hospital in its onward march for good.

C h a p t e r   21.

"THAT IRELAND"

The Ninth General Chapter and elections were held at Maryfield on October 3rd, 1952, the Archbishop of Southwark, Most Reverend Dr. Cowderoy, presiding. The results, as in 1936, were a completely new group, except for one. They were: Mother M. Geraldine, Mother M. Lewis, Mother M. St. John, Mother M. Aloysia (re-elected) and Mother M. Agnes Joseph. All had been trained by those who had known Mother Magdalen Taylor, or had been trained by those who did know her, and who had passed on her spirit. Even among the delegates to this Chapter were three Roman Sisters who knew her well, or at whose Vow ceremony she was present in the Roman Church. These were Sister M. Raphael and Sister M. Odilia, whom she had sent out as novices, and Sister M. Agostino, who went out as a young first vow Sister.

Our dear outgoing Superiors had remedied much of the damage and destruction of the War years, and here special mention must be given to Mother M. Germanus, whose great and marked love for the Sacred Heart of her Spouse, and whose practical devotion to Our Lady and to the Congregation gave her the courage to take risks and chances. A simple local book-keeper in her young years, a local Superior in Liverpool in after years, where she was remarkable for her great charity to the poor, Mother M. Germanus had gained that experience which matures and broadens one's outlook and which teaches that every human being has equal rights in this world. Having had the responsible office of Bursar-General since 1923, and having been elected first Mother Assistant in 1936, and re-elected to the same position in 1945, hers was the God-given choice of being a very special help to three successive Mothers-General, and their loyal and obedient co-worker withal. Mother M. Germanus never sought the limelight, in fact she was of a quiet, retiring nature, sometimes mistaken for coldness. The ego was absent in her person. As Superior in Paul Street, Liverpool, her first thought after breakfast was, with the help of a Sister, to prepare thirty sandwich parcels for the very poor who came to the Convent door each morning. For the young and able-bodied she would try to find "jobs". One such man, when hearing of her change from Liverpool, said: "That Superior has saved my life, and my soul from hell."

After the 1952 Chapter, Mother M. Germanus lived at Raheny, Dublin, where she was given the office of Local Superior. Still very much alert and active, she supervised the building of the schools and of the Convent which replaced the Old Manor House. Mother M. Germanus was a real mother to her new Community, and was loved and appreciated for her interest in each Sister and her attention to her spiritual duties. Her great devotion to the Sacred Heart and to our Blessed Lady were an inspiration to all. She came from Dublin to Maryfield, Roehampton, for the 1959 Chapter, and to her great joy was present in the Chapel at the re-interment of Mother M. Magdalen's remains on September 24th. She died at Raheny on January 23rd, 1965, in the 67th year of her religious life, having laboured for God and for souls almost to the end.

From 1952 to 1965 the growth of the Congregation in that Ireland, and especially in that Dublin, beloved of their Mother Foundress, was a great consolation to the Poor Servants of the Mother of God. To the Irish nuns and soldiers of the Crimea she owed her Faith, under God. To Irish vocations in the early years she owed the growth of her Institute. As early as 1875 the S.M.G. Sisters were working in their first Apostolic Boarding School, as well as in the National School in Carrigtwohill, Co. Cork. In 1888, it will be remembered, the Foundress took over the great work for aged ladies at Portland Row, Dublin, at the invitation of Archbishop Walsh; also at the pressing invitation of His Grace of Dublin and of the Catholic Guardians, she gave her "Yes" in 1899 to the question of another great charity — the taking of the responsibility of Rathdown Union Workhouse, for many years now replaced by the Loughlinstown District Hospital. Two similar charitable institutions were taken over at Youghal, Co. Cork, soon after the Foundress' death — a workhouse and a mental hospital. As heretofore stated, the former became St. Mary's District Hospital when the workhouse system in Ireland ceased to operate, and the Sisters had to be withdrawn from the mental home in 1963 for personal reasons, to the regret of the Most Reverend Dr. Ahern, Bishop of Cloyne, the clergy and the dear people of Youghal.

In 1952 the call for teaching Sisters in Dublin came through the Very Rev. Monsignor Fitzpatrick, who, with the authority of His Grace, the Most Reverend Dr. McQuaid, asked Sisters for the parish school at Raheny. His Grace gave permission also for a new day Secondary School. In the meantime, while councils, estate agents etc. were planning and purchasing new localities for building purposes, Dublin's Archbishop and His Grace's advisers were busy acquiring sites for churches, schools, parish halls and convents on each new Estate, while S.M.G. Superiors were preparing and replacing both University College, Dublin, and Carysfort-trained Sisters to take over.

On the morning of the solemn opening and blessing of the new Raheny Convent with its fine Chapel and schools, an incident occurred which, though considered very ordinary for such an occasion, resulted in an unexpected blessing within a few weeks. After luncheon, a lady came to the Mother Superior and, without explaining her purpose as a reporter for the "Irish Independent", asked some questions relating to the Roman Convent, the Trinità dei Monti, etc. Next day a surprise telegram from a nun-friend in the West read: "Come down, postulant." Of course the invitation was gladly accepted, and, after an interview with His Grace, Archbishop Walsh, of Tuam, and His Lordship, Dr. Brown of Galway, and having promised to abide fully by the decision of the Synod of Maynooth, the fruits of the visit were nine aspirants instead of the telegraphed "one". All nine have happily persevered to Final Vows, and are doing great work for God and souls.

The next move in Dublin was to Chapelizod in July 1954. A deceased lady benefactress in the city left a rich gift to the Congregation in her will "to extend the good work of St. Joseph's,

Portland Row." The lady was always in sympathy with this charity and loved sending gifts of fruit or cake to the Home, but this windfall at her death was a pleasant surprise, and meant for her that her name be inscribed in the archives of the Congregation for a special Mass yearly at Maryfield, Chapelizod, and to be prayed for daily in our every convent, in the prayer for "deceased benefactors."

His Grace the Archbishop of Dublin advised the purchase of the property "Culmore House", standing in its own grounds, which was advertised for sale and was admirably suitable for its purpose at the time. His Grace came himself one happy evening to bless every nook and corner of the house. He gave the necessary Canonical permissions, named a chaplain, and called the building "Maryfield".

"Maryfield" has for long had to refuse applications for lack of rooms, but as its history is being written, there is the long-wished-for news of its future extension and adaptation, when it is hoped "to extend the good work" for aged ladies according to the wish of the deceased benefactress and to the joy of its present Superior, Sister M. Constance.

In 1954, on September 18th, and while still busy with the Chapelizod House, an S.M.G. Community took possession of an already existing private school, having its own fine, spacy playing-field, in Banstead, Surrey, with the full authorization of our kind Archbishop of Southwark, Dr. Cyril Cowderoy, in whose diocese the Sisters have worked since Mother Magdalen's time. Reverend Canon Moriarty, the Parish Priest, and a zealous Catholic layman who saw what the Sisters had accomplished in the Hayes Parish, approached Head Superiors with their problem in the spring of the year. A thorough inspection of the building by our architect, who was experienced in school planning and in all that was necessary for its success, revealed many defects, which, however, were remedied in time for the re-opening in September. A neat little Chapel was fitted out, and soon there was regular community life. To the great apostolate of the school was added the visitation of the poor, the sick and the lonely. Instruction of converts played a major part in the activities, and soon great interest in the Sisters' work was taken, even by many non-Catholics who also became generous neighbours.

The Catholic school fulfilled a great need in Banstead in its first years. The annual Diocesan Religious Examinations have been most encouraging, and much sooner than was expected, the school ranked as "Efficient" after what the Sister Principal, Sister Anne Patricia, and her two trained S.M.G. Sisters described as a "strenuous General Inspection" lasting two days, from 9.0 a.m. to 4.0 p.m., by two of Her Majesty's Inspectors in 1964. In the Sisters' overflowing gratitude for this blessing on the Catholic school, they wrote: "External success is very evident, and the work is esteemed by parents, clergy and the Education Authority alike, but no one, as says Browning, can really measure earthly success, so, together with our limitations and without any illusions, we leave all in humility to the mercyful bounty of the Heavenly Head Master, to Whose honour and glory the work of the Congregation is dedicated."

The Banstead school, through its many and difficult vicissitudes, has had a phenomenal growth over the years. Beginning in a humble hut on the Brighton Road in 1939, with a roll of six or seven children and two lady teachers, the work was encouraged by the Reverend Dr. Dockery, whose untimely death by a German bomb in 1940 prevented his seeing his zealous aims fulfilled at Banstead. His successor in the parish, however, the Reverend Father Ryan, was able to buy Court House, which was built on the site of an ancient Manor used in feudal times for a hunting lodge by many of England's kings. Banstead's Anglican Cathedral once belonged to Southwark Diocese, and is mentioned in the Doomsday Book, so the town and district are rich in history.

The Banstead Catholic School of 1969 is in the process of more evolution which will make history for the Church in this ancient parish and town. Now the school is to be again extended to meet the requirements of the Department of Education and Science, with a view to its becoming State-aided, as has been the case with others of our "Private Efficient" Schools. Head Superiors are fully aware of the great necessity of building, given the fact that as many as ten housing estates with their hundreds of houses are going up all around. As to the means, the great Foundress has left the example of "knocking" at the door of the Bank of God, according to Dr. Manning's assurance and after the manner of the great St. Teresa and her sixpence.

This will mean a great extension of their apostolate for the S.M.G. Sisters from many points of view. Mother Magdalen Taylor will see from Heaven her Sisters carrying on her zealous work not only in the school but outside it: wherever there is a poor, sick, lonely or straying soul to be helped, either spiritually or temporarily, or both, there will be a Poor Servant of the Mother of God to be found.

In the late 1950's, the Mother General heard from the Superior of the Roman House that the Congregation was about to be asked for yet another foundation in the Archdiocese of Dublin. Difficulties loomed largely for the moment, but on considering the crying need and who it was that hinted at the hope of its being remedied, there could be no refusal. The small but very historic town of Castledermot in Kildare had already got its fine new primary school, its up-to-date technical school, its beautiful, if rather old galleried church and its chapels of ease some distance away at Moone and Levitstown, but it lacked its own secondary school. This void was becoming a cause of great concern, not only to His Grace, the Archbishop, and the local clergy of Castledermot and of many outlying districts, but to the parents, who dreaded the possible risks and results of early or late road-travel for their children.

In the 1959 General Chapter, all the Mothers of the 1952 government were re-elected, and the Castledermot question was almost the first item on the agenda to be discussed. On His Grace's return from Rome, an interview was arranged at Archbishop's House, Dublin, and on the day following, a journey to Castledermot and a visit to the parish priest finished the decision. The site was there, extending from the Church and the parochial house to a fine old stately ruin of a Franciscan Monastery, that voiced the silent history of a tragic penal past. Soon the architect and his draftman were chosen, the responsible builder got his workers ready, and by May 30th, 1960, the Sisters took possession as a community. Children began to pour in, although the official opening was not until 1961. That was a day never to be forgotten in the annals of the house. As his car appeared, the Archbishop was welcomed by the local men's band in picturesque costume on the outskirts of the town, and the townsfolk themselves walked after His Grace's car in reverent and ordered procession. The school-children formed a guard of honour lining the entrance to the new convent and school, and the Sisters filed up nearest the entrance door. The sun shone out in buoyant, gleeful glory. Surely the smile of God was over all: another Tabernacle had been set up, and education was secured to Catholic University entrance level. One could not but look forward to what it all meant. The Lord had come to "set His tent" in the midst of beautiful, aspiring youth, there would be annual retreats and repeated conferences, doctrinal preparation, theses and oral examinations; yes, and dramatics, sales of work, bazaars and raffles; nothing would be left undone to help the poor and to encourage priests and messengers of the faith in missionary lands. Meanwhile each girl herself would be attaining maturity — the great characteristic of dignified womanhood, which, with the help of God's grace, makes her aware that all she possesses is from His Divine Bounty, either to be used as a mother in the upbringing of a future well-trained, happy religious family, or as a nun, chosen by God for some Congregation in His Church, to mother not one but many families and lead them to His yearning Sacred Heart, pierced on the Cross for their purchase.

On that happy day, after His Grace had blessed the Chapel, convent and school, and the ceremony of cutting the white ribbon was over, all assembled in the Chapel for Holy Mass. The Reverend Father Fahy, P.P., was celebrant, and His Grace presided in the sanctuary. A glorious congregational "Magnificat" finished the sacred scene, which, as the Minister of Education said afterwards, "gave it all a magnificent wind-up." Luncheon for all followed at mid-day, and the primary school-children had an evening party on the lawn.

Such is the story of Castledermot Day and Boarding School, and of its happy official opening in 1961.

The beautiful marble altar and tabernacle were gifted by a Mr. Frank Cullen Brophy of Arizona, a friend of the Florence Sisters since World War II. He and his wife visited the Castledermot Convent and school afterwards. His was a great history.

An ancestor had been hanged for his Faith and patriotism on what was called the "Brophy Tree". Hence his love for Castledermot and Kildare, "the land of his staunch Catholic ancestors," as he liked to say.

The marble flooring, with the predella steps and beautiful altar-rails were the gift of Mother M. Aloysia's relatives.

Shortly after the Castledermot Convent and school were securely working, another parish, with its Church and school, was predicted. The Cameron Estate, not far from Raheny, was purchased for building purposes, and it soon became news that the site for a new Church, convent, and primary school was part of the extensive building scheme, the name of the locality to remain "Edenmore". Soon houses began to appear as if by magic, so did the families to live in them, and shopping centres were not behind hand to serve the rapidly increasing population. The Archbishop, ever alert to the spiritual needs of his people, consulted with his Vicar-General, Monsignor Fitzpatrick. The decision was that, pending the construction of a new school and convent, temporary contrivances could serve, and that if a few Irish-trained teaching Sisters could live with the Raheny Community and go out to Edenmore each morning, it would more than solve the problem. The solution worked, and was blessed in the solving. Monsignor himself, on damp or rainy mornings, often motored the Sisters to school, until on April 8th, 1965, all was well, and the Sisters took possession as a community of the newly-blessed Convent, with its neatly furnished Chapel and beautiful Tabernacle, where their Divine Guest had come to stay.

In addition to their principal work of teaching or nursing, the Sisters in all the Irish convents, as in every country, carry on the parish apostolate and help the clergy as much as they can. They visit the sick, the poor, the lonely, get up subscriptions for the missions, help where they can with food, clothing and other necessaries, above all else do they pray and strive to instil into all whom they come to serve, whether in school or outside it, a great love for Holy Mass and frequent Communion. Thus and thus only, with the great strength of Divine Grace, can young people, especially of this disturbed age, resist the many temptations of our time.

The "setting out" for school at 7.30 or 8.0 a.m. on week

mornings was for years an obligation for the teaching Sisters. In Carrigtwohill, in Clongowes Wood, as well as in Rhyl and in Selkirkshire, in the Foundress' time the Sisters had to walk good distances to and from school. In Brentford for well-nigh sixty years the school Sisters walked to and from the Parish school, as they also did and still do at Portslade, and in some parts of the Clifton diocese. Of course, for longer distances as at Liverpool, where their own children of the Home go with them or are dropped at the various schools of the city, they now have a commodious school-bus which eases an otherwise difficult problem.

The first general Novitiate House at St. Mary's Convent, Roehampton, Surrey, must have its say at this point. Built on a large scale, according to the dying wish of the Foundress, sixty or eighty novices was the minimum in the early 1900's. The older house, already alluded to as "three houses knocked into one" became the large orphanage, and later still, after World War II, when the adoption system was introduced for children, it became a home for mentally defective, retarded and irresponsible girls. The condition of these poor girls is always sad; and the fact of their not realizing this themselves, makes one sympathise with, and love and understand them all the more, as the Sisters do who are specially trained for this charitable work.

The four-storied St. Mary's Convent itself has now become the Community centre from which groups of Sisters go out each morning to teach in four diocesan schools, viz. Our Lady of Victories, Putney, Our Lady Queen of Heaven, Midway, Sacred Heart, Roehampton, and St. Agatha's at Kingston-on-Thames.

The wide apostolate which has ever been connected with their vocation as Poor Servants of the Mother of God goes hand in hand with their school work. The poor, the lonely and the sick, in their homes or in hospitals, lapsed Catholics and those who have gone astray are all visited regularly, while the instruction of converts and catechism classes for those who have to attend non-Catholic schools are part of the week-end work. All of this work is appreciated by our kind Archbishop, Dr. Cowderoy, and his responsible clergy, for all of whom it is a pleasure to work, so co-operative and zealous are they in their great efforts for God and for souls.

Chapter 22.

VATICAN II AND VITALITY

The delegates for the eleventh General Chapter of the Poor Servants of the Mother of God assembled at Maryfield, Roehampton, in the last week of September 1966, and the election of its new government was presided over on October 3rd by the Most Reverend Archbishop Cowderoy of Southwark. The results were: Mother M. Azevedo, Mother General, with Mother Margaret Mary, Mother Agnes Joseph, Mother Rose Thérèse and Mother Maria Annunziata as Assistants. With the unanimous consent of the delegates and of the outgoing Mothers, Mother Agnes Joseph was again re-elected to her particular office of charge of the English Schools, to the appointment of teaching Sisters at the School Managers' meetings, and seeing to the Sisters' religious programmes and the various academic requirements of our time. All her former work she was to carry on until a successor took it over, the which was committed to Mother M. Basil at the beginning of 1969.

At this point it is well to mention that a great nun, Mother M. Lewis of the 1952 election and re-elected in 1959, died in November 1965, to the great grief of all. When the Mother General with the consent of her Council put the matter before the Sacred Congregation of Religious, as to whether a temporary appointment, (as allowed by the Constitutions) should be made, pending the forthcoming Chapter's choice in 1966, the answer from Rome was: "Carry on in God's Name until the next election." So in God's name and with Our Blessed Lady's help the Mothers carried on, and all went well in the assurance that it had the blessing of the Holy See.

Another dear Mother of the re-election of 1959 was Mother

M. Aloysia, who likewise took her flight to God a few years afterwards, and was replaced by Mother M. de Ricci. Mother M. Aloysia was a great spiritual soul, of a very simple and lovable nature, and one who went straight to Our Lady in every difficulty. After her death many Sisters wrote in their obituary notes of how she had helped them during her various visitations. She always prefaced her little admonitions and talks with a kindly smile which made them feel her sincerity, as she opened the conversation with: "Now, child," or "My dear child, did you talk that over first with Our Lord?"

The dear Mother General and her Council of the present régime have had, and are still having a busy time in this important period of the Church's Renewal. With courage and with full trust in the Holy Spirit's action throughout the Congregation, they have asked themselves, as has every Community in the Institute: "What would the Mother Foundress do, and how would she act, were she living to-day?" Surely she who gave our dear Congregation its very distinctive spirit, and laid, with God's help and Our Lady's, its solid foundation, and who, with the advice of her spiritual directors, searched throughout Ireland, Belgium, France, Germany and Poland for all that would help and inspire, and after all this experience concluded: "The more I see of foreign Institutes, the more certain I am we must found our own," would now ask herself: "Into what side-paths have we deviated since 1869?" Please God, her children could answer: "With God's grace and Our Lady's help, into no serious pitfall." But as each one looks into herself in the grace and the light of the Holy Spirit, she feels and sees the great need of a more intense renewal of her interior life with her Divine Lord, so that the ever-increasing intake of the divine graces of her Baptism and of her whole sacramental life, as well as of her holy vows and her fidelity to them, strengthened each morning by the graces of Holy Mass, may be a continuous offering to Him, to buy back, as it were, with His own gifted coin, the souls for whom He died. The Sisters' many-sided apostolate, with the help of His grace, will thus be enriched by the renewal of their own interior spirit of union with God.

One may ask the "Why?" for those extra chapters in this biography after the death of Mother Magdalen Taylor? Would not an appendix or two have sufficed, as in the first "Life" by Father Devas, S.J.? The answer is: "Not only is the aim of the book to make the English convert Foundress better known in our time, but in accordance with the oft repeated emphasis of the Council, 'On maintaining the spirit of the Founder or Foundress,' these chapters on the different foundations and their works since 1900 show, that every work of charity which she opened up during her lifetime, has since her death been multiplied in the life of her Congregation. In its hospitals, including general, maternity and spastic, schools at all levels, orphanages, homes for the mentally handicapped and the irresponsible, the unwanted and deprived, homes for the aged and infirm, where the Sisters themselves are qualified nurses, nothing has been left undone that would forward her plan for alleviating human misery."

"The Sisters are permitted to receive the rich into their hospitals and other houses as a means of gaining aid for the poor." This rule has been faithfully observed also. It has been said of St. Joseph that he was "every inch a Jew." He had to maintain the Son of God and His Holy Mother, and, while he would gladly complete some article of carpentry for a poor neighbour, or construct a small fishing boat gratis for a poor fisherman, he would certainly charge full price where he knew he could justly demand it.

While, however, advocating and herself originating every possible means of helping the poor, Mother Foundress says in a letter dated December 1891: "Yes, Our Lady is indeed good to us, for she allows us to perform all the corporal and spiritual works of mercy," but she warns in another place: "Our Lord has called us, not merely to teach children, or nurse the sick or visit the poor, but to be nuns — real nuns."

Each Sister's response to this call, made according to the spirit of the Congregation, has continued and developed the original response of the Foundress, which first caused the Congregation to come into being.

Again in 1892, Mother Foundress warns the Sisters: "Never let us be led astray by the excitement which accompanies our good works, to forget that a religious is first of all called to be a religious, a being consecrated to God, whose first contract with God is personal holiness, and that if works of zeal are not founded on a full interior life of union with God through prayer, obedience and humility, they are nothing before God."

Mother's great devotion to the mystery of the Incarnation made her design, as it were, her idea of its great theological importance for salvation, and instruct the Roman artist how to get her idea on to the canvas. The Archangel had given his message, Mary had put her question, the Holy Spirit had descended and the Word was made Flesh. What a moment of grace for Mary and the world! She had become the immaculate Christ-bearer,and her first act was to bring the good tidings to others, to help and comfort St. Elizabeth.

This is what Mother Foundress prayed for in her life, that she and her Sisters would ever be Christ-bearers — His witnesses to all with whom they came in contact, of every creed and class. In the Rule it says: "The greatest festival will be the 25th of March — feast of the Annunciation — the day on which the astonished angels saw their God descend from the Heavens to be made man to become our Brother." When it was argued that the greatest feast and miracle of the Church was the Resurrection, Mother would lovingly reply: "There could not have been a Resurrection if there were no Incarnation and Death of God made man." And in the "Community Intentions" of the Congregation, drawn up by the Foundress, she makes the prayer of Père Oliér her own: "Oh Jesus, living in Mary, come and live in Thy servants, in the spirit of Thy holiness, in the fulness of Thy might, in the truth of Thy virtues, in the perfection of Thy ways, in the communion of Thy mysteries. Overthrow every hostile power to Thy Spirit, for the glory of the Father. Amen."

In another important paragraph, the spirit of the Institute is clearly stated as: "Life for Jesus Christ, labour for Jesus Christ, zeal for Jesus Christ, and all things through Mary — His most sweet Mother and our Mistress."

Referring to the Angelus, the Holy Rule says: "And first at the sound of the bell in the houses of the Institute, and in the most profound silence and with great and loving devotion, the Sisters will devoutly recite the Angelus, remembering that 'the Word was made flesh and dwelt among us.' Happy those whose devotion to the Angelus shall never fail."

The Feast of the Sacred Heart is the next mentioned, when the Sisters are reminded that "Our Lord has deigned to ask of us (this feast) as a reparation for the injuries He receives," and still referring to the Sacred Heart, the Holy Rule reminds us that "the Congregation was solemnly consecrated to the Sacred Heart on the 28th December, 1873, by its first Mother General, the Foundress, Mother Magdalen Taylor, and that act of consecration must be publicly and solemnly renewed every year on the feast of the Sacred Heart, Friday after the octave of Corpus Christi. All will desire and try to console Our Lord by their devotion for the pains of disappointed love which His Divine Heart suffers from the indifference of ungrateful men."

The third particular feast of the Congregation is Our Lady's Maternity, when (to quote the Rule again) "All will then rejoice in our most sweet Mother's happiness and glory in the possession of her Divine Son, and they will expect great graces from her hands." And in the following paragraph the Sisters are reminded that "Devotion to the Sacred Humanity of Jesus Christ, proper to the Congregation, naturally brings with it the devotion to the Blessed Sacrament, and the Tabernacle will be the home of their hearts, and to visit It their chief earthly joy."

When one considers the prayer-life of Mother Magdalen, and that her great and solid devotions were: The Incarnation, the Sacred Heart, and the Motherhood of Our Lady, one understands her great desire to multiply Tabernacles, and the secret of her great maternal heart, wherein every form of poverty and misery found shelter and succour. What a blessed example she has given her spiritual daughters in their sincere work of spiritual renewal in their centenary year!

After having given a general idea of the spirit and devotions of the Congregation, and of the Foundress as a Mother to her spiritual children, it will be seen how well her idea was grasped from the first, by those Sisters whose good fortune it was to see how their magnanimous Mother put her hand in the Hand of God from the beginning. Like the great St. Paul, she knew in Whom she trusted. The Jesuit Father Porter had said once, perhaps when some heavy cross had to be shouldered by Mother Magdalen: "Plod on — you don't see what is beyond!"

Great advisers were hers from the outset; God provided

reliable spiritual guides in Dr. Wiseman, working through Dr. Manning, in the new venture of 1854 and the Crimean campaign. The sending of Catholic chaplains and Sisters from England and Ireland to see to the spiritual and corporal needs of the dear dying Catholic soldiers was a novel move for the England of the Reformation. It would soon mean the "defection" of two lady volunteers, Miss Stanley and Miss Taylor, from their former beliefs. The Spirit breatheth where He will. Soon and sudden did both ladies succumb to His action, and within a week Father Woollett saw Fanny Taylor a Catholic. He returns later and continues her instructions, the which were to be taken on and continued for almost a whole year by Dr. Manning himself.

In God's designs, Fanny was to get to know Mother Frances Bridgeman and her nuns in the Koulali hospital wards. She witnessed the utter dedication of the Sisters to their work for the sick and wounded. She herself will get to love and pity her poor patients. She will write their home letters. They will teach her the Rosary.

At home in London once again, she is begged by Miss Stanley to write "Eastern Hospitals and English Nurses." She will have Dr. Manning, Father Gallwey and Father Clare to help and advise her. She pays a first visit to Ireland, writing for "The Lamp" and makes a circuit almost of the whole country, which leads up to her production of another book, "Irish Homes and Irish Hearts." Her "Tyburn" results in a meeting and a life-long friendship with Lady Georgiana Fullerton.

The Divine Hunter is now on Fanny Taylor's track. She will be advised, or rather seek advice, to enter with the Daughters of St. Vincent de Paul. Father Gallwey sees her strong attraction, and knowing of her great love for the poor both before and after her conversion, encourages her. Fanny thought she was at the end of her "seeking". God, through Père Etienne and the Paris Superior spoke the definite "No" that could be spiritually interpreted from the war-cry of World War I: "Your King and Country need you!" Surely her King, her Lord, and her poor England needed this valiant daughter to help in the restoring of His Mother's Dowry!

Dr. Manning is delighted that Fanny is back. He reads Père Etienne's letter to her. Now he, Fathers Gallwey and Clare, and Lady Georgiana decide that Fanny should visit European active congregations for experience' sake, to see if any could offer affiliation for a branch in England. She goes to France, Belgium, Germany and Poland, and concludes with the decisive phrase: "The more I see of foreign Institutes, the more certain I am we must found our own."

Her "own" is founded, and the Feast of Our Lady of Mercy, September 24th, 1969, will for ever be a blessed anniversary for the Poor Servants of the Mother of God. This memoir of their beloved Mother and Foundress tells the complete story of its growth and foundation and of its unique spirit: "Life for Jesus Christ, labour for Jesus Christ, zeal for Jesus Christ, and all things through Mary — His most sweet Mother and our Mistress."

In this period of the Church's Renewal, the Poor Servants of the Mother of God, Head Superiors, Local Superiors and each individual Sister is occupied prayerfully and sincerely to come to a full knowledge of how their Mother would react to the call of Holy Church to-day. Certainly this great woman, this valiant lover of Christ, would utter her "Fiat" of obedience, and offer herself anew for every sacrifice that her Lord would ask. She herself in life would go to his slum house to nurse the poor man in London whose doctor knew he had not the wherewith for hospital fees. In her early years after her Crimean experience, she would coax the poor boys of the slums to her night school for Catechism and the three R's and then provide a supper. She herself would canvas for "jobs" for such, and teach them the love of work. They were called "Tailor boys", but Fanny Taylor was winning them for God, and heeded not the criticism of armchair Victorian ladies. Dear Mother Magdalen rejoiced exceedingly in after years when these boys reverently approached the altar rails with their wives and children to receive their Eucharistic God, to Whom she was the first to introduce them in earlier days.

What lesson did her own Sisters learn from this dutiful and practical Mother? These last chapters of her biography show how well her elastic spirit was understood and imbibed, and then exercised by her Congregation. Mother Magdalen opened a school wherever she could. "Suffer the little children to come to Me" was Our Lord's plea. She knew little children draw their elders to God. She trained her Sisters for hospital work from her earliest years, so have Superiors ever done in her imitation.

Apostolic boarding schools were another choice where aspirants to her own or to other Congregations were prepared. At Pope's Leo XIII's gracious request, she ventured the Roman convent and school for the "Poor rich." The spiritually poor were and are the poorest of all. With the sound and practical advice of her Religious Superiors of the Congregation of Propaganda, she and her God-given adviser, Father Dignam, S.J., inserted in the Holy Rule of the S.M.G.'s: "The Sisters . . . are permitted to receive the rich into their hospitals or other houses as a means of gaining aid for the poor." The Foundress never yielded to human respect. She herself would accost the rich and plead for the poor. Sir J. B. Leach of St. Helens said of her that "That courageous woman never used an intermediary." He, a non-conformist, yielded to her persuasions as to where his duty lay with regard to the poor. He was one of her best friends all her life, as were his sisters, after his death, who left the Providence Hospital and the poor all their money.

One necessarily asks oneself here: "Did not and does not Mother Magdalen's spiritual life, and that of her daughters, suffer some mitigation and danger from all this activity in their apostolate?" Over and over again did their great Mother warn her Sisters, as does their Holy Rule, that secular teachers, trained nurses, social workers etc. etc. can do all this work and perhaps accomplish it much more proficiently than can nuns, but — and this "but" is a challenge — if a Sister's work is not stamped with the hall-mark, the trade-mark of love for her Lord, overflowing from the strength and grace of her own heart's possession of Him, it is of no value. On her Vow Day she gave herself to Him who had called her "from the beginning." He chose her for Himself, as He chose her companions whom she will call her Sisters, who will live the common life with one another under a lawfully appointed Superior who represents her Mother General, who represents Christ's Vicar, who is the voice of God on earth.

"That they may be one" was Christ's prayer for His

disciples. This "oneness" must first of all exist in the sisterly love and sincerity of the Religious whose unifying, strengthening force comes from the Tabernacle. One in Him and with His Mother, their "Queen and Mistress", and in the unity of their family spirit, the Sisters are safe. Then, to quote Dr. Butler's Catechism of our school days, "Our neighbour is all mankind, of every description, without any exception of persons, even those who injure us or differ from us in religion." Mother Magdalen Taylor's "neighbour" depended neither on creed nor class. Her all-embracing charity born of her love for the Blessed Sacrament embraced the world of souls that she might win them for God. Let us hope that an increase of zeal and of perfect charity will be the fruit of Renewal in each Sister's heart during this special time of the Holy Spirit's work in and for the Church.

Nor did Mother Magdalen's splendid spirit of prayer and work for God and souls exclude all joy or fun from her convents, nor does it interfere with the Sisters' life to-day. The Foundress, as was seen in earlier chapters, loved to gather her children in large numbers for retreats, and loved to see them enjoying one another on the days that followed. Concerts, plays, soirées, outings, all forms of happy innocent relaxation were and are part of their busy, active lives. Mother Magdalen loved to encourage Local Superiors of neighbouring houses to visit one another, with a companion or two, on their saint's feast-day, and to bring some little present as a mark of interest and affection.

Respect for the Hierarchy and for all God's priests, especially for those who are our confessors, chaplains, or otherwise connected with us is insisted upon in our Holy Rule. The kindest and most gracious and respectful hospitality must always be shown to each and every "alter Christus" in all our houses, as we would show it to Christ Himself.

As has been already said, this biography is written for the purpose of making our beloved English convert Foundress better known in the coming centenary year of the birth of her Congregation, but it has for its special aim the making clear to those Poor Servants yet to come what a truly wonderful Foundress their Mother was. In the prayerful hope that the story of such a dedicated life may reach and influence many in their "seeking" for God and His Will in their lives, especially in those blessed times of Vatican II when the Holy Spirit is lavish of His gifts of grace, it is thought well to finish this book with some paragraph of Mother Magdalen's own letter from Rome to her Congregation for the occasion of the Silver Jubilee, March 25th, 1894:

"I see our first little houses — our hard work, our hard days, when we had little to eat and much to suffer. I see our first little chapel, where we received the holy Habit, and made our Vows. And now I see our great house in Rome — our large school, and our numerous other houses, with our orphans, sick, patients, old women and others — and I am wonder-struck, and I feel no one can help saying: 'Lo, the Finger of God is here!'"

If the "Finger of God" was there, to bless the Congregation in its Silver Jubilee year, surely Mother Mary Magdalen's Sisters can say in their Centenary year: "The Hand of God is here!"

For steadfast in His kindness towards us,
And the fidelity of the Lord endures forever.

(Psalm 116)

L. D. S.

ALPHABETICAL INDEX

273

Lamp, The, 43, 75, 178, 179.
Lancashire, 105.
Lateran, Treaty, 136.
Lavigne, Père, 25.
Leach, Sir J.B., 202, 269.
Lee, Most Rev. Dr., Bishop of Clifton, 233, 234.
Ledochowski, H.E. Most Rev. Dr., Archbishop of Posen, 46, 77.
Leo XIII, 36, 90, 91, 96, 99, 167, 173, 204, 240, 269.
Le Puy, 216.
Leslie, Shane (Life of Cardinal Manning), 20.
Lewis, Mother M., 212, 253.
Liège, 54.
Limerick, 80.
Lime Kiln Lane, 149.
Lincoln's Inn Fields, 85.
Lincolnshire, 1, 7.
Livesey, Rev. Fr., 88.
Lloyd, Rev. Fr. Wm., 140.
Londonderry, Lady, 123.
London Bridge, 22, 32.
Loreto, 95, 124.
Lost and Other Tales, 180.
Lourdes, 19, 98.
Louvain, 94.
Lucas, Herbert, Rev. Fr., S.J. 133.
Lucy, Mother M., 68, 178, 224, 232.
Lumozzi, Fr., S.J., 198.
Lyons, 94.

Mackay, Rev. Fr. Peter Paul, O.P., 133, 199.
Madeleine, Mother (Marie Reparatrice), 125.
Maher, Rev. Fr. W., S.J., 216.
Manning, H.E. Cardinal, 20, 21, 23, 31, 33, 34, 35, 37, 40, 41, 42, 44, 45, 46, 49, 51, 53, 60, 62, 76, 77, 86, 96, 99, 113, 114, 117, 174, 208, 258, 267.
Manzoni, Professor, 223.
Marie Anne, Sister (Notre Dame) 110.
Marie Reparatrice, Society of, 72, 95, 126, 129.
Maresca, Padre, 118.

Margaret Mary, Mother, 262.
Margate, 84.
Martha, Mother M., 234.
Maryfield, High Point, U.S.A., 241, 242, 243, 244, 245, 246.
Maryfield, Roehampton, 208.
Marseilles, 29.
Mazzella, H.E. Cardinal, S.J., 206.
Mazzini, Signor, 136.
McCarthy, Denis Florence, 178.
McQuaid, Most Rev. Dr., Archbishop of Dublin, 145, 255, 256, 258, 259, 260.
McSweeney, Dr., 145.
Measures, Mr. R.H., 139.
Mercy, Sisters of (see Crimea).
Merry del Val, H.E. Cardinal, 19, 167, 168.
Middlehurst, Mr. & Mrs. Peter, 112.
Miller, Rev. Fr., O.M.I., (afterwards Vicar Apostolic of the Transvaal), 187, 191, 192, 201.
Mistrangelo, H.E. Cardinal, 122, 138.
Modeste, Brother, 55.
Month, The 178, 200.
Montessori, Madame, 9.
Mortlake Cemetery, 198, 201, 208.
Most Pure Heart of Mary (Feast of), 72.
Mount Argus, (Dublin), 15.
Murray, Miss, 186.
Murphy, Mr. James, 143, 144.
Murnane, Very Rev. Canon, 199, 216.
Mussolini, Il Duce, 223.

Natal, 14.
Newburgh, 67, 102.
Newman, H.E. Cardinal, 8, 12, 43, 48, 59, 178, 179.
Newry, 44.
Nicholas Nickleby, 9.
Nightingale, Florence, 21, 24, 122, 177.
Norfolk, Duchess of (Minna), 67.
Norton, The Hon. Mrs., 178.

Norton, Virginia, U.S.A., 246, 247, 248.
North Carolina Medical Care Commission, U.S.A., 244.
Northampton, Diocese of, 239, 240.
North Hyde, 116.
Nugent, Very Rev. Monsignor, 149, 150, 183, 220.

Oakley, Rev. Fr. Frederick, 14, 143.
Oblates of Mary Immaculate, 187.
Oblates of St. Francis de Sales, 95.
O'Connell, Daniel, 1, 12, 143.
O'Connor, Don The, 231.
O'Connor, Mary 211.
Odilia, Sister M., 138.
O'Donnell, Very Rev. Canon, 143.
Offerings for Orphans, 177.
Orange, Martyrs of, 179.
O'Rielly, Most Rev. Dr., Bishop of Liverpool, 109.
O'Sullivan, Most Rev. Dr., Bishop of Kerry, 231.
Oxford Movement. 12, 16, 27, 48.

Packenham, Charles Reginald, 15.
Parker, Most Rev. Dr., Bishop of Northampton, 239, 290.
Paray-le-Monial, 98, 187, 191.
Paris, 10, 186, 192.
Parocchi, H.E. Cardinal, 126, 167, 168, 195.
Passionist Fathers, 149.
Patricia, Mother M., 230.
Patrick, St., 152.
Paul VI, Pope, 104.
Paul Magdalen, Sister, 180, 199.
Paul Street, 221.
Pazzi, de, Mother M., 230
Pearl in Dark Waters, 177.
Peeler and the Goat, 86.
Peers-Smith, Rev. Fr. S.J., 199, 211.
Pembridge Square, 228.
Percy, Lord Eustace, 88.
Percy Street, 114.
Père Caussade, 168.

Père Olier, 162.
Pereira, Hon. Mrs., 67.
Pera, (Constantinople), 23.
Petrus, Mother M., 233.
Peter Robinson's, 180.
Philadelphia, 249, 250.
Philomena, Mother M., 164, 165.
Phoebe, Sister, (Emma Taylor), Miss Sellon's Sisterhood, 9.
Pitt, Susan, The Hon., 178.
Pius IX, Pope, 42, 60, 90, 136.
Pius X, Pope, 133, 243.
Pius XI, Pope, 179.
Pius XII, Pope, 208, 209.
Pincio, Piazza di Spagna, 95, 127, 240.
Plymouth, 9.
Polish Journey, 51.
Portland Row, 14, 143, 179.
Porter, Rev. Fr., S.J., (afterwards Archbishop of Bombay, 48, 93, 124, 266.
Portslade Manor, 217, 218, 219, 260.
Portsmouth, 14.
Posen, 55, 82.
Potatoe Famine, 14.
Prassedes, Sister M., 134, 137.
Pre-Raphaelite Brotherhood, 17.
Prisca, Mother M., 232.
Propaganda, Congregation of, 97.
Providence Hospital, 117, 118, 121.
Pusey, Dr., 16, 27, 43.
Putney, 87.

Quakers, 8.
Queen Mary's Hospital, 36.
Quercia, La, 171.
Quin, Very Rev. Canon, 185.
Quirinus, Sister M., 138.

Ragged School, 41, 91.
Raheny, 255.
Raphael, Mother Agnes, 111.
Rathdown Union, 183, 185.
Rathdrum, 232.
Regina Prophetarum, 167, 168, 172, 173.
Regis, Sister M., 140.
Retreats by Father Dignam, 181.
Richard, H.E. Cardinal, 148, 228.